The Hidden History of

EWYAS LACY

in Herefordshire

With best wishes

Priscilla

The Hidden History of
EWYAS LACY
in Herefordshire

by

Priscilla Flower-Smith

LOGASTON PRESS

LOGASTON PRESS
Little Logaston Woonton Almeley
Herefordshire HR3 6QH
logastonpress.co.uk

First published by Logaston Press 2013
Copyright text © Priscilla Flower-Smith 2013
Copyright illustrations © as acknowledged 2013

ISBN 978 1 906663 81 0

Typeset by Logaston Press
and printed and bound in printed in Spain
by Graphy Cems

*Cover illustration: Looking across Longtown to the Black Mountains and the Cat's Back,
courtesy of Jenny Houston*

Contents

Acknowledgements

Excitement mounted as we descended the steep hill into the Olchon Valley on our first visit to inspect a house seen only from a picture little bigger than a postage stamp. For once we were not disappointed as it was a paradise, with acres of peaceful fields, woods, a stream and even a stretch of river. As an added bonus there was an ancient house to be restored to life, a house built when Shakespeare was a boy and which saw the final years of Queen Elizabeth's reign. Our time in the Olchon Valley was brought to an end by illness but it will always remain a perfect place to us and these pages are in a sense my tribute to it.

Heartfelt thanks are due to the following for their help over the past two years: first and foremost I have my husband to thank, as without his help this book could not have been written. He took over from me many of the main domestic tasks such as shopping, and, as he had shared the work of obtaining and transcribing the documents from the first, was able to discuss problems and make useful suggestions, especially technological! My second tribute has to go to my friend Jonathan Barry at the University of Exeter, who patiently oversaw the thesis that led me to this point and who subsequently enabled me to have a two-year Research Fellowship to develop the themes in these chapters. I also have to thank the members of the group working on the wills and inventories of Uffculme who gave me that heady first experience of working with probate documents.

Another group deserving of gratitude is the Longtown and District Historical Society, not only for their generous purchase, helped by the Heritage Lottery Fund, of the copies of the wills and inventories from the National Library of Wales at Aberystwyth, but their constant support and encouragement from the first, especially that of their President, Jenny Houston.

In addition, I am grateful to the staff of Hereford Record Office and the National Library of Wales, in particular Rhys Griffith and Miss Samuel, respectively. Sue Hubbard kindly transcribed the Michaelchurch Escley wills and the Woolhope librarians, Miss Jonson and Mr. Gwillim Rees efficiently found the extra papers that I needed from the Woolhope Transactions. Sadly, it is too late to thank Jim Tonkin for his inspirational afternoon lectures on vernacular architecture, but both he and Muriel were generous with their help, as was Dewi Williams with his work on the Longleat Papers.

For photographs I must thank the generous help of Jenny Houston for those on pages 3, 41, 47, 48, 49, 52, 71, 76, 77, 95, 99, 100, 101, 102 (top), 104, 105 and 151, Logaston Press for those on pages 1, 53 and 155, whilst I have contributed those on pages 2, 5, 39, 40, 50, 55, 56, 57, 73, 74, 75, 78, 81, 83, 102 (bottom), 106, 108, 109, 113, 120, 121, 152, 153, 154 and 170.

Finally, I must thank Karen and Andy Johnson, my publishers, for having the courage to take on an unknown author and skilfully shape her work until it becomes readable.

Preface

Much of the information in this book is the result of extensive research into the wills and associated inventories of the inhabitants of Ewyas Lacy in the years between 1547 and 1858. It has allowed a detailed look at how people lived, the nature of farming life, the gradual growth in number of personal possessions, the establishment and the range of goods they supplied. The wills even tell us something of people's emotional and moral lives, of affairs and of heartbreak.

A visit to the National Library of Wales in 2001 showed there to be a large number of probate documents held there for the Hundred of Ewyas Lacy. Until the Act of Union in 1536 this borderland was treated politically as though it was in Wales, and control of probate matters continued within this system until 1858, when responsibility for probate was transferred from the ecclesiastical authorities to Hereford Probate Registry Office. In 2003, with the aid of a grant from the Lottery and Longtown Historical Society, copies of the probate documents were obtained from the National Library of Wales for the ten parishes and townships of the Hundred: Clodock, Craswall, Llancillo, Llanveynoe, Longtown, Michaelchurch Escley, Newton, Rowlestone, St Margarets and Walterstone. A small area of Cusop once included in the Hundred was not part of this survey, as it was not part of the original manor of Ewyas Lacy. Although only a tiny settlement now, Clodock was the most important historically and was the mother church for the four chapelries of Craswall, Llanveynoe, Longtown and Newton. Today, Longtown is the better known.

Eventually, over a thousand sets of documents were received spanning almost three centuries, from 1547 to 1858 (the last inventory was made in 1857). These sets were all listed, the 721 wills transcribed by my husband and myself, précised and put on a website (lhsarchive.org.uk). It is these, together with the 719 inventories, that are the main source for most of the information that follows. Since that time many of the pre-1660 wills have been discovered at the National Library of Wales and, thanks to my husband, have been transcribed, together with 153 National Archive wills from Kew.

The number of pages per set varied from about seven or eight to only two. They might include a will, an inventory, plus administrative documents. We were fortunate if we had all of these; very often the set consisted of either a will or an inventory and little else. It helped if a bond was included in the administrative documents, as, if the will was absent, it was easier to ascertain the family connections from the names of the administrators of the probate who were 'bound' to obtain an inventory of the goods of the deceased, or produce other information to the church court. A relative rarity were Grants of Administration giving relations or close friends of the deceased the power to administer the estate if there was no executor named, or if the executor had died during probate, or were minors.

The administrative offices associated with Brecon Cathedral
where probate matters would have been dealt with

Wills have been made from very early times, but inventories were only required by law from the early 16th century. Ewyas Lacy Hundred is exceptionally fortunate that, unlike in most other dioceses the archdeacon's court at Brecon required them until the early 19th century, and wanted them in duplicate during the 18th century. Not all the wills had inventories attached, and vice versa. Of the inventories that have been transcribed, there are 61 for the 19th century – a unique survival.

There has been an explosion in the study of inventories in recent years, and most parts of the country have now been covered to some extent. There are too many to name all the authors of these individually; suffice to mention the names of Margaret Cash, Mark Overton, Margaret and Peter Spufford, F.W. Steer, Joan Thirsk, Nancy and Jeff Cox and Barrie Trinder for their studies of Devon, Norfolk, Cambridgeshire, Essex, Lincolnshire and Shropshire respectively. I am indebted to them for opening up aspects of this subject to consider when writing this book.

So far, little has been done to explore the probate papers of Herefordshire. Some years ago a study was made of Herefordshire inventories (3,000 representing 20% of the total) by Jim Tonkin, Chairman of the Woolhope Club, and with them he included 178 Ewyas Lacy inventories which were held at the National Library of Wales.[1] This latter was a fairly selective group, with a particular focus on the buildings and their contents. In his study he states that prior to 1660 all the inventories for Ewyas Lacy appear to have been lost, though there were copies for the years 1570-1589. (We were eventually able to recover many of these from the National Library of Wales.) On the other hand, Ewyas Lacy is fortunate, compared with Hereford diocese, in that far more of its inventories survive into the 19th century. In the Hereford diocese inventories survive only until 1771, and after about 1760 give virtually no detail. This equates to survival levels elsewhere in England.

Information from the documents for Ewyas Lacy, and comparisons with studies elsewhere, allow us to consider questions such as: What influence did their isolation and proximity to the Welsh border exert on the lifestyle and farming methods of the people in their customs, innovations and language? How convenient was access to transport systems for their surplus goods? Over the 300-year period did stocking densities increase, the numbers of livestock rise, and the range of crops grown vary, (as Overton found they did in Norfolk from the 13th until well into the 17th century)?[2] Was there a growth in luxury goods in the inventories and wills? What was the likely influence exerted by the chief landowners of the district? What was the position of women in local society, and what part did faith play in the life of the community?

By tackling these and other questions through using wills and inventories it is hoped that this study might serve to introduce probate documents to a wider audience, and demonstrate how immensely valuable they can be in genealogical and other ways. They throw light on relationships, show how matters developed over the centuries and, while not 'bringing people back to life', they at least remove them from the obscurity in which they have lain for too long.

If it sounds as though I have only used information gleaned from the probate records, this is not the case. I have made use of all the available strands of information including census records, court rolls, leases, parish registers, and taxes, including hearth and land taxes, which exist for the Ewyas Lacy Hundred. By using a combination of these sources I hope I have caught something of this distinctive community on the Welsh Marches, balanced on the edge of the modern world, and between two different cultures: the Welsh and the English. Indeed, even today, in out of the way places it is still possible to catch the flavour of that former world, as anyone who has read Bruce Chatwin's *On the Black Hill* will know.

Despite the extensive research there are still many questions left unanswered in a broad sweep of the subject, such as this has necessarily been. The reader may wish to know more about the diseases that carried off so many people, especially children, during the period, and why there is no record of any physicians. Others may wish to explore the subject of apprenticeships, or how much pewter or brass people's homes contained. It is hoped that the addition of these wills and inventories to the multitude of other available sources will now make this possible.

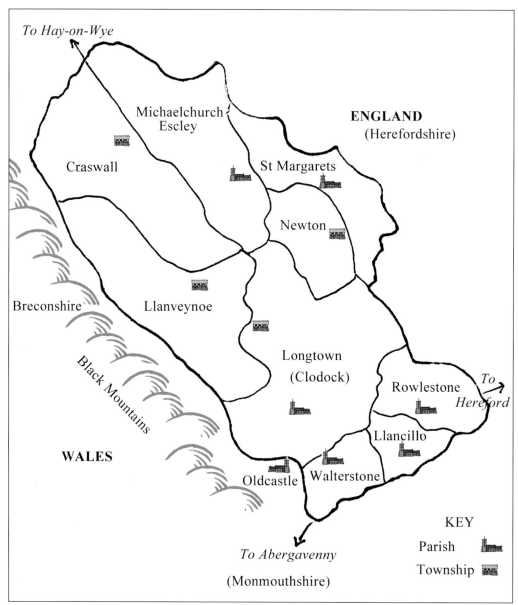

To Hay-on-Wye

ENGLAND
(Herefordshire)

Michaelchurch
Escley

Craswall

St Margarets

Newton

Breconshire

Llanveynoe

Longtown
(Clodock)

Rowlestone

To
Hereford

Black Mountains

Llancillo

WALES

Oldcastle

Walterstone

To Abergavenny

(Monmouthshire)

KEY

Parish

Township

Map showing Ewyas Lacy Hundred, with its parishes and townships

1 THE EARLY HISTORY OF EWYAS LACY

The situation of the Hundred of Ewyas Lacy is a grand one, settled as it is under the towering backdrop of the Black Mountains on the edge of Herefordshire. These hills run along the length of the Hundred with the wildest and roughest terrain under their lea, where the ruin of the 13th-century de Lacy castle at Longtown still stands. Long before the castle was built there is evidence of the Bronze Age in a burial cyst in the Olchon Valley, and an Iron Age hill fort at Walterstone. Later, it was thought that there were Roman remains in the vicinity of Clodock, but evidence seems to suggest that the Roman army marched no closer than through the Golden Valley to the east of the region.

West of the Golden Valley was frontier territory, and though a quiet place now, it was for centuries a place of violent clashes between the Welsh and their English neighbours over the border. Still a wild area today, echoing to the cries of buzzards and ravens, before the Norman Conquest this district was a Welsh commote known as Ewias. Hundreds were already an established feature of much of England by the 10th century, but the region west of the Golden Valley remained beyond the reach of Anglo-Saxon administration.

Celtic remains are abundant across the Hundred. One interesting relic of the 9th century is a stone slab, found under the nave of Clodock church during restoration work in the early 20th century, with a dedication in Latin to the memory of the wife of Guinndas, 'a native of this place'. The slab was subsequently found in a cupboard when Clodock vicarage was being demolished in 1959, and a rubbing was sent to the Society of Antiquaries for identification. The church which houses this stone is itself a memorial to early Christianity in this place and was founded in memory of the Celtic saint Clydawg, a son of the King of Ewias, who was murdered near the site in the 6th century.[1]

The 9th-century stone that commemorates Guinndas in Clodock church

Another important Celtic saint, St Beuno (c.600 A.D), was given an impressive site for a church above the Olchon Valley at Llanveynoe, by the King of Caerwent. Beuno is mostly associated with north Wales and is supposed to have

Llanveynoe church

died at Clynnog in the Lleyn peninsula in around 648 AD. The present church of St Beuno and St Peter is a replacement of 13th century date. Two memorial stones, discovered during the 19th century and dating possibly from the 9th or 10th century, or even earlier, were incorporated into the church wall during the building of an extension to the church in 1912. These have formed a fascinating focus for conjecture ever since as they indicate a very early, possibly monastic, cemetery. A short-arm-cross of Celtic origin, the only one of its type in the county, was discovered lying under the churchyard wall by Alfred Watkins in 1929 and re-erected in the churchyard. Another cross was discovered as recently as 2005 almost hidden on the north wall and opposite another set into the south wall, bringing the total number of ancient stone crosses in and around the church to five. The short-arm-cross can be placed in the context of what we know of early Celtic Christianity which had been adopted by most people in this area by the 5th century. This was before St Augustine brought the Roman tradition of Christianity to Britain.[2]

After the loss of influence of the Celtic church at the Synod of Whitby in 664 over the question of when Easter should be held, this area came under the diocese of Llandaff. However, after a dispute between Urban of Llandaff and Bernard, the Norman bishop of St Davids, as to which see had jurisdiction, the two sides presented their case before the archbishops of Canterbury, York and Rouen at Rheims in 1133 and Bernard emerged the victor. From thenceforth all the parishes of Ewyas Lacy came under the spiritual governance of the diocese of St Davids until the 19th century.[3]

Offa, who was King of Mercia from 757, made an attempt to mark a boundary between his kingdom and the Welsh by building a massive dyke, though the Wye appears to have formed the southern part of this border beginning from just north of Hereford. In 1055 Welsh soldiers sacked Hereford and laid waste to the neighbouring Golden Valley.

Firm government was only imposed when this Welsh region, governed by Welsh law, was given, after the Norman Conquest, to the de Lacy family to govern in the 11th century:

witness the castles that were built along the Welsh border and the remains of motte and bailey sites scattered around the Hundred as at Llancillo, Rowlestone and Walterstone. Ewias became the Hundred of Ewyas Lacy under courts Baron and Leet administering customary law. Longtown Castle was built in the 13th century but there are the remains of an earlier motte and bailey castle beside the road to Clodock church, at Pont Hendre; possibly the one mentioned as captured by the Welsh in 1146. Longtown Castle was probably built as a replacement, probably no later than 1223. It had the distinction of being paid a visit by Henry III on his way from Hay to Abergavenny in early September 1233.[4]

Longtown Castle stands on a spur overlooking the Olchon and the Monnow valleys in a rectangular enclosure, or bailey, of around 3 acres. The site's rectangular shape earlier led people to suppose that the castle had been built on the site of a Roman fort, but so far there is complete lack of any archeological evidence to support this. A dig in 1869 produced what may have been footings of medieval date and these were thought to be Roman at the time. The castle keep has an unusually early circular shape. Not only were these cheaper to build but they were an improvement on the previous square or rectangular design as missiles tended to bounce off the curved stonework.

The keep has three projections on the outside, first, a spiral staircase linking the main floor to the upper storeys, then a chimney flue for the main floor, and a waste chute for a garderobe on the upper floor. There is a round-arched gateway flanked by semi-circular turrets leading from the outer bailey. This must have been a scene of much activity in its heyday during the 13th and 14th centuries, when the area around the castle must have been humming with activity. In addition to possibly wooden buildings in the inner bailey, which have disappeared, the de Lacys set up a borough, and burgage plots were laid out below the castle. A triangular market place was established in the shadow of the castle, and St Peters, a chapel-of-ease, was built just to the south. Later, an ale house was built next to the chapel, so the area must have continued to be a centre of activity until well beyond the medieval period. Less attractively, there was a gallows just outside the castle which was in use up until the 19th century.[5]

Longtown Castle, with the keep on its motte and the wall and gateway to the inner bailey

The Hundred must have seemed quite a cosmopolitan place to any visitor of the time as the place was full of people speaking not only Welsh but Latin, Norman French and English. Hugh de Lacy issued instructions to his servants 'whether French, English or Welsh'.[6]

The castle's last major defensive action was probably at the time of the Owain Glyndwr rebellion after which it was virtually abandoned, and there is nothing to suggest that it was used during the Civil War.[7]

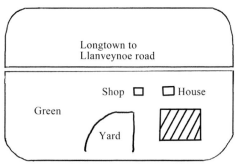

A redrawn map of Longtown Castle in 1718 showing the presence of a shop and house

The de Lacys were concerned not only with military security, but with spiritual safeguards too. In 1222 they founded a religious house at Craswall, which they dedicated to St Mary, staffed by ten chaplains and three priests and a prior. They gave the foundation to Grandmont Abbey in Normandy where their ancestors were buried. This grant was well supported by gifts of land from Henry III and subsequent kings. The Grandmontine Order was established by St Stephen of Thiers in the Limousin in around 1078, and moved to Grandmontine in 1124. The most austere of all monastic orders, the Grandmontine monks, or hermits as they chose to call themselves, wore the roughest of clothing (sackcloth next to the skin) covered by a brown tunic, were vegetarians and did not keep sheep or cattle for fear of antagonising the farming community around them, living rather on alms for their existence; all shared the same cubicle style accommodation. One of their duties was to offer prayers and masses for the de Lacy family.[8]

During a visit made by the Woolhope Club in 1904 a coffin was discovered containing a large skeleton which crumbled away on exposure to the air. Placed in a prominent position in front of a step leading to the high altar, it was thought that it might well have been the remains of a member of the de Lacy family.[9] When a Mr Llewellin visited the site in the early 20th century it took him three attempts to find it, so remote from civilization was it. (This could be said of the whole area of the Hundred during much of the three centuries of the probate documents. The roads were appalling and communication slow which ensured that much of the territory had become isolated, and was described so by visitors in the 19th century.)[10] Considerable decay of the stonework has taken place since the early 20th century, as brambles and ivy grew up over the stones and sheep wandered amongst them, but has now been halted due to the efforts of The Craswall Grandmontine Society and the support of English Heritage.

With the Act of Union in 1536 the district became part of Herefordshire.[11] As a result of the process that led to the Act, the countryside was more peaceful, and with the dissolution of the monasteries ownership of land became more widespread; the gentry, in particular, profiting by it in the 16th century, with heavy investment in land and grand houses. The population figures, after earlier rapid growth, stabilized and were kept in check by outbreaks of the plague.

Relative peace and prosperity in the first three decades of the 17th century was followed by the turbulent years of the Civil War. There was a skirmish at Ewyas Harold on 13

November 1642, when the first soldiers were killed in the district. Later, in 1645, when King Charles was being hunted through Herefordshire, Parliamentarian guards were quartered at Rowlestone.[12] The years after the Restoration, in the late 17th century, saw a depression in agriculture, with landowners finding it difficult to find tenants, let alone be paid the rents they asked for.

One of the many mountain streams flowing into the Olchon

Herefordshire's roads were notoriously awful, and being land-locked, the county could not easily rely on the sea for transport. Even so, the area is home to a multitude of streams and waterfalls which make their way down from the Black Mountains to the three main rivers of the Hundred – the Olchon, the Monnow and the Escley – and thence into the river Wye and the Bristol Channel. In the past, transport would have been down the rivers, notably the Wye, which was fed by the Monnow, to Bristol and beyond.

Despite a further depression in the 1730s and 1740s because of poor harvests which led to food shortages and high levels of mortality (confirmed locally by the Clodock parish registers), by the mid 18th century populations were again growing rapidly, with London in particular drawing in all the produce it could to feed the numbers flocking to it from the surrounding countryside.

During the century that followed, from 1750 to 1850, agricultural output (including cereal and livestock) more than doubled, with the Napoleonic Wars an especially prosperous time for farmers, though, as bread became more expensive from 1795, people began using potatoes instead. John Duncumb, who wrote an account of the agriculture of Herefordshire in 1805, claimed that 'potatoes were gaining ground every year ... They are applied to fatten pigs with great success'.[13] The 1790s were tough times generally. Bread was not only more expensive but also in short supply and there were riots nationwide. New taxes came into force as the cost of the war against the French mounted. Yet despite heavy taxes on carriages, servants and hair powder (made from wheat), landowners remained a prosperous section of society. William Cobbett, writing scornfully of 19th-century farmers, described the aggrandised farmhouse with its parlours, carpets, pianos for their daughters and expensive furniture. Did this apply to Ewyas Lacy? Profits translated into a boom in building as houses were extended or rebuilt, all of which we may, or may not, find evidence of in the wills and inventories.[14]

It has been suggested that as there were about a hundred burgesses in Longtown by 1310, there were probably around 500 people then living there. It would be surprising, given the lack of statistics on the population before the census returns that commenced in 1801, if we were able to give a firm figure on levels of population for Ewyas Lacy during the intervening years. Historians have tried with varying success to compile figures, using the taxes of Henry VIII in the 16th century, the hearth tax of 1664, Bishop Compton's census

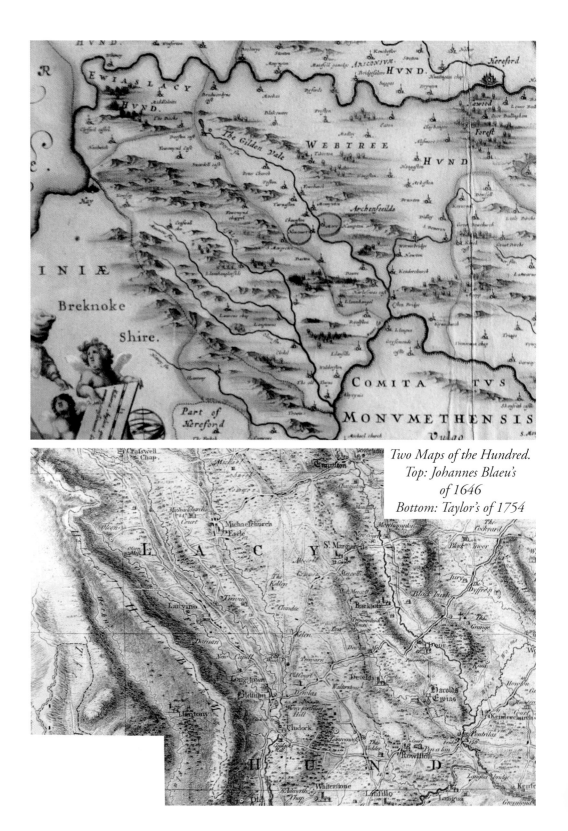

Two Maps of the Hundred.
Top: Johannes Blaeu's
of 1646
Bottom: Taylor's of 1754

and figures sent in by incumbents of the parishes in 1707. Accuracy is difficult because there are gaps in almost all the figures. Henry VIII's tax omits the poor, St Margaret's parish does not appear under Ewyas Lacy's hearth tax but under Madley's, and the Compton Census leaves out half the Hundred. It seems, however, that the population must have fluctuated from roughly 2,000 in the mid 16th century to about 3,000 in the mid 19th century (when the figure for England and Wales had grown from 5 million to 17 million).

The focus of this region was towards Wales and the Welsh border counties, partly because of their close proximity and the origin of many of the inhabitants, and partly because ecclesiastical control came from that direction. Nevertheless, wills from the National Archives show that there were numbers of local gentlemen with contacts with the wider world to the east, people like William Cecil of Alltyrynys, cousin of Sir Robert Cecil the son of Lord Burleigh, who was probably the most powerful man in the kingdom in the late 16th century. Sir Robert was mentioned in William's will in 1597. Apart from people like Cecil, there were, particularly in the latter part of the 17th century, few large landowners to give leadership. The earls of Abergavenny never lived on their estates in Ewyas Lacy; these were administered for them by a steward during the 300 years under review. Nicholas Arnold, another owner of a manor and advowsons (the right to appoint the local clergy, often enabling a landowner to benefit members of his family), lived a few miles away at Llanvihangel Crucorney, and his property was sold on to the Earl of Oxford in 1720, together with other parts of the Hundred.[15] The advowson for Clodock changed hands several times, at one time being in the ownership of the Vaughans and latterly possessed by the de Winton family of Glasbury. The right to reclaim income from the benefice in the form of tithes was sold to a Herefordshire landowner, George Cornewall of Moccas,[16] who also owned land in Michaelchurch Escley. In around 1700 another part of the manor of Ewyas Lacy was obtained by absentee landlord John Jeffreys of Brecon, and a further part was owned by Sir John Williams, who did not live in the Hundred. However, the Heralds Visitation of Herefordshire in 1634 shows that there was scarcely a parish in the Hundred that did not have a resident armigerous family in the early 17th century, some, like the Scudamores of Llancillo, and the de la Hayes and Vaughans of Walterstone, with links to greater families in the area. Junior branches remained in the area for decades.

The will of Henry Thomas ap Richard of Clodock in 1563 mentions a debt of £20 owed by Rowland Vaughan of the neighbouring Golden Valley. There was no lack of entrepreneurial activity taking place at the end of the 16th century in the Golden Valley: Rowland Vaughan's experiment on 300 acres of water meadows along the river Dore must have been noted by his neighbours.[17] Was he borrowing the money for his new venture?[18] My guess is that a few men in the district would have espoused the latest techniques but that the mass of farmers would have farmed pretty much as their fathers had before them.

Mark Overton and Bruce Campbell consider in their paper on farming in Norfolk[19] that the greatest rise in technology and productivity of the six centuries studied took place after 1740, due to such factors as a better fed and more hard-working labour force, the elimination of peasant smallholdings and the replacement of open field agriculture by independently owned larger farms. Apart from the absence of open field systems in Ewyas Lacy, the presence of small mixed family run farms seems to have militated against much of this progress, abetted by the absence of good road systems and efficient marketing organizations. G.E. Mingay writes that, in England, family farms formed nearly half the farms in 1830, and that the situation was relatively unchanged by the mid 19th century, when this study ends.[20] I would suggest that in Ewyas Lacy this figure would be considerably higher, especially in the earlier period.

Anne Kussmaul's interesting study of marriage seasonality[21] suggests that there was a change from arable to pastoral farming by the latter half of the 17th century in this region. With the decline in grain prices in the mid 17th century a pastoral region would have specialized in farming what it knew would do best – animal husbandry was the order of the day at Ewyas Lacy, especially cattle rearing. This generally meant late spring marriages (from May and tapering off by July), as confirmed by the bishop's marriage register. Over the first four decades of the 18th century, in the combined parishes of Clodock, Longtown, Craswall and Llanveynoe, out of 58 entries (there were usually just two or three marriages a year, sometimes only one or even none) the favoured month for a wedding was May (with 15), with eight in June. However, there was another cluster of marriages that took place in the earliest months of the year, with eight in January and ten in February, trailing off in March when lambing and calving would begin. The times of Advent and Lent appeared to be observed, with no marriages in December before the 29th.

Mingay claims that travellers to the county by the mid to late 18th century saw increasing numbers of a breed of cattle known as Herefords. These were a cross between the indigenous breed and Dutch blood.[22] Remarkably, there is a mention of what are almost certainly Herefords, if not then described as such, much earlier, in the will of John Harry Maddock of Clodock, on 30 April 1611. In his will he leaves to 'John David Phillipp my Cosen one Bull of twoe yeare olde coloured redd', and in the next line, 'unto Thomas ap Iein my Cosen twoe heifers of twoe yeare olde the one coloured redd the other redd with white face'. There is another reference, not quite as specific, in widow Johan Myles' will of 1693, where she mentions a red bullock.

Sheep farming trailed well behind in popularity, oddly, considering the dominating presence of the Black Mountains and their rough terrain. Both Joan Thirsk and Mark Overton claim that sheep are under-recorded in inventories, but was it the case here?[23] That hardy sheep, the Ryeland, was being bred by the latter half of the 18th century, mainly for wool and to subsist on the poor hill pasture of Herefordshire and the other counties hugging the Welsh Border.[24] It seems unlikely that the local farmers would have spurned such a useful animal. It will be interesting generally to see whether stocking densities increased over the 300 years of this study, as Overton says they did in Norfolk.

Cider was a vital product of Herefordshire, in which it was a foremost producer and supplier to a wide area, including Bristol but chiefly London. Lord Scudamore of Holme Lacy had been making cider as early as 1667;[25] there is evidence from the inventories of large quantities of cider being made at Ewyas Lacy also.

Anne Kussmaul also mentions that a resident of Herefordshire in 1677 asserts that clover was already being grown here;[26] however, there are only a few late 18th-century references to this crop in the Ewyas Lacy inventories.

Apart from clover, what other crops were being grown by the farmers in the parishes around Clodock? Oats and barley were more likely to be grown in the wetter west of the country, and there is evidence of this in the inventories for Ewyas Lacy. Naturally, oats and barley feature often as these were fetching high prices. By the end of the 18th century 9,000 tons of grain and meal were sent annually from Herefordshire to Bristol, down the Wye, together with 2,000 tuns of cider.[27] Hereford was the main town, but had a small population even by the latter half of the 18th century, so surpluses were forced outwards to larger conurbations. Were there surpluses from Ewyas Lacy, and if so, in which direction did they go?

The river Wye was the main vehicle, apart from the pack horse, for the transport of surplus goods, and complaints were made that even that was difficult to navigate at times. Manufactured items and coal were not imported until a canal was completed from Newent to Ledbury in 1798. The arrival of the canal meant that goods could begin to be exported to the Midlands and the North as well as Bristol and London, and indeed, goods could come the other way too.[28] How far did the Hundred benefit from the arrival of the canal, seeing that it was so far from it and with such poor roads, often deep in mud even in the 19th century according to contemporary accounts?

Welsh Connections

Ewyas Lacy's close proximity to the Welsh border was bound to have an influence on the Hundred, quite apart from the fact that it had once been considered a part of Wales. The geographical alignment shows in a number of ways. There are numerous Welsh names for farms and fields and the district is peppered with names like Cwm, Wern or Tyr attached to farmhouses, or Ty for a cottage. Cae means field, so Cae Croon means round field; Gwrlod means meadow.

Even more telling is the predominance of Welsh surnames in the area. Names like Price, Powell and Watkins abound, many of whose owners may have migrated over the border originally looking for better pasture. With this came the prevalence of patronymics, where names are taken from one's father or ancestor. In Michael Faraday's paper on Herefordshire taxes he comments on the fact that in spite of a steady decline, there were still an exceptionally large number of people with Welsh names using this system in the mid 16th century.[29] This would apply even to daughters. A clear case occurs in the will of William George, whose daughters were Anne and Catherine William. One bequest in his will, dated 1631, was to Howell ap David. However, in the same will the testator also named a Hugh Powell and his daughter, Catherine Powell, indicating a declining use of patrimony. The custom, which seems to die out in the first half of the 17th century, accounts for the sometimes confusing use of what might be thought of as Christian names both fore and aft. An extreme example is that of a yeoman, Lewis John Thomas Williams, in 1665.

For centuries English land measurement was ignored in favour of 'customary Welsh measure' in this border country. There are many examples of this in the Court Rolls, and in the wills and inventories up until the 19th century. Lewis John Thomas Williams left a cottage and 2 acres of 'welsh measure' in Llanveynoe. In Lewis Jenkins' will of 1670 he mentions a messuage called Blackhill 'containing 6 acres of welsh measure' in Craswall. Not until the 1730s was English measurement given and it seemed necessary in 1740 to explain the difference between the two in a lease, viz. 'one messuage together with 25 acres of customary Welsh measure (that is to say) a hundred acres of Winchester measure'. That this measure was variable is shown in an 1812 lease to James Jones of Longtown of '4 acres Welsh' which was translated into 10 acres. The Welsh 'cyfar', meaning 'acre', occurs in many of the Abergavenny leases. As late as 1775 it was used to describe a 'rough close called Cae Coch, of 15 covers in Craswall township'.[30]

Gavelkind, or equal inheritance, also operated in this district. Chambers' *Twentieth Century Dictionary* describes gavelkind as an old Saxon or Welsh form of tenure by which an estate passed to all the sons equally. In her study of Monmouthshire wills, Judith Jones noticed the use of gavelkind in Monmouthshire in the early 17th century, even on the anglicized borders.[31] In neighbouring Ewyas Lacy this system seemed to apply not only to sons but to daughters also. Among the many examples, in 1708 Walter Harry's estate passed, after his wife's death, in equal parts to the four youngest children, two sons and two daughters. In this instance it applied only to the youngest children, but there are several examples of the system applying to all the children. In the 1740s Noah Symonds left his estate, after his wife's death, to both his sons equally. The grandchildren, three girls and a boy, of Rowland Jennings, a gentleman of The Wayne, inherited his estate in equal shares in 1748 (his son, Rowland, having died 6 years before) and they were all made executors.

There were other connections with Wales too. For many centuries and until the mid 19th century Welsh ecclesiastical courts, rather than those at Hereford, dominated probate affairs. This involved the watchful eye of the archdeacon of Brecon, supervised by the bishop of St Davids. Most wills went to the probate court at Brecon which entailed a long and difficult journey over the hills for the executors (though now only an hour's journey by car). This was where the local clergy had a part to play as surrogates for the courts, but people still made the journey, unless they were sick or aged, and the clergy pleaded on their behalf. The wealthier members of the community tended to prefer to have their wills probated by the Prerogative Court of Canterbury, meaning their wills can be found at the National Archive, at Kew.

Hereford market was too far away for many to carry their goods so it was natural that they should go either to Abergavenny, in Monmouthshire, for those in the southern part of the Hundred, or Hay-on-Wye for those in the north, such as those who lived in Michaelchurch Escley.

A type of dialect known as 'Herefordshire Welsh' existed in the area in the 19th century and a Welsh inflection remains today amongst some of the older generation. This comes through earlier in some of the wills. One example is that of William Rogers, yeoman, in 1739, where the name Richard Davis is written phonetically as 'Richet davice', and 'good shoes' becomes 'good shoos'. A few of the administration papers actually state that the substance of the will had to be explained to the dying man in Welsh, for instance that of Lewis Powell, husbandman in 1749, or David Price, yeoman, three years earlier. A century earlier, in the 1650s, the Revd John Delahay wrote to the ecclesiastical authorities to protest that the living of Clodock had been promised him and that as he spoke Welsh he would be better understood by the local people 'of whom the majority spoke only Welsh'. Letters from a subaltern at the start of the Civil War seem to confirm this as he writes that the Welsh language was still spoken by many even in Hereford.[32]

2   PROBATE

Let not Ambition mock their useful toil,
Their homely joys and destiny obscure;
Nor Grandeur hear, with a disdainful smile,
The short and simple annals of the poor.
(From Gray's 'Elegy in a Country Churchyard')

On 18 October 1745, a yeoman called David Price lay dying in his house at Craswall. Although he had been ill, it had not occurred to him before to make his will, or perhaps he was afraid of the finality of it. Thomas Price, then a middle-aged man of 37, happened to be out when he was sent for to 'draw' the dying man's will and testament. On hearing of the request from his mother when he got home, he immediately went and took down David Price's instructions in Welsh, read them back to him in English and explained the will in Welsh which was 'very well Approved'. David Price, in the sight of two witnesses, then made his mark (a wavery scrawl). He had cut it a bit fine, for he died that night.

The two witnesses were able to sign their names, so it may have been because of his weakness that David Price could not. The witnesses were Thomas Williams the elder, aged 55, and Thomas Williams the younger, aged 27, two hoop makers working nearby for the testator's brother Robert. Thomas Williams the elder says in his statement that on the 18th the testator's maid came to where they were working, saying that her mistress wanted to speak to them at the house. They were then taken upstairs where Thomas Price produced the will, which the testator signed, and which they then witnessed.

There are many interesting features arising from this sad little scene, but the one I want to concentrate on is the clear process we are given of will-making, starting with the anxious testator, and his or her friends or workers being called to write or witness the will. Then follows the necessity of having it read over to the testator, often in both English and Welsh. In this case we also have the depositions made by three witnesses, adding both clarity and detail to the events.

That we have such detail is because the will was contested by Robert, the brother of David Price. Robert was contesting the will as almost everything, including the lease on David's house and land that he held of Lord Abergavenny, was left to Ann, the dying man's 'well beloved wife', who was also made the executrix. Robert had been left five shillings, so it may be that the bone of contention was the land. The inventory, valued at only £20, was taken on 23 October, only five days later; this was not unusual. His clothes were worth, for a yeoman, a fairly substantial £1 10s. The appraisers were Thomas Price (in all probability the same man who drew up the will) and John Jenkins.

In the event, Ann Price got justice, as the will was finally passed for probate on 26 May 1746, seven months later. In the meantime no fewer than ten people had been drawn in – the bishop of St Davids, the deputy registrar at Brecon, Richard Reece the vicar of Clodock and the original seven who met round the deathbed: David Price, his wife Ann, the maid, the greedy brother and the three witnesses. The bishop had to write to the clergy of Ewyas Lacy – who at that time were Richard Reece, Phillip Price, John Price and Thomas Higgins – to 'instruct and empower' them to get Ann Price to take an oath to the truth of the will, that she would administer his goods 'towards the payment of his Debts and Legacies ... as far as his Goods Cattle and Chattells will extend', to take an inventory and make an account which had to be exhibited at the Archdeaconry of Brecon. The irony was that the original reason for making wills had been to avoid family quarrels; unsuccessful in this case.

Thomas Price, who drew up the will, had been involved with another contested will two years earlier for Lewis Powell, a husbandman of the same parish. He had taken instruction 'by word of mouth' and the will was contested, again by a brother, William Powell, in spite of there being simply one beneficiary to whom Lewis left all his goods and chattels. Once again Thomas Price had to write the will in English, and then explain 'the substance of the same in Welsh'.[1]

In these two cases the dying had set about making their wills in the correct way. However there were two other situations that could make life difficult for the surviving members of the family: first, if the deceased left no will at all, dying 'intestate', or second, if he or she left a 'nuncupative' will, where the instructions were given verbally by the testator on his deathbed and there was no signature. One example of the latter is the will of William Brood, a bachelor of Michaelchurch Escley who died in 1670 leaving only his clothes and a bond due to him of just over £15. Another was that of David Maddocke, a yeoman of Llanveynoe in 1673.

Wills

Wills have been made since time immemorial, were positively encouraged by the medieval church, and could be made by females over 12 and males over 14 – the age of marriage. It seems that our attitudes to will-making have not changed much over the centuries as it is considered that in the past only about one third of the population made a will, pretty much the same proportion as make wills today.[2]

Quite apart from their legal significance to the testator's family, surviving wills are useful in a number of ways since they are the most numerous of personal documents to survive, supplying information for the social and economic historian over a considerable period of time. They give occupations and status, throw light on agricultural practice, give an idea of the relative importance of various groups in the community, open up information on relationships and families useful to the family historian, and indicate patterns of ownership of household goods and the early introduction of luxury goods. The ones from Ewyas Lacy are especially valuable, as most previous studies have been of urban areas.

On the other hand there are considerable limitations to studies of wills as they cannot be taken entirely at face value. For instance, they survive for only a relatively small proportion of the population (probably only 20-40%), with a bias towards prosperous males. The wealthy needed to make wills to ensure that their property went to the people of their choice, though this does not mean that others did not make a will. Another bias is that of age as the tendency was to make a will only at the end of one's life. Historically, women were less likely to appear as will makers as, unless they were widowed, they had little or nothing to leave. At Uffculme in Devon only about one fifth of the surviving wills were made by women, and this figure seems to be true of Ewyas Lacy too.[3]

A further missing ingredient is usually the mention of any freehold estate, as that went automatically to the heir or heiress by law. Copyhold land (see also p.51) descended according to the custom of the manor.

In David Price's case we have already seen the process by which a will was made, and the wills generally followed a pattern, probably guided by the experienced will maker at the time. To state that the testator was 'of sound mind' was important as, for obvious reasons, lunatics could not make wills. After giving the date, there was a religious preamble which could vary in length from about half the will (for wills in the 16th and 17th century), dwindling to a mere line or two by the 19th century. Then came the bequests to the cathedral at St Davids (Ewyas Lacy was then in the diocese of St Davids), to the parish church, the family and the poor, with the residue of the estate mentioned last, together with the names of those entrusted with the management of the will, the executor (male), or executrix (female), very often adding that any bequests were on condition that all debts and legacies should be paid. An additional provision, where young children were involved, was the appointment of a guardian or overseer of the will, like Simon John when William Powell Madock died in 1631 leaving his 'reputed' son Harry, who was a minor, as his executor. In 1649 John Price, a gentleman of St Margarets, made his young son his executor, while making his wife his son's guardian.

If the testator was able, he then signed the will watched by the witnesses, who then signed themselves, or made their 'mark'. These marks can be an interesting study in their own right as they range from a simple cross to something much more elaborate. In 1697, for example, a gentleman, Walter Delahay, made a mark like an agitated spider instead of signing as one would expect a gentleman to do. Some managed at least the first letter of their names, others up to three letters.

Unique to Ewyas Lacy, but used sparingly, is the mention of 'Standards', which seemed to equate to heirlooms, or pieces of furniture (usually) to be left in the house and considered as being attached to the freehold as if a fixture. This was possibly done to affirm one's position, or newly arrived status. Bedsteads seemed the favourite choice for this and these were chosen by David Nicholls of Craswall in 1728, Noah Jenkins of Clodock in 1766 and Philip Beavan of Newton in 1731, all yeomen. However, Edmund Thomas, Esq. of Michaelchurch Escley, who had the distinction of having his will proved at the Prerogative Court of Canterbury, required, in July 1744, that, while his wife had the use of all the contents for life, half the plate and furniture was to stay with the house.

Wills sometimes literally cut people off 'with a shilling'. This seems to have been a legal device whereby someone in the family who might otherwise have contested the will, was left with a shilling; he could not then claim to have been excluded from the will. One of the clearest examples of this lies in Thomas Seaborne's will of 1842 where he bequeathes his son, Thomas, '1/- to cut him off the property'. A century earlier, in 1730, Thomas Mabe, a shoemaker, clearly annoyed with his son Foster who owed him money, left him one shilling, and in 1797 a husband, John Jones of Craswall, left his wife only one shilling if she remarried.

This last bequest shows that considerable leverage could be used in wills to try to make people do the testator's bidding, especially where marriage was concerned. Attempts to control not only wives but daughters from beyond the grave were numerous. In 1575 Harrie Powell, yeoman of Michaelchurch Escley, left instructions that his daughter Katherine was to get £60 on the date of her marriage – but only if she married with the consent of the executors. William Phillips of Fair Oake in St Margarets was even more emphatic in his will of 11 May 1728, stating that he was leaving a messuage at 'St Wainyards' to his granddaughter, Joan Phillips, when she reached the age of 21, with the proviso 'that if she shall be stoborn and undutiful to her parents' and contract marriage 'without thyre consent undervalling her Fortune', her father and mother were to take the profits. In one case, that of Edmund Thomas, Esq. of Michaelchurch Escley, his will in 1758 consisted of five pages of complex instructions covering virtually every eventuality within a trust controlled by four trustees.

Who were the people who physically wrote the wills? Most likely they were people of standing in the community who were recognised as being skilled in this area, often clergymen, but perhaps by the 18th century this task was more often taken by other professional men such as the manorial steward. An example is that of the will of Thomas Price, a yeoman of Llanveynoe, which was written by Job Gilbert, Abergavenny's steward, in 1740. As befitted Job Gilbert's powerful position in the community, his own will was proved in 1749 by the Prerogative Court of Canterbury. There is at least one example of a will written by the testator themselves, in this case a woman, Constant Tomlins of Clodock. From the late 17th century there were publications available for the guidance of will writers. One by George Meriton was cheap enough at 1s 6d to be purchased by most country gentlemen and even yeomen.[4]

In the 17th century the task was almost invariably undertaken by the clergy, whose involvement was crucial in such a remote district as Ewyas Lacy. They undertook various tasks that followed the making of the will, such as administering the oath required for a nuncupative will, and acting as surrogate for the church courts in the case of people unable to attend. In 1671 John Delahay, vicar of Clodock, and William Allen, curate of Michaelchurch Escley, administered the oath for the will of Edmund Thomas, gent of Michaelchurch Escley. Four years later, William Allen again administered the oath, this time for John Maddocks of the same parish. Charles Probert, one of the most active vicars of Clodock in the 19th century, supervised the probate of William Jenkins' will as well as undertaking the writing of letters to the court on the part of the bereaved. He also was not only witness, and executor, but writer of the will of Thomas Penry, a Longtown innkeeper in 1856. Sometimes vicars were too preoccupied to write their own wills. One such was the vicar of Clodock in 1814, the Revd Thomas Bowen, but his death may have been sudden.

Executors were able to 'renounce' this onerous task and appoint someone else if they were physically disabled, or did not want to be held liable for the debts of the deceased. An example of the first case was Jane, the widow of Harry Rees of Clodock in 1662, who was unable 'to ride or go' and who appointed John Pugh to act for her. This substitute would usually be a close relation. On rare occasions, money was left in the will to pay the executor for their trouble. In 1640 Thomas Powell of Llanveynoe was careful to allow his executor, Charles Jennings, to keep 'all his charges and expenses' out of the goods left. John Symmonds, a bachelor of Craswall who died in 1768, paid Philip Parry, father of his goddaughter, to whom he had left 'six yearling ewes', £4 'for his pains' in executing the will. He was, no doubt, unwilling to burden his elderly parents, John and Mary, with the task, though he left them his leasehold cottage and land. In 1857, Hannah Williams of Newton Cottage left £10 to each of her executors 'for their trouble' in supervising her complex will.

The tasks undertaken by the executor were many, and must have been daunting even for a young person, let alone the elderly on whom the burden would generally fall. After swearing an oath as to the validity of the will, which was usually organized by the vicar of the parish, letters of 'admonition' were issued by the court giving permission to 'administer' the deceased's estate. Then there was the long and difficult journey of 20 miles over the hills to Brecon, via Crickhowell or Hay, by cart or on horseback, by the grieving widow or other relation. Even today the journey to Brecon by car takes about an hour on good roads.

Intestacy was a real headache as the executor or administrator then entered into a bond with another person, possibly a relative, for about double the value of the estate, as a guarantee that the estate would be dealt with efficiently. Then the wife, husband or kinsman would be instructed to administer the estate, and provide an inventory of the goods and an account to show that all debts had been settled. After 1600 the bond gave the names of two bondsmen and this was formalised in 1670.[5] As far as bonds are concerned, the puzzle is that the amount of surety bore no relation to the value of the inventory. In a ten-year sample taken of bonds for pre-Restoration Clodock the sureties varied widely, but, for one year in particular, the surety was always £100, or £200 for inventories worth from only 10s to £51 3s 6d. It is a mystery that anyone would be prepared to stand surety for such amounts, unless they were notional.

One aggrieved executor, Phillipp Thomas Prees of Michaelchurch, left details of some of the problems and the costs that he faced in 1646 on behalf of the testator, Abraham Powell. One of the reasons for his agreeing to be executor was that Prees was owed sums of money from the estate. He writes to the court that he had had the expense of having the will engrossed and sealed, calling 'John William Prichard to waive his caveat'. Then he had to draw two inventories, pay 2s for a bond and then 'for this accompatants paines and travel in goeing to Brecon at three several times' he asked to be allowed expenses of 6s. In all he paid out, in charges, a total of £1 19s 3d. The money owed him amounted to £1 19s 7d so he had recouped a net amount of 4d. However, as in addition he had paid £4 7s 8d for all the funeral expenses and the goods and chattels were only worth £4 17s 4d it is not clear how, after legacies were paid out, he was going to be paid unless there was further money to be obtained from the estate.

An inventory was usually considered a sufficient check on the executor or administrator but in some cases, especially where the deceased had died intestate (leaving no will), or when a minor was involved, or when they had been specifically asked for, accounts had to be produced within a year or two after the administrator had been granted probate. The format for an account was fairly standard. It began with the total inventory value, then listed the disbursements including any payment for medical costs, any debts including a payment to the woman who cared for the deceased and prepared them for burial, and funeral expenses. All these debts were then subtracted from the credits. The accounts presented to the church court served two purposes: firstly, they relieved the administrator of further responsibility and secondly, they ensured that everything had been done in accordance with the dead person's will or, in cases of intestacy, to the satisfaction of the church court. In most dioceses the need for such accounts is for less than one case in a hundred, and the position in Ewyas Lacy seems similar. Under the Administration of Intestates' Estate Act of 1685 Act, an account prepared for the church court was only necessary when there was a dispute, or the relations asked for it, and these cases dwindle in number after the 17th century.[6]

Church Courts

The final destination of all these wills was the two main church courts, in the case of Ewyas Lacy either the Registry of the Brecon Archdeaconry, or the Prerogative Court of Canterbury. Ewyas Lacy is exceptionally fortunate, not only to have so many surviving probate documents, but to have them survive well into the 19th century. Survival of documents is a chancy business. One only has to remember the fire that destroyed most of the documents in the Houses of Parliament in 1834, or the bombing raid on Exeter in 1941 that destroyed almost the entire collection of wills and inventories for Devon, to realise their insubstantial nature. At Ewyas Lacy, the executor of Thomas Prichard of Rowlestone relates, in a deposition of 16 December 1729, that the will was mangled and torn by mice, having been placed in a cupboard for safe keeping six years before.

Despite the separation from Wales in the 1530s, all Ewyas Lacy's ecclesiastical business continued to be dealt with by the Diocese of St Davids, and the Archdeaconry of Brecon in particular. This continued until probate was transferred from church courts to civil probate registers, in this case Hereford, in 1858. For some reason the archdeacons had been prevented from carrying out visitations since 1665, which made contact with Ewyas Lacy especially difficult when the bishop himself spent much of his time in London. So it seems unlikely that people saw much of the archdeacons unless they had to visit the church court at Brecon themselves. There is an interesting description of one of these 19th-century Brecon archdeacons just before the responsibility for probate changed to Hereford, in Romilly's *Visits to Wales*: Richard Davies is recalled as being a handsome man, then in middle age, who had served as a major in the Militia from 1805 until his death in 1859. Some of the clergy had houses allocated them at St Davids in Pembrokeshire, and Davies' still stands in a quiet lane not far from the cathedral.[7]

The one exception to sending the probate records to Wales was if the testator owned land in more than one diocese or county, or had died abroad or at sea, in which case the documents would go to the main registry at the Prerogative Court of Canterbury, in London. There also seems to have been a certain snob value to dealing through the latter, as it may have been considered superior. The only other exception was during the Interregnum, when the church courts were abolished after the Civil War and everything had to go through Canterbury; there are no probated Ewyas Lacy wills held at the National Library of Wales between 1652 and 1660.

Inventories

Whatever his shortcomings as a husband, Henry VIII gets full marks from historians for his insistence on inventories being required by law from 1529. They had been made before then, but not in such numbers.[8] Unlike the Prerogative Court of Canterbury, who seem to have destroyed most of their inventories (those for Ewyas Lacy have either not survived or are so damaged as to be virtually unreadable) inventories for the Hundred at the National Library of Wales have survived in large numbers. Inventories are attached to most of the wills for Ewyas Lacy, in the 18th century assuming even greater importance as not one but two copies were made. By the 19th century there are fewer probate documents. In fact, it was interesting to discover that in the largest group, that for Clodock parish, inventories were far more numerous than wills (179 compared with 126), an indication, perhaps, of the large number of people who died intestate.

Inventories of the deceased's goods were usually drawn up within a short time of the death, generally within a few days, by people called 'appraisers' who would be the relations, friends or even creditors of the deceased. Hugh Morgan of Rowlestone's 1636 inventory states that it was drawn up by the 'parishioners and neighbours there'.

Similar limitations apply to inventories as to wills in that they were only compiled for a limited number of people nor can they be taken as an indication of the testator's true worth, interesting and full of detail though they are. The 1685 inventory of Philip Prichard of Rowlestone was valued at only £38 3s though he was able to leave monetary bequests of £200 in his will. In 1756, Milburne Prichard, possibly a descendant, of Vedow in Rowlestone, had an inventory valued at less than £20, though he owned at least two estates besides the one at Vedow; at Werndee and at Orcop. John Price, a gentleman of the Upper Cwm 'in Craswall', left only £46 13s in his inventory, but bequeathed four freehold estates in his will in 1804.

Also, the inventories will not necessarily show all the items that have been bequeathed as these may well already have been taken away. At the Wern in St Margarets some items such as the Great Bible, a table and bedstead, bequeathed by William Lewis to his brother John in his 1709 will, are missing from the inventory. One development that had taken place by 1635 was that items once considered moveables such as wainscot and glass were now fixtures, as were cheese and cider presses, and other heavy things such as malt mills and anvils, connected to a particular trade. In addition, by law, some of a woman's belongings such as her bed and personal items should be omitted from the inventory, but not everyone knew that. Fruit trees are omitted as they, legally, are supposed to come without any effort of man, as was hay, oddly enough. Hay, though, is quite often mentioned. Crops grown after breaking the ground went straight to the heir so need not be mentioned, though they often were, while saffron, hemp and hops could go to the executor as they were sown. Other items excluded were tea or tobacco and spices as they had no resale value.[9] Manure or dung heaps, and firewood were also supposed to be included; in Ewyas Lacy the first item was not often mentioned, firewood never.

The subject was a minefield, which is why probate needed the supervision of someone with training in the law, however superficial, or at least access to the law. For social and economic historians it is frustrating that there are many small things, usually labelled 'Trumpery', that are not considered worthy of mention, such as books, ornaments, or musical instruments.

The most dangerous omission as far as historians are concerned is that of the debts owed *by* the testator, although those owed *to* him are included. This can give a completely false impression of his or her wealth, and this is where an account, if there is one, comes in useful. Debts are usually noted down as either 'desperate' or 'specialty'. 'Desperate' speaks for itself, but in the case of the latter there would be a signed bond or bill that ensured its payment. It is probable that in such a close community as Ewyas Lacy even desperate debts were paid if at all possible. In the case of one widow, Joane Prees of Craswall 'relict of Thomas Lewis Prees' in 1637, she paid all his debts of whatever kind, even though it may have left her destitute.

Details from the Will and Inventory of William Walbieff of Clodock

William's will was dated 27 October 1648, His first wish was to be buried '... according to my rank within the parish church of Clodock', before detailing a number of bequests: 12 pence to the Cathedral church of St Davids; an indecipherable amount towards repairs to Clodock church; 20 shillings to the poor of the parish of Lanhamoulth, Breconshire (almost certainly this was Llanhamlech, the parish from which the Walbieff family originated) and 10 shillings to the poor of Longtown. To Robert Walbieff, his brother, he left £6 'to buy him a nagg' and 'to his dear wife Elizabeth ... all goods, cattell and chattels ... and all my household goods and stuff'. His wife was also to be his executor. (Elizabeth lived on until the 1660s in a house with four chimneys in Longtown.) The will was witnessed by Hugh Lewis, Paul Thomas, Phabian Phillipp, Magdalen Morgan, William Symond and Symond Graham John.

His inventory (with modernised spelling and numerals) is given below.

Item	£	s	d
Imprimis in ready money	6	0	0
Item his apparel	6	0	0
Item owing unto him by Roger Landon	5	12	0
Item owing unto him by John Symonds	6	8	0
Item in silver plate, two salt cellars and six spoons	2	10	0
Item one standing bed with a tester in his chamber over the buttery		8	0
Item two feather beds and bolster two blankest, one coverlid	6	12	0
Item in the same chamber one low bedstead one table board with a livery cupboard two chairs and 9 low stools with two [indecipherable] Andirons with one pair of tongs	2	0	0

18

Item	£	s	d
Item in the same chamber one table carpet and a carpet for the livery cupboard & one cushion		8	8
Item in the chamber over the Hall two bedsteads with one tester with three feather beds two bolsters three pillows two rugs three blankest two pair of curtains & valences	5	10	0
Item in the same chamber one press one coffer one little 'coobert' table three trunks one chair one little stool	2	0	0
Item in the maiden's chamber two bedsteads two feather beds two bolsters one pillow one coarse tick one rug one coverlet one table one old trunk one old coffer three small boxes	1	13	4
Item sixteen pairs of sheets one large damask table cloth two diaper table cloths five flaxen table cloths twenty diaper table napkins twelve flaxen table napkins twelve coarse table napkins four pillow beers	5	0	0
Item in the chamber in the gatehouse two bedsteads with one tester one pair of curtains with an old valence one feather bed two coarse ticks four bolsters with one old decayed 'vries' [frieze?] one coverlet two blankets with one little old table	1	10	0
Item in the parlour two tableboards two press cupboards one chest three chairs one little chair nine joint stools	1	10	0
Item in the hall one great table one little table two old chairs two benches		6	0
Item wooden vessels in the kitchen and elsewhere	1	0	0
Item in pewter of all sorts	1	13	4
Item brass of all sorts	2	13	4
Item In the Day house or Milk house two old tables		1	4
Item four iron spits or broaches one iron dripping pan two gobbards one pair of andirons one pair of tongs one fire shovel		7	0
Item hemp and flax		5	8
Item hay spent for the cattle	1	6	0
Item forty bushels of all sorts of corn and grain in the house threshed and winnowed	5	0	0
Item corn and grain in the barns unthreshed	5	0	0
Item six flitches of bacon & two quarters of beef	1	14	0
Item small lean hogs		13	4
Item seven kine	14	0	0
Item four oxen	10	0	0
Item two steers	3	0	0
Item five yearling and two-year old beasts	3	0	0
Item one bay mare	7	0	0
Item one grey mare and two old decayed lame horses	3	0	0
Item four and forty sheep remaining of a greater flock	2	10	0
Item corn now growing in the field	3	6	8
Item fire irunds [irons?]		10	0
Item implements of husbandry	1	5	0
Total	120	13	0

His assessors were Hugh Lewis, Phabian Phillipp, Henry Powell, Symond Abraham, John Jenkins, John Symonds, Edward Powell, John Watkins and Rees Prichard. The number of assessors for his inventory indicates the importance of William Walbieff. Much of his wealth seems to have derived from his wife Elizabeth whose first husband, James Watkins, died intestate in early 1645 with no heirs and so Elizabeth inherited. She must then have married William who moved into her house.

There has been some question in the past as to whether the values given in inventories were genuine or deflated, but now the general consensus of historians is that they were second-hand prices that could be fetched at local markets.[10] This was important, as the goods very often had to be sold to pay debts. In the case of specialised or shop goods the aim was to get values from those with inside knowledge in such matters, such as other shopkeepers.

Visiting the house of the recently dead must have been a distressing experience for the neighbours as they had to make a thorough search, even to searching in the pockets of the dead man's clothes, which they also had to assess, for any cash. There is a hint of the distaste felt by one appraiser after the death of James Price of Clodock in 1776 when 2s 6d was added to the bottom of the inventory list as 'Found in deced's pockets'. There are, however, records of the neighbours being given a meal during the course of their visit and this may have been quite common.[11]

Though they might have little to include in their inventory, paupers also made wills, especially if some little property was involved. Just before the outbreak of the Civil War, in 1640, Philip Griffiths of Clodock made his will. His inventory listed goods worth less than £1, including one broken pot worth 2d, one pair of 'ould' sheets, a suit worth 12d and a goose with six goslings and 'one henchicke'. Accentuating the pathos was the rare inclusion of 'one shrowd'. Walter Watkins, a yeoman of Longtown, left an inventory in 1708, written on a scrap of paper that was endorsed 'pauper', and valued at only 13s. His four children were left only 1s each, but his wife had some leasehold land on Maescoed Common which was probably the reason for the making of the will.

Another common misconception is that wills and inventories need only be for estates worth £5 or more. No estate inheritance tax was payable, but as it probably cost around 5s to make a will and a further 30s for the probate, this limited the number of people who could afford it. The court's administration fees were based on the value of the estate, with three bands used. When valued at £5 or less they could be exempt except for 6d to the registrar for copying the will and another payment when letters of administration were required. There was a set charge of 3s 6d when values were between £5 and £40, with over £40 costing 5s. The impression given was that the courts discouraged those with less than £5 from making a will, which is probably why the idea has arisen that none *need* be made for under this amount.[12] As far as Ewyas Lacy costs are concerned, when broken down they seem to be as follows, and seem to confirm that slightly different costs were paid according to the value of the estate. For John Prosser of Llanveynoe in 1679 it cost £1 10s 'for probate' and in the same year it cost yeoman Richard Francis, £1 for 'admon fees'. Three years earlier, it cost Richard Powell, a tanner of Michaelchurch, only £1 for probate and for William George of Rowlestone, only 18s. In one sad case of a 'pauper' whose estate could be processed free, the courts, in order to save money, wrote on a piece of paper that had already been used to save the ½d tax on a sheet of new paper. In 1778, farmer Evan Baynam had to pay 5s for making a will.

Funerals were far more expensive, and varied considerably in cost, from the £1 funeral charge for Jane Prichard, a widow of Michaelchurch Escley, or £3 for John Prosser of Llanveynoe, both in 1679, to something much more elaborate. One of the most detailed descriptions appears in the accounts for James Jones of Michaelchurch Escley in 1759. His executrix spent 12s on cake, 9s 6d on cider. A shroud and hat bands came to a total of £1 12s. Then there was the expense of gloves for the mourners – 19 pairs at 1s each. Making the shroud and shrouding cost 2s 6d, the coffin cost 8s, the parson and clerk got 2s 6d for taking the funeral service and the nurse 2s. The total amount paid out by his widow, in legacies and funeral expenses was £59 4s 4d out of an inventory worth only £66 3s. It is hoped that she was able to rely on other means. In the same year in the same parish, Henry Estland, a yeoman, spent only £13 on funeral expenses including the usual cider and cake out of a total inventory value of £34. The account included spice, which may have been used to mull the cider, as the funeral was held in December. In the account of Thomas Prichard of Clodock there is a note of payment 'to the ringers – 10s'. Earlier in the 17th century, a will made in April 1646 in the closing months of the Civil War records beer rather than cider being given out at the funeral, in the account of Phillipp Thomas Prees.

The final stage was the grant of probate, generally made much faster than today, and in Latin until 1733. This can usually be found at the end of the will.

Details of the 1770 Will and Inventory of Elizabeth Prosser of Newton

Elizabeth's will was dated 5 February 1770. She left £5 each to her nephews Thomas and John Gilbert and niece Elizabeth Addice, sons and daughter of her brother, Clement Gilbert. To another nephew, Edward Gilbert, who was also her executor, she left everything else, and he was to pay all her debts and funeral expenses. The witnesses were Rebecka Meed and Henry Marsh.

The inventory given below is dated 4 April and the appraisers were Benjamin Prosser and John Thomas. Probate was given the following day.

Item	£	s	d
The deceased's wearing Apparel	3	0	0
money in Purse	26	12	2
one feather bed bestead & Appurts	2	10	0
one feather bed	1	5	0
Linen Yarn & some flax unspun	2	0	0
Some Hurden yarn		15	0
About 5 Bushels of wheat	1	12	6
About 4 Bushels of Barley		10	0
13 pair of sheets & a little piece of New Cloth	3	5	0
a small Remnant of Cloth		7	6
8 Napkins		10	0
one Chest		5	0
8 old Boxes		12	0
2 trinds		2	6
a spinning wheel		2	0
a hair sieve and sash[?]		1	6
6 Bushels of Oats		12	0

Item	£	s	d
One bed and Appurtenances	1	5	0
one Woollen & one Linen Wheel		3	0
12 old Bags & one Winnowing sheet		9	0
1 half Hogshead & podering Tub a kipe [probably a fiddle for distributing seed] & Seed Loose*		10	0
Carpenters Tools of all sorts		5	0
Two Riddles & two seeves		1	0
two small pillows & a bag with a Quantity of Feathers		3	0
some old hoops		2	6
a pad		4	0
a press	1	1	0
One bed and Appurtenances	2	10	0
Twelve Cheeses	1	0	0
one Cheese press		5	0
a Table		5	0
a Dresser		1	0
Eleven cheese vates & butter prints		7	6
a small Barrel & Tunpail [?] and Butter Tubs		5	0
three Tablecloths		3	6
Earthenware		2	0
a Cheese press		7	6
six chairs		2	0
seven pewter dishes		12	0
14 plates		7	0
24 Trenchers 8/6 three Brass kettles 1ˡᵇ	1	2	6
One Brass Morter 2ˢ two brass Candlesticks 1 Bras spoon & skimmer		4	0
Two brass pots two Iron pots		8	0
a warming pan 1ˢ a chamber pot a cullender & dripping pan 3/6		4	6
3 porringers patty pans & spoons 2ˢ a Table & cubboard 1ˢ		3	0
a cleaver & chopping knife		1	0
2 spits & dripping pan 4ˢ four candlesticks & Gridiron 1ˢ		5	0
an Ironing box gads & 2 heaters 4ˢ a frying pan & maid 1.6		5	6
a fire shovel tongs & Irons sway & hooks		3	6
a Gun 5ˢ a pile & lanthorn		6	0
3 pails 3 gauns one Boul [tear] a Bellows 1ˢ		3	0
2 Hogsheads 2 Barrels	1	10	0
3 Tubs 1 Chees Cowl 5 Milk Vessels & a butter Tub	1	1	0
3 small Barrels		6	0
Sythes Mattocks Bills Axes & ring Beetle		4	0
A freok [?] & wash Tub		1	6
3 young Bullocks	8	8	0
5 Cows	20	0	0
2 heifers	4	0	0
a mare	5	0	0
a pig		10	6

Item		£	s	d
a Dung Cribb		1	10	0
one plow Harrow and Yokes			15	0
Horse Gears			2	6
	Total	101	12	2

One thing all the wills and inventories have in common is the way in which they open up the details of the changing seasons at Ewyas Lacy from, in the early ones, the geese being reared at Michaelmas, or the corn still unthreshed in the barn at the end of the year and the hay-wains filled with hay in the summer. Style and content certainly changed over the centuries, the earlier ones more detailed, the latter more formalized as the professionals took over. One of the most striking changes is the reduction of religious preamble in the wills, coupled with a reduction in or total lack of charity giving as the state took over the care of the poor.

As time progressed few seemed to give regular sums for the maintenance of the churches – the once common payment of 6d or 12d to St Davids Cathedral ended by the 18th century. Another change is the level of comfort and 'modern' goods that appear in the inventory of David Smith, a cordwainer (shoemaker) of Longtown dated 1813, with its potatoes and coal, knife box and looking glass (see below). It reflects the more peaceful times for the nation too, as the sword and dagger worn by Roger Powell, 'gent of Clidock' changes to David Smith's homely clock and corner cupboard. The inventory is also interesting for the amount of credit he had allowed his customers, almost £80.

The Inventory of David Smith of Longtown, 3 January 1813

He appointed his widow, Elizabeth, to administer his estate, and the appraisers of the inventory were John Price & Henry Harris

Item	£	s	d
Wearing apparell	2	10	0
Money in the House and in his pocket at his Death	13	5	0
Nine chairs 3 Tubs 4 Pewter Dishes 6 pewter Plates	2	0	0
Four Iron potts two tea Cettles fryling pan & Earthen Ware		14	0
Knife Box Corner cubbord & 12 Pewter Spoon		6	0
1 Cask Sotting [Salting?] Stone 2 Baggs & some Earthenware		10	0
A Flox Bed Bedstead & Appertenances	1	0	0
2 Tubs Lasts and Seates[?]		7	6
4 Beds & 5 bedsteads	8	0	0
13 pr of sheets	1	18	0
A Clock and Case	3	0	0
A Sett of Bed hangings 2 pr Blanketts 1 Counterpane	2	15	0
2 Chests 2 Boxes 2 Tubs & Looking Glass	1	0	0
2 Casks Pikes & Rakes and old Bords		7	6
A quantity of Pitch some Hopps a coffer & box	1	0	0
A quantity of Leather	2	0	0

2 pails Ring-Beatle & Stone [?]		5	0
12 Hurdles and some Stubbs [?]		10	6
4 Store Piggs	4	4	0
A Mare	15	0	0
A Quantity of Hay	12	5	0
A Copper Furnace	5	14	0
A Quantity of Cheese and Butter		10	6
4 Hogsheds	8	0	0
6 Chairs	2	2	0
Cubbord Coffer & 2 Bottles		18	6
Maltmill	1	1	0
Warming pan & old Iron		4	6
Money due on the Books at the time of his disease	78	9	7
Goods Sold by Oction [Auction?] to Discharge the Debt	15	3	2
A Quantity of Coal	1	0	0
Potatoes flax & Hemp	1	10	0
Total	187	10	9

3　THE LANDOWNERS OF EWYAS LACY

11th – 13th century

The advent of the Normans meant that the heavy hand of the military, under the lordship of the Lacy family, descended on Ewyas as castles were built, first at Pont Hendre in Clodock, and sometime between 1200 and 1223 at Longtown. The castle at Longtown was built by Walter de Lacy II, whose lordship covered the modern parishes of Clodock, Craswall, Llancillo, Llanveynoe, Longtown, Michaelchurch Escley, Newton, Rowlestone, St Margarets, and Walterstone (and at this stage Dulas also). As sheriff of Hereford until 1223, his main responsibility was to protect the county against attacks by the Welsh, and being able to hold Longtown and the valleys below the Black Mountains was crucial to his purpose. Relations with the Welsh were at their worst during the time of Prince Llewelyn in the 13th century, culminating in attacks along the march at Kinnersley, Whittington and Builth; in September 1233, Henry III himself visited the area, probably to check the defences.[1]

On Henry's mind might also have been Walter's 1225, or earlier, foundation of Craswall's Benedictine Priory a few miles to the north of Longtown Castle, in a remote place 1,200 feet up the mountain; the ruins of which became so covered in vegetation that the vicar of Clodock had difficulty in finding them in the early 20th century.[2] Hugh II, his father, had re-built Llanthony Priory and, in a similar concern for his soul, Walter followed his example; both foundations were generously endowed from the de Lacy estates in Ireland. Craswall Priory was one of only three English Grandmontine establishments, no doubt inspired by Walter's visit to Grandmontine in France when in the company of King John in 1214. Founded for the well-being of the souls of himself, his wife and son, Gilbert (who pre-deceased him), the priory was to have a 'corrector [or Prior], three clerks and ten lay brethren'. However, it experienced endless problems from the first due to Walter's indebtedness to the powerful Jews of Hereford, and the priory eventually needed Henry III's intervention to protect lands transferred to them from Holme Lacy.

On the whole, Walter II had been a loyal subject of the Crown under the reigns of Richard I, John and Henry III, yet it is sad to think that he died a disappointed man, blind and without money or de Lacy heirs, in 1241. His lands were divided between his two granddaughters, Matilda and Margaret, who married Peter de Geneva and John de Verdun respectively, with the Verduns inheriting Longtown Castle and Ewyas Lacy manor. Marriage to heiresses was always considered a useful method of acquiring land. Little is known of the later descent of the manor until the 15th century when the Neville family acquired half the manor through the marriage of Elizabeth Beauchamp to Sir Edward Neville, third Baron Bergavenny.[3] George, the 15th baron, was created Viscount Neville and Earl of Abergavenny in 1784, a year before he died, and thus this part of the manor was subsequently held by the earls of Abergavenny. (His father, William, the 14th baron, who died in 1745, was the first to be styled Lord Abergavenny, rather than Lord Bergavenny. There seems to be no particular reason for the elevation of George, Lord Abergavenny the year before his death, unless it was the fall of the Whig Ministry in 1783 after the loss of the American Colonies, and George III's attempts to gain support for the Crown by giving away peerages by the dozen.)[4]

Unlike the smooth descent through the earls of Abergavenny who continued to own their half of the manor until the early 20th century, the other half of the manor had a fragmented life.

Turmoil in the 16th century

A method of acquiring land, other than marriage, was by being in the right place at the right time. At the Dissolution of the monasteries, the first people to buy the clutch of possessions, such as monasteries, nunneries, advowsons and tithes previously given to the monastic orders, were those courtiers close to the king. The plaintive words of Viscount Lyle, a kinsman of the king, in 1536 that he wished the king would 'help me to some old abbey in mine old days', echo down the centuries. With Thomas Cromwell's help he was granted Frithelstock priory in Devon in 1537, but three years later Henry, unpredictable as ever, had him arrested and thrown into prison, where Viscount Lyle died before he could take advantage of the gift.[5]

Others were more successful. John Thynne of Longleat in Wiltshire (who began his career as a kitchen clerk in the royal kitchens), as steward to the earl of Hertford, Henry VIII's brother-in-law, was in a position to acquire properties across England in Gloucestershire, Oxfordshire, Dorset, Shropshire and Herefordshire, much of it monastic land and church livings. In 1540 he paid £53 for 60 acres of land and a tumble-down priory which became the site of Longleat.[6]

In most cases this monastic property was paid for, but in some cases it is not clear how it was acquired. In 1563, handsome Robert Dudley, earl of Leicester, Queen Elizabeth's favourite, was given, amongst others, the manor and castle of Kenilworth together with

11th to 13th century	The de Lacy family
15th century	Neville Earls of Abergavenny (Known as 'Bergavenny' until 1730)
16th century	Earl of Leicester (Longleat) Arnolds of Llanvihangel Crucorney
17th century	Henry Neville, Earl of Abergavenny Ralph Hopton, Esq. Arnolds of Llanvihangel Crucorney
18th century	Earl of Abergavenny Jeffrey family of Brecon (they bought half the manor c.1700)

The Lords of the Manor

estates in the west Midlands, including Ewyas Lacy.[7] In 1566 his agents made a rental survey of the latter manor. They stated that the boundary of the lordship lay west of Hatterall Mountain and included Maescoed Forest, and named three valleys – Cwm Olchon, Afoncwm (meaning river valley, so it must have been the Monnow) and CwmEsgle (Escley) – as having very good meadow and pasture, well enclosed and manured and 'inhabited by freeholders and copyholders'.

The other half of the manor was owned by Lord Abergavenny, whose properties were said to be in good order with the exception of the castle, whereas the earl's were not. It seems clear that the earl of Leicester wanted to sell his land rather than keep it in hand, as his agents claimed that when the tenants were made a good offer they could not be bothered to accept, preferring to rely on the generosity of the customs of the manor. They must have regretted this later as the agents suggested that the earl raise the rents from 3d to 2s a Welsh acre, 'at least'.[8] (Remember that in the 18th century, 25 acres of Welsh land was considered the equal of 100 acres of Winchester, or English, measurement.)

The earl of Leicester's share of the manor passed at the end of the 16th century to Robert Hopton of Witham Friary in Somerset. (The Hoptons had also benefited from the Dissolution, buying the friary from Henry VIII in 1544 and adapting the buildings.[9]) Robert Hopton's wife, Jane, was the daughter of Rowland Kemeys of Monmouthshire which may explain the family's interest in this part of Herefordshire. The Hoptons' eldest son and heir, Ralph, had an energetic early career. When aged 24, in the middle of studying in the Middle Temple, he went with an expedition to rescue Elizabeth of Bohemia from Imperial Catholic forces in Prague, then carried her to safety on the back of his horse. Inevitably, he was caught up in the Civil War and fought for Charles I, in spite of having some sympathy with Parliament. Appointed to the Council of the Prince of Wales in 1645, he was forced to surrender to Fairfax in March 1646, and joined the prince in exile, where he died in 1652.

His estates, confiscated by Parliament and given to the regicide, Major General Thomas Harrison in about 1653, were finally returned to his four Hopton sisters in 1672. The Ewyas Lacy property eventually passed to Catherine, who had married Thomas Wyndham of Somerset, and Elizabeth, daughter of another sister, married to Sir Trevor Williams of Pontrilas.[10]

This half did not remain with the Hopton family for long, as in about 1700 it came into the hands of John Jeffries, a very rich and ambitious politician. He, and his elder brother, Jeffrey, inherited their wealth from their uncle, a tobacco merchant and Tory alderman of London, and with it Jeffrey was able to buy another Dissolution plum, Brecon Priory. The younger brother, John, became MP for Radnorshire from 1692 to 1698, and Breconshire from 1702 to 1705. In a fruitless attempt to become an MP for Herefordshire in 1699, he bought up land in the county, including Ewyas Lacy. He died in 1715 and his estates passed

16th and 17th century	Arnolds of Llanvihangel Crucorney
18th century	Earls of Oxford (the Harley family of Brampton Bryan)
19th century	Sir George Cornewall, and others

The Patrons of the Living

Kentchurch Court circa *1870, home of the Scudamore family*

to his dissolute son John, who seems to have run through his father's fortune. His heir, Walter, had to buy back the manor from the Chancery Court.[11] The last member of the Jeffrey family died in 1811, and the estate passed to a cousin, who married John Wilkins of Brecon.[12]

The origin of ownership of other manors in the Hundred is sometimes murky. Duncumb states that Llancillo had been leased by the Scudamore family, of Kentchurch and Rowlestone, 'at a nominal rent', long since discontinued, and 'the manor is now vested in that family'. We are also told that the Warwick estates in the Marches were forfeited to the Scudamores in 1452, during the Wars of the Roses.[13] Rowlestone, anciently part of the manor, was leased or sold to a branch of the Scudamores of Kentchurch, who sometimes lived there until the middle of the 18th century. When the two properties were united in the Rowlestone branch they moved to Kentchurch.[14]

The great tithes and advowson of Clodock and many of the other parish churches and chapelries, including Llancillo, had been bought from Henry VIII by Sir Nicholas Arnold, Chief Justice of Ireland, for £160 when Llanthony Priory was dissolved. Clodock later had a different trajectory, the patronage, or advowson being owned by vicars and rectors of the parish, the Reeces, the Vaughans[15] and, in the 19th century, the Wilkins family of Maeslough, in Breconshire. The priory at Craswall had already been dissolved by Edward IV as an 'alien' priory of Grandmont, in Normandy, and its lands had been given to Christ's College, Cambridge in 1462.[16]

One of the opponents to Ralph Hopton during the Civil War was Edward Harley of Brampton Bryan, a Parliamentarian, whose descendants, almost a century later, came to own property in Ewyas Lacy. In 1720 Edward Harley, of Lincoln's Inn and Eywood, in Herefordshire, bought the advowsons of Walterstone and 'Ewyas Lacy' from Nicholas Arnold, together with the great tithes in Walterstone, Rowlestone, Llancillo, Craswall, Clodock, Longtown, Michaelchurch Escley and others within the Hundred (for instance tithes of corn and grain in Old Court and Trelandon). All these had originally been given to Llanthony Priory for its support.[17] Edward, who had married Sarah Foley of Whitley Court in 1685, died in 1735, and his son, Edward became the third earl of Oxford.

The Arnold family, settled at Llanvihangel Crucorney in Monmouthshire, on the borders of Ewyas Lacy, had owned land in the region since the Dissolution. John Arnold married Margaret Cooke, eldest daughter of William Cooke of Highnam, Gloucestershire in 1666, was High Sheriff of Monmouth between 1668 and 1689, served as an MP between 1681 and 1698, and in 1683 was also a JP for Monmouthshire. He was a leading Whig in the 1670s and 1680s with Presbyterian sympathies, and an associate of Sir Trevor Williams and Sir Edward Harley. His son and heir, Nicholas, was married to Lettice Moore, daughter of Sir Edward Neot and Dame Elizabeth Salisbury. The settlement on her included the manor of Newton, and a £500 marriage portion. His mother, Margaret, married John Dutton Colt as her second husband after his father's death in 1703, taking her very generous jointure with her to the Dutton Colt family. Portions and jointures could be an expensive problem to landowners if widows, or wives, lived long as they tied up the property and prevented its descent to the heirs.[18] (The portions given by the bride's father to the prospective bridegroom was not the wife's property but, in return, the husband was expected to make provision for her on his death – hence the jointure.)

Profit from the Estate

Conditions favoured the landowner and the producer of goods rather than the consumer in the 18th century. Growing prosperity, a rising population and increasing exploitation of land all led to profit for the landowner. Profits could be made even from the waste from quarries, turf cutting, grazing and burning lime. Landowners also drew on their estates for food for the manor house, and food would be sent to them when resident in London or elsewhere.

Agricultural innovation could be one way of increasing the revenue from an estate and several landowners in the county with interests or farms in or near Ewyas Lacy were, from the late 16th century, trying new ideas in farming. These included Rowland Vaughan of the Golden Valley, who was interested in irrigation, and Sir Nicholas Arnold of Llanvihangel Crucorney, who was instrumental in improving the breeding of English horses.[19] This interest was continued during the following three centuries by lords Oxford, Scudamore and Cornwall. The first Lord Oxford, on his estates at Brampton Bryan, was keen to introduce flax in 1691. During his years of retirement, from 1718 to 1724, he had 15 acres under turnips and he increased his sheep flock from 413 to 615, on estates which were regularly limed and manured.[20] Improving the property by liming the soil was not a new idea, but had been practised from early times. When the earl of Leicester took over his Ewyas Lacy estate in the 16th century, his agents were keen to tell him that lime was plentiful there.

Towards the end of the 18th century Sir George Cornwall of Moccas, who bought the tithes of Rowlestone from the earl of Oxford and had property elsewhere in the Hundred, besides introducing turnips and swedes, bought a wheel plough in 1783, a seed drill in 1785, a threshing machine in 1802 and a plough from Scotland in 1815.[21]

The Lord's Courts

Through the control of the manorial courts, changes in land tenure were introduced as landowners changed from the old copyhold system (see below) to greater profitability from fixed rents on leaseholds and to rack rents, with a sharper eye kept on estates through the employment of professionals like stewards and attorneys.

The lord controlled the affairs of the manor through his steward and bailiff; the former ran the courts, whilst the latter collected the rents. At the end of the 16th century, the steward of Lord Abergavenny's Ewyas Lacy manor is said to have been William Cecill, and the bailiff Lewis Gilbert. A century later, in 1701, the steward was Bennett Delahay, and by the early 18th century it was Job Gilbert, then John Gilbert; towards the end of the century it was listed as Robert Morgan Kinsey.[22] The steward, by the 18th century, was usually a local solicitor or attorney. Their duties were many and varied, and included disciplining the tenants for misbehaviour, acting as clerk of works when buildings were erected, appointing court officials such as the bailiff and keepers of the livestock pound, and collecting heriots when due. (A heriot was a payment to the landowner on the death of a copyholder. It could consist of 'the best beast' or second best in the early days, but was later converted to a cash payment.) Most of all they were responsible for keeping the manorial courts on behalf of the owner, who was normally absent.[23]

There were three types of courts held in the manor. One, 'customary', was for copyhold tenants only and was presided over by the lord's steward; the second, 'court baron', was administered for freeholders only, though in practice both were dealt with at the same court; whilst the third court was a Court Leet held only twice a year, commonly around Easter and Michaelmas. This involved a twice yearly inspection by the sheriff of the county of the system of tithings, including the ten men of each tithing responsible for good behaviour.[24] The importance of the latter declined during the Tudor period because of the expansion of national courts such as the Quarter Sessions and this must have massively undermined the power of local landowners.[25]

The most important court was undoubtedly the Court Baron, which was usually held on a three-weekly or monthly basis. Ewyas Lacy is fortunate to have a copy of the records of this dating from the early 18th century giving valuable information on the freeholders, the tenants and their holdings. The court was governed by the custom of the manor and its task was to deal with offences against it, also with debts and disputes between tenants, in which it acted as a safety valve. It also recorded changes in ownership of tenancies, and imposed fines (see below).[26]

Tenants were usually of three kinds: freeholder, leaseholder and copyholder. In the description of the manor made to the earl of Leicester in 1566, the tenants were described as being 'above 300 persons very tall men the most part freeholders ... some copyholders there be'. The freeholder, although he owned his land, still came under the jurisdiction of the courts and was expected to attend and occasionally act as a juror. He, or she, still paid rent to the lord, although this became a negligible amount over the process of time, but often held leasehold land in addition. Copyholders, at this time holding their grants for only 21 years, could be stung for an increased rent when the leases fell in at the end of the term.[27]

Leaseholders held a lease from the manor, sometimes for a period of 99 years, and sometimes by what was known as a three life lease, by which three names were included in the lease, usually members of the same family. Such was the case with James Parry's lease, which was held in the names of James Parry, 32 years old, Mary aged 30 and James their son aged 3. The lease would run out on the death of all the names, but what generally happened was that on the death of one of them he or she would be replaced by a new 'third life' on payment of a small 'fine'. If the tenant was purchasing a holding from the lord, the fine was the major part of the deal, the rental comprising only a few shillings. The heriots associated with each lease could be the sting in the tail, as they were paid out on the death of the tenant. In James Parry's case the fine was £120 (a not inconsiderable amount at that time) and the rent was 3s 9d p.a. The heriot due was the second best beast. An example of what would happen later is entered in the court roll for 1754 when John Price came to court and 'recited' the entry of 27 April 1710 concerning '2 acres of Welsh called Teer Jack Vawr for two lives'. As the only life surviving he wanted to add two names. He was aged 'about 56 years' and sensibly wanted to add his two sons James Price aged 8 and William Price aged 4. For this he was charged seven guineas, with 6d rent and 5s as a heriot (the heriot was by this time sometimes commuted to a cash value).[28]

A copyholder was in the privileged position of merely having to produce his 'copy' of his holding which was enrolled in the manor records. Copyholders could pass their holdings to another tenant as is shown in 1737, when the lord granted permission for 'Thomas Jones, tenant of the Township of Llanveynoe re copy of Court roll dated 15 Nov. 1733 ... to the intent that the said Lord should grant the same to John Watkins of the same township, husbandman'. This 'customary' tenure, and that of a 'three life' lease, was so secure that the tenants regarded it as being as good as full ownership. Copyholds in particular were looked on as a disadvantage by a lord of the manor and these were beginning to be turned into short term leaseholds in many manors as the copyholds fell in. All copyhold was abolished by the Law of Property Act in 1922.

For centuries the courts for this part of the manor were held somewhere in Longtown Castle grounds, but by the end of the 17th century they were held in a house said to be owned by Sir Trevor Williams, his wife, a Hopton descendant, and Thomas Windham. In that case, where were the courts held for the Lords of Abergavenny? The Courts Baron in 1733 state 'the Court Baron held for the said manor under the said Lord [Abergavenny] at the Castle of Longtown'. As the castle was then in a ruinous condition and had been for some considerable time, they may have had the use of the same house. Certainly, a lease for three lives given to John Watkins, cooper, in November 1692 states that he had the lease of the castle site at Longtown with one 'ancient house ... excepting the liberty of stewards to hold Ewyas Lacy manorial court within the house as accustomed'.[29] As this was a lease granted by Lord Abergavenny there may have been a second house being used by the other part of the manor.

The Abergavenny courts continued to be held at 'the castle' until the 1850s, then in 1852 the court was held at The Bear Inn in Crickhowell, no doubt a move promoted by Baker Gabb, the steward, as his lawyer's office was in nearby Abergavenny. One could imagine that inns were more comfortable and convivial anyway. Indeed, there is a give-away statement in volume two of the court rolls, on 9 May 1816: 'The Court Leet and View of Frankpledge together with the Court Baron and Customary Court of the Right Hon. Henry, Earl of Abergavenny' was 'held at the Castle of Longtown ... and from there adjourned to the dwelling house of Thomas Parry, innholder'. It was still only May, after all, and would still have been cold.[30]

Manorial Receipts

Reserved out of any grants of land was anything that could be exploited to the lord's advantage at a later date. A grant of 1858 of land to John Griffiths of Olchon in Llanveynoe notes that 'reserved out of this grant all timber, Quarries and minerals'. Other items were mills, both grist and fulling, that existed on the estate, and woodland. Even wood in the hedgerows belonged to the lord of the manor.[31]

The planting of woodland not only represented for the landowner a love of his land, but also was an expression of faith in the continuation of his family for generations to come. Where this was absent it perhaps demonstrated a lack of interest in the future of the estate. Woodland was a prime source of income for the landowner; as much as 10% of his revenue in any one year could be gained from it, and even more when there was a financial crisis. There was a constant demand for wood from the estate alone: houses needed building materials (a larger house could use as many as 120 oaks), and bark was required for tanning.[32]

The Scudamore family of Kentchurch, when in financial straits towards the end of the 18th century, were selling off timber on their estates in Rowlestone and Llancillo, including 126 oak trees growing at Goytree, Old House Lands and Rowlestone Park. In 1786 John Scudamore had declared that one of the ways to escape the financial mess he was in was 'Cuting Timber'.[33] By the late 18th century, concern was already being expressed by more thoughtful landowners that too many woods were being cut down as a quick cash crop for landowners in financial difficulties, especially by landowners who spent much of their time in London and rarely visited their estates.[34]

During the Napoleonic Wars there was pressure of another sort – an enormous demand for timber for the Navy, as no fewer than 2,000 trees were required for each ship built. Nelson himself toured the country in the summer of 1802, amongst other reasons in order to ascertain the woodland that might be available. At one point he, together with a party including Sir William and Lady Hamilton, was not far from Ewyas Lacy, enjoying a hero's welcome in Monmouth. During the following month he made notes in his own hand on what was available as he visited, or was in the company of, local landowners.[35]

Towards the end of the Napoleonic Wars, at Brass Knoll farm in Llanveynoe, 50 'maiden' (unpollarded) oaks were sold in 1813.[36] In the same year, in the parish of St Margarets, there was a massive sale of timber for the Navy on the Whitehouse estate.[37]

Landowners further down the social scale showed great concern for their woodland and regarded their trees as a precious asset. During the Civil War, the 1644/45 will of Thomas Prichard of Rowlestone makes it clear to his heir that he should not give or sell the wood, 'nor commit wilful waste'. In the following century the will of Constance Tomlin of Clodock, written in 1766, left her farm at 'Bulgfa' to the tenant for the term of the 99 year lease, under the condition that he 'keeps the estate in all respects the Land Buildings Hedges Gates and Stiles in good repair and Husbandlike ... when the coppices are eighteen years Growth I desire Tho: Jones to fell it and make the most of it reserving all the Timber & yong oaks as will not damnifie the underwood as it may grow for the use of the premises Hearafter'.

Money could also be made out of coppice wood every 12 or 14 years, which could produce a better return, at £12 to £22 per acre, than ordinary land. Much of it was sent down to Bristol and elsewhere to make hoops for barrels.[38]

Any industrial interest could also be a massive source of income to the lord, but this was unusual in the Hundred where agriculture was the chief form of income. One landowner family in the region, the Scudamores of Kentchurch, was more fortunate as they had an iron forge at Llancillo, and made money not only by leasing it out but also by selling the wood to fuel it.[39] Towards the end of the 17th century the forge was leased to Paul Foley of Stoke Edith, who shipped its products down the Monnow to Bristol, via the Wye. Duncumb states that an iron forge was worked in the parish of Llancillo for several centuries 'but has lately been destroyed'. This was written in the early 19th century. We know that it was worked until at least 1755, when Elizabeth Russell, wife of Thomas Russell, 'forgeman of Llancillo', was listed as one of the lives in a copy of the court roll.[40] There is also a will and inventory for Giles Griffit or Griffiths, a 'hammerman' of the mid 17th century.

Details of landlords' income

By the end of the 17th century, greater landowners like the Harleys were considered to be worth £1,500 per annum. Some of the value accruing from the ownership of tithing alone could be substantial. That of Llancillo and Rowlestone were worth, in 1731, £50 p.a., but values could go down as well as up.[41] By the end of the 18th century, in 1799 this was let, on a 21 year lease, to Philip Griffiths for £46. The total amount from tithing from Ewyas Lacy property came to £211. This may today seem very small beer but when one considers that Lord Oxford had many other manors all producing similar amounts, and the average salary for a professional man would be between £50 and £100 p.a., it all adds up. Apart from the odd capon or pullets due from the tenants, there was the value of the heriots, a best beast or a sum of money, which was valued at the end of the 18th century at £20.[42] In 1823 Lord Abergavenny received £1,764 5s in 'Fines from the Hundred', and in the previous year £36 17s had fallen to him in heriots from the same source, and for chief rents £35 7s 2¼d.[43]

This income was not always easily come by. A depression in farming could mean that it was difficult to find or keep tenants. The years after the Restoration and until the 1690s were such a time and there were later depressions when landowners were forced to reduce rents in order to keep tenants happy, if, indeed, they could let farms at all. Generally, though, the 18th century was a good time for landowners at all levels, but not so good for the landless as there was little or no inflation where wages were concerned.

Out of his income the lord of the manor had to pay his officials (Lord Abergavenny's steward was paid £100p.a. in the 19th century). There was also the cost of holding the Court Leet (which came to £5 4s 6d in July 1823) and there were other expenses, apart from having to serve his county in various capacities, as JP or MP. For instance, the Scudamores, Duncumb says, held the manor of Llancillo 'by their service as judges in the county court'.[44]

Land had to be maintained at a certain level to be profitable and that involved the landlord in costs. Writing to Sir George Cornewall about one of his recently acquired farms in Craswall, his valuer says that, apart from the wood which (as usual) was kept in hand, the farm was worth £40 p.a. but, 'this farm wants a deal of money laid out in Ditching and Draining the lands before it can be let at a fair value'. A later hand has written 'let at £45'.[45]

There were other hazards involved in buying land. One year into the negotiations, in 1805, it seemed that Sir George was having second thoughts about acquiring the tithes from Lord Oxford, as they were offered to Col Cotterell, Sir George feeling that it was 'too much expense'. Col Cotterell replied saying that he had considered it but since then he had decided to purchase another estate 'which would be more desirable to me'.

The dispute over the value of the tithes acquired from Lord Oxford dragged on for about eight years with some hard words being exchanged. Half way through the negotiations people could not be sure to whom their tithes should be paid. In a rare letter from Lord Oxford to Sir George, in March 1806, he writes that while he agrees to employ another man to help, he hopes that it will be worth while as 'Mr Harris [the surveyor] not only gave up a years purchase in your favour ... but also made greater allowances than he would otherwise have done' and he 'hopes this business may soon be settled between us'. Four years into the negotiations Sir George's valuer was stating that 'seeing no prospect of obtaining better information respecting the value of the Clodock tithes ... I send you my opinion respecting that property ... were there any Degree of Industry amongst the people of the Country ... the Tithe would be exceedingly cheap at Mr Harris's valuation, even at 30 years purchase ...'. Looking at past valuations listed on the books was no good apparently. In 1808 Sir George's steward wrote to him saying another surveyor was needed to give a more accurate valuation of any individual estate in case he wanted to sell it off at some later date; if he went by the book list he 'would suffer great loss in some cases'. There was such a variation in value as 'those that are very poor and mountainous, are rather too high and the richer and more improvable Estates too low'. Another reason for the delay was that the valuers had to wait for the crops to grow. Lord Oxford and Sir George must have felt it was like watching paint dry. Eventually a reasonable level of value was decided upon with the steward writing to say, in February 1808, that he felt that the sum of £11,162 10s was a fair price, taking into account that 'the property at best is of so unpleasant a kind, and attended with so much Trouble'. Even then there was trouble from some of the new tenants, who complained of being 'ill-treated' by their new leases.[46]

During the 18th century some estates were in a parlous state because of the debts of their owners. In 1724, two years after inheriting the Earl of Oxford's estate on the death of the first earl, the new earl wrote to his uncle begging for advice about a debt of £1,880, stating that since inheriting the estate he had had to apply all he received to pay debts, adding 'this is a very true but a melancholy account'. He complained of his predecessor's financial mismanagement but doesn't want any reflection on his memory, however, adding 'It is now two years since his Death and I am much pressed for money by several of the creditors'. A weakness for books and manuscripts, shared by both the first and second earl, may have hastened their downfall. Even as a student Lord Harley was notorious for his expenditure on books, and a few years later, on the death of Lord Sunderland, he paid £10,000 for his library. In 1723, a correspondent wrote to tell him of another death: 'Do you know how his books are disposed of? If they should be sold, perhaps there might be some pickings for your Lordship.'[47] On the death of the second earl in 1741, his widow sold the entire collection, and the manuscripts went to the British Museum. By the end of the 18th century matters were even worse for his successors and everything had to be sold. The tithes and other property, according to Duncumb, were sold 'to such proprietors of the lands as chose to become purchasers, and the residue purchased by George Cornewall, Esq.'[48]

Others towards the end of the century, like the Scudamores, were also in dire financial straits. Writing to his man of business, Mr Bird, from Kentchurch, about ways of paying off his debts, John Scudamore says in a letter of 23 March 1785 that 'having already had too much business with Jews I will not treat any more in that manner [presumably by loans from them] ... I will by the sale of the purchased Estates, regranting leases for lives, renewing Copyholds, and Cutting Timber, etc, discharge my debts, as fast as I can.' A month later his wife writes to the agent laying out the full horror of John Scudamore's debts and how they are to settle them. The total sum amounted to £29,865, an amount that would be horrifying today, how much more so then. She adds 'In this include the Mortgage on the Campstone and unsettled estates ... his other debts ... will make up the amount to at least £31,000'. The solution was to sell 'the Lincolnshire and London estates [which] would jointly sell for £20,000 – certainly not more than £21,000'. The Lincolnshire estates she had brought with her on marriage so this was a great sacrifice. John Scudamore's blood relations don't appear to have been very sympathetic. His brother wrote early in the year giving advice from Kensington Square, when he heard of the steps being proposed 'for relieving himself from the heavy load of debt (which I must say his own improvidence has brought upon him) ... in Justice to your Creditors give up everything you are possessed of into the hands of proper Trustees ... and be content with whatever they shall allow you out of it for your own support ...'. Unfortunately, the very day before his brother was gambling a horse in a sweepstake; perhaps the family had used up their store of sympathy. As some of the property was entailed (legally tied to the heirs in a way that could only be broken by an Act of Parliament), the core of the estate was saved from the wreckage.[49]

It has to be remembered that the landlords, whilst creaming off much of the profit from their estates, were also creating employment. Although none of them lived in the Hundred, the best had a patriarchal attitude towards their tenants and tried to help them when turned to, and encouraged local industries. Even Lord Abergavenny, with land in no fewer than seven counties, kept an interest in his Welsh border property. A letter of August 1853 mentions Lady Neville giving a prize for the best specimen of Welsh blue cloth of Welsh wool, and she also wanted applicants to compete for prizes 'for articles of manufacture most beneficial to the country'. To put this generosity in perspective, however, another undated 19th-century letter from Baker-Gabb, the steward, to the tenants asked them to reserve their votes in favour of the Neville family at the next election.[50]

The most geographically distant of the landowners were the Abergavennys who, at least by the 19th century, resided chiefly at Eridge in Kent. The Harleys had lived at Brampton Bryan for centuries, but they were at the other end of the county. The Hopton family's roots were in Somerset. The Arnolds and Scudamores were the closest, the Arnolds on the Monmouthshire border, adjoining Ewyas Lacy, and the Scudamores at Kentchurch a few miles away.

The families that lived in the county or close to Ewyas Lacy and had the closest contact probably provided the greatest benefit as they were serving the community as JPs and MPs and knew the people and the terrain, but also, importantly, had contact in turn with London and the City. Even the more remote landlords could be said to contribute as they transferred a greater awareness from their contacts with the wider world. Their marriages, too, brought contacts on a wide scale as they acquired property in distant counties. This is a factor, for instance, in the innovations brought about and introduced by the Harley and Cornewall families. It must be remembered that, in the main, these people were in the business of land ownership for financial gain and concern for their tenants was driven by the urge to maximize their investment as well as their sense of duty towards them.

An interesting conclusion reached from this study is that almost all those landowners who acquired church property failed to profit from it in the long run. The earl of Leicester's family died out with his death. The lands of the Hoptons passed into other hands towards the end of the 17th century and the Arnolds at about the same time were bankrupt, their property eventually passing to the Harleys. Sir Trevor Williams was fined £20,000 for offending a county magnate, and spent some time in prison, as did John Arnold for the same offence (Arnold was a notorious troublemaker and an embarrassment to his friends).[51]

4 The Gentry

William Harrison's view in the 16th century was that the gentleman must be educated, have a profession or military rank, sufficient income to free him from manual labour and 'he shall *for money* have a coat of arms bestowed upon him by the heralds'. So what it all boiled down to in the end was money – he says nothing about ancient lineage, or even, as Lord Burghley did, of 'ancient riches'.[1]

By the end of the 17th century the boundaries between the different groups of gentry was becoming somewhat hazy. The top level of county magnates or landowners has been discussed in the last chapter, so the groups considered here will be the middling gentry and the minor gentry. The former (the lesser esquires and more prosperous gentlemen) might hold office as Justices, had annual incomes of between £250 and £350 p.a. and were entitled to bear a coat of arms. Men of this status were rare in Ewyas Lacy. The minor gentry included those called 'Mr' – doctors of medicine, merchants and stewards to the greater landowners – who might aspire to the minor posts in their counties such as local positions of authority as Chief Constable of the Hundred or Grand Juryman, and own a large house or mansion. These parish gentry would be likely to live in houses with between five and eight hearths, but the size of a house did not necessarily equate to the owner's wealth.[2]

There were certain features that linked the middling gentry group: first, family connections by marriage or by birth, secondly, size of estate, and thirdly, sufficient income to be freed from the necessity of earning a living. It is dangerous to be too pedantic as the gentry were not a closed caste and one man might call himself a 'gent' in his will only to be disabused of this opinion when his neighbours came to write his inventory. So these groups cannot be easily pigeon-holed. Indeed, there was a very fine line between each status, which sometimes overlapped. Occasionally even the local appraisers writing the inventory could not be sure. A man might consider himself a gentleman but then be downgraded to 'yeoman' by the appraisers, or in the case of Thomas Price of Michaelchurch Escley call himself by the grander title of 'victualler' but be reduced by his contemporaries to 'aleseller' on his death.

Sometimes it was the other way round: a man considered by his peers to be a gentleman might be wary of claiming this. Throughout the period under review there was rapid social mobility, as some examples will show. Case histories can be difficult to construct for men at this level, but wills, inventories, hearth tax records, deeds, surveys, church memorials and letters can yield a rich harvest.

Downward mobility of younger sons of the aristocracy was almost inevitable given that (in spite of small sums being shared equally between the families in most cases), the lion's share would still go to the eldest son and many estates were entailed. Avenues of advancement open to people in other areas, such as court preferment, the professions, and commerce were not easily available to the relatively isolated people of Ewyas Lacy.

Once or twice in a century heralds came from the College of Heralds in London to all the major towns in order to ensure that no-one was taking status to which they were not entitled. All who claimed gentrihood had to go to their nearest town with appropriate documents of proof, and between 1590 and 1640 about 4,000 grants of arms were made.[3] There is a delightful description of one young man, at the end of the 17th century, going to his nearest town to meet the heralds, proudly clutching his 'parchment in which [was] my coat of arms'. He was disgusted when he got there because, as he says, he saw no JP 'nor could learn of anyone else who went'. As a result he felt that the Heralds' visit was more to grant coats 'to new upstart families than review the ancient gentlemen's coats'.[4] It was the beginning of the end, and this practice died a natural death with the explosion of social mobility in the 18th century.

In the Herald's Visitation to Herefordshire of 1531 the only recognisable local name is that of Henry Delahay of 'Halterennis'. Just over a hundred years later, at the Visitation of 1634, the picture is very different, with Ewyas Lacy names scattered freely amongst the pages, including those of Vaughan of Walterstone, Gilbert of Clodock, Thomas and Parry of Michaelchurch Escley, Watkins of Craswall, and Scudamore of Llancillo. Unlike the 1531 Visitation that of 1634 records the names of more local, or lesser gentry. At this level were people who could produce a coat of arms, and often had close familial links with, though they lacked the wealth of, the greater gentry. The Vaughans, who were connected with, or descended from, Sir Roger Vaughan of Tretower, are mentioned as being at Walterstone, but appear at Llancillo 30 years later, after the Civil War, as gentlemen. One turns up as the vicar of Clodock in the early 18th century. These are clearly not the main branch of the family but a cadet line, as were the Scudamores of Llancillo, one of whom, James Scudamore, was Chief Constable of the Hundred in 1663.[5]

In general, it was their more cultured lifestyle that would have made the local gentry stand out: their expensive clothing, generally from £1 to £3 in value, and their possession of large dwellings filled with furniture and books and containing a study, in which was probably a desk. This group could merge, however, with the minor or parish gentry, who lacked the wealth of the others but were considered gentry by their contemporaries. Stone calls these parish gentry 'men whose interest and powers were limited to the boundaries of one or at most two villages, most of whom had no education beyond that at the local grammar school'.[6] It was almost certain that they would be able to read, write and do accounts and were the people most likely to write the wills for others. In some counties they would at least be expected to serve on the Hundred Jury and as churchwardens, have a minimum income of £20 p.a. and live in a house with at least five hearths.[7] Jim Tonkin found that the smallest houses in Herefordshire were found in Eways Lacy and this level of income and size of house needs to be adjusted downwards for the area as there are gentlemen in most of its parishes with houses of only three hearths.[8] The best source of information comes from the hearth taxes of the 1660s, where Alltyrynys, home of the

Alltyrynys in the 1970s

Delahays is listed as one of the largest houses, if not the largest, in the district, with eight hearths. James Scudamore, gent of Llancillo, had only three, but wise householders had at that time stopped up some of their chimneys in order to escape the tax. In the 1665 hearth tax for Llanveynoe, John Gilbert is shown as having three, with two others 'stopt'.

Some of these applicants failed in their bid for gentrihood. At Ewyas Lacy at the Herald's Visitation of 1634 there were ten disclaimers (refusals), the third largest group in the county. The Heralds rubbed in the humiliation by making them say 'We Whose Names are here under written being lawfully Summoned ... to make proofe of our Armes and Gentry doe hereby acknowledge our selves to have noe right or Interest in Armes or Gentry'. Among those who signed, or marked, were Hugh Morgan of Rowlestone, David Howell Probert of Michaelchurch Escley, Charles Jennings of Newton, Roger Morgan of Walterstone and John Thomas of Llanveynoe. Hugh Morgan was listed as a yeoman when he died two years later, probably of mortification, whilst Charles Jennings' rejection was predictable as he was the son of Thomas Jennings, the tanner of Newton. Upward and downward mobility was probably greater amongst this group than amongst the county elite whose position was founded on a firmer base of wealth, land and contacts.

It is interesting to follow the progress of some of these families who successfully gained an entry into the Visitation of 1634 and study the route to success or failure. One tactic was to move away to the towns. The Cecil family are a prime example of this. One of them went to Court and prospered in the reign of Queen Elizabeth, while the rest of the line remained behind and withered away, or became merged with others of the parish gentry, in their case the Delahays. The Revd Charles Robinson is very scathing about the Cecils in his *A History of the Mansions and Manors of Herefordshire* with his remark that not only was their name not found in a list of principal inhabitants of Herefordshire in 1431, but they never attained the posts of sheriff or knight of their county. However, in 1458, Richard Cicile was appointed Forester of the then royal manor of Ewyas Lacy. It was the younger of his two sons, David, who settled in Lincolnshire and was grandfather of Robert Cecil, Elizabeth's chief statesman. Once in high position the family were able to progress to even greater wealth.[9] However, links remained with the Cecils of Alltyrynys during the 16th century at least. William Cecil, Esq., in his will of 1597, after leaving 2s to the cathedral church of St Davids, 20s for the repair of his parish church at Walterstone, and lands to his son, Mathew 'to provide education' for his 'reputed son John', requested that if Mathew has no heirs then any household stuff was to go to 'The Right Honourable Sir Robert Cecil, knight'.[10] This was the younger son of Lord Burghley and his right-hand man, later to be elevated to the title of Earl of Salisbury after courting James I. William Cecil was, no doubt, adhering to Lord Burghley's maxim of always having someone of influence in your pocket, saying 'keep some great man thy friend ... otherwise in this ambitious age, thou shalt remain like a hop without a pole'.[11]

The Cecil coat of arms as depicted in stained glass in Walterstone church

Education was an important dividing line between the gentry and the rest. In a rare mention of education in the probate documents, John Cecil of 'all Tynys' instructs his wife in his will of 1551 to maintain their son Philip 'at school for the next six years'. Richard Parry, 'gent' of Longtown in 1622, asks for the income from his estate to be used for the education of his six daughters, and presumably his son, Rice. Edmund Thomas, Esq. of Michaelchurch Escley, in his will of 1744 leaves his nephew, Edmund Lewis, £20 for his education until the age of 18. If he went on to university he would then have £30 p.a. until he had his degree.

Other requirements for success as gentry were good marriages, either to heiresses or into families of higher status. John and Judith Gilbert's grandson, John, who was left Brass Knoll in the Olchon Valley in his grandfather's will of 1708 (which does not appear to have survived), was initially called a yeoman. He married Anne Vaughan, inherited Dulas Court from his uncle, William Parry and was called a 'gent' in a deed of 1745. He thus restored the status held by his grandfather, John. A magnified example of this advancement was when a Scudamore of the junior line, living at Llancillo, was able to regain the family seat at Kentchurch when the main line died out in the first half of the 18th century. Rees Parry of Michaelchurch Escley at some time in the 16th century had married Julyan Gwatkin, a sole heiress, of Pontrilas. Julyan's mother was the daughter of Sir William Herbert of Colbrook in Abergavenny.

Brass Knoll in the Olchon Valley in 2007

It was probably a downward move to marry a member of the clergy in the 17th century unless they were likely to be promoted. John Hoskyns' daughter, Elizabeth, married John Delahay, vicar of Clodock in the early to mid 17th century.[12] He was a kind man, but his prospects of advancement were not great.[13] Even in the early part of the 18th century there was a vast gulf between the great landowner or peer and the lower level of clergy. This is illustrated by a letter from Dr Stratford, Lord Oxford's old tutor and friend and himself a clergyman, about 'Auditor Foley', a cousin. He writes on 15 December 1728 regarding his daughter's disastrous marriage to the parish clergyman: 'I hope the father bears it like a man ... the parson is inexcusable, the Auditor had been not only his patron, but kind friend, too'. They could be treated like friends but not be accepted into the family.[14]

The poor box in St Devereux church

A feature of gentility was generosity to others, especially the poor, though this is not to say that the yeomen were far behind in this. Much of the repair of the fabric of the churches was due to the generosity of the yeomen, but such generosity was automatically expected of the gentry class. The Delahay family of Walterstone, apart from generous bequests to their servants, regularly left 40s to the poor in their wills, viz Gabriel Delahay in 1648, Helena Delahay in 1650 and John Delahay in 1675.

The Gilberts, one of whom, William, was listed in the Visitation of 1634, were a vast and mostly prosperous clan who spread across at least three of the townships: Clodock, Craswall and Llanveynoe. The Gilbert Charity left in 1658 by Lewis Gilbert of 'The Brynn', who was an uncle of John Gilbert of Brass Knoll, is still a source of funding today. His will reads: 'To nephew, John Gilbert, the unexpired term of the lease on the tenement and several parcels of land called Kaer Onn, Kay (an Anglicised form of the Welsh 'cae', meaning 'field') Werne, Kay Hendre, Er Enys y Kandire here, Free Keven y Kay Mayne and Kay Odden all situated in Llanveynoe ... in consideration of which John and his heirs, is to pay, for the remainder of the term of the lease, £6 annually to the overseers of the poor, the churchwardens and constables of Longtown and Llanveynoe'. This, initially, was to be used to place out 'two children of the poorest sort as apprentices' from the two townships, but over time the charity and the lands held in trust by it changed and adapted. In the Charity Report the indenture covers five closes in Longtown which by 1815 were known as 'Poor's Land'.[15]

In the 16th and 17th centuries the gentry probably put money regularly in the 'poor box', or left money to it in wills, as did Thomas ap John in 1589. He left 'to the poor mans box of Clodock parish – 6d'. This was the only mention of it in the probate documents, as the 'poor box' was eventually driven out by the increasing amount paid, instead, to the poor rate.

A year after Lyson Thomas' listing in the Visitations, 20 shillings was left in his will of 1635 towards 'the making upp of a top of the old decayed steeple' at Michaelchurch Escley, also generous sums of money and mourning gowns, not only to his servant maids but another six mourning gowns to the six poorest women in Michaelchurch Escley. He added a phrase to the gift that rescues two of them from obscurity: 'Margaret verch [daughter of] Lewis and Ilby Vache [small] be two of them'.[16] He also had high level contacts within the county as John Scudamore, Viscount Sligo of Holm Lacy was to be the recipient of his best bay gelding, and he asked his heir to present a 'great gilt bowl and cover to the Dean and Chapter of the Cathedral Church' (of Hereford). He also appears to have travelled widely beyond his parish as he mentions the possibility of dying 'farr remote', and expects a tomb to be erected over him.

This practice of placing memorials in churches was a distinguishing feature that linked the upper level of lesser gentry to the middling and greater gentry; and many would also expect to be buried in the chancel or at least in the church near their ancestors. In 1597 William Cecil, Esq. asked to be buried in the parish church of Walterstone, 'where my ancestors are buried'. Hugh Lewis, gentleman, was more specific in 1657 when he requested that his burial be 'where my father heretofor was buried in the South East side [of Clodock church] and in the seat where the new pulpit is now erected'. A year later, in 1658, Lewis Gilbert of the Brynn simply asks to be buried 'in the parish church of Clodock', as does Simon Jones in 1665. There are very few, if any, such requests during the 18th century, then a touchingly humble one from Mary Symonds of Craswall in 1856, asking to be buried 'as near as conveniently may be to the remains of my late beloved Husband in the parish church of ... Michaelchurch Escley', or if objections are raised, then 'in the churchyard there'.

There was a certain degree of culture shown at this level, together with the expectation of owning certain goods such as paintings, jewellery and fine linen. Helena Delahay of

Alltyrynys in 1650 bequeathed several items of jewels and silver, including her silver tankard and her 'great silver salte' to her son, John, and to her 'daughter Delahay one Holland tablecloth and dozen of Holland napkins'. To her granddaughter went 'my London barred chest of fine linen and my hamper of London pewter'. In nearby Trewin, in 1719, her relation, Mary, wife of Thomas Delahay, left a dazzling array of jewellery, including earrings and rings set with diamonds and emeralds, diamond lockets, in addition to masses of plate.[17] At Longtown, the heir of Richard Parry gent, Rice Parry, in 1640, had some elements of refinement in that he had silk bed curtains and a very early looking glass, though his father, in 1622, had nothing in his inventory that would set him apart from any prosperous farmer.

Musical instruments are puzzlingly absent considering the region's closeness to Wales. There was a strong tradition that harpists gathered at Llanwonnog in the 16th century, during the residence of a well-known Tudor poet, James Parry, who lived between c.1531 and 1627. He wrote a poem praising another Ewyas Lacy inhabitant whose will we have, Captain John Prydderch, a gentleman who served in the Low Countries and lived at a mansion called The Park in Longtown at the end of the 16th century.[18] There are, however, two mentions of harps that might well tie in with all this activity at Longtown, coming as they do towards the end of the 16th century. The first occurs in the inventory of Thomas ap Richard alias Taylor of Craswall in 1580, and the second two years later in that of Ievan William David of Michaelchurch Escley. The other musical instrument, a violin, appears at the end of the 18th century in the inventory of Mr John Prichard, a gentleman of Rowlestone who also owned several paintings, probably inherited from his grandfather.

Many gentry families who had been able to pass on estates without difficulty in order to keep their name going in the 16th and 17th centuries struggled by the following century to find male heirs. Worsening demographic conditions in the late 17th century and early 18th meant that, unlike the 16th century when there was a quiverful of surviving children, there are numerous cases in the 17th century of numbers of daughters in the family and only one son or no sons at all. Lawrence Stone even suggests that in families where daughters predominated, perhaps the next generation were likely to produce more daughters in their turn.[19] Another possible theory is that by the 18th century more young men, instead of staying on their estates, were heading for the cities where disease such as smallpox was rife. The Civil War does not seem to have been a factor, unless it destroyed the stability of society, breaking the continuity of life in the community. As a result, there may have been a loss of confidence leading to a tendency not only to marry later (on average in the 16th century at 21; by the end of the 18th at 29), but abstain from marriage altogether.[20] This phenomenon, though, would be less likely in a farming community such as Ewyas Lacy. There does seem to have been a preponderance of heiresses in the first half of the 17th century. Richard Parry, gent of Longtown is one example. He died in 1622 leaving two sons and six daughters, all of whom had to be provided for in the way of dowries, jointures and so on, an expense that could sometimes entail selling off the patrimony. There was also a branch of the Gilberts affected in this way in the 18th century. John and Judith Gilbert of Brass Knoll had only three daughters, so their land, in the 18th century, passed to grandchildren who lacked the attachment to the estate; within 40 years of John Gilbert's death Brass Knoll had passed out of the family's ownership.

The law had always been an avenue of social mobility. Job Gilbert, 'gent' of Craswall, was an attorney who had his prospects advanced when he became Lord Abergavenny's steward in the early 18th century. With the expansion of trade and commerce there were now other avenues for advancement. With Thomas Jennings' purchase of Myles Hunt's house, formerly the property of one of the Delahays, a man with tanner connections and forebears, had moved in the 1660s onto land that had belonged to an earlier elite. In 1661 his brother bought Merry Hurst, an important property in St Margarets, and Cae Court Melyn in Longtown. A clue that they were 'new men' is the appellation 'Mr'. They appeared to sit uncertainly on the edge of gentrihood but were highly respected in the community. Such was 'Mr' Rowland Jennings of 'The Wayne', a descendant of tanners, who had the confidence to take the clergy and churchwardens to court when crossed, and who was, by the time of his death, listed as gentry.[21] Another was 'Mr' Thomas Harris, the mercer in 1786, whose descendants were gentry and contributed a good deal to the church at Clodock in the 19th century.

With increasing travel by coach and rapidly expanding towns, towns were the melting pot into which young and impoverished gentlemen's sons could disappear, and from which they could emerge as successful clergymen, lawyers, doctors or merchants. John Rogers, the vicar of Clodock in the 19th century had three sons. One of them, Aaron, followed his father's calling by becoming a vicar; Moses became a surgeon; and one of his daughters, Pheobe, married Henry Thomas Harris (almost certainly the grandson of Thomas Harris, the mercer). After their widowed mother's death these children were seriously wealthy as John Roger's considerable property was sold and placed in a trust invested in Government stocks.

There was clearly a recognised lifestyle that went with gentrihood. In summary, it involved having a certain level of education, and enough money to pay for extra luxuries like a large house, servants to run it and fine goods to furnish it, with sufficient money to give to charities at the end, together with a tomb or memorial at the chancel end of the church, or at least within the precincts.

By the end of the 17th century and throughout the 18th there was a rapid increase in the numbers of 'new' gentry enjoying this life-style. One of their first moves was to invest in land whenever it became available. Thus their wealth would generally come from the land, rather than trade, land which they would often not farm themselves but lease out to others.

5 AGRICULTURE

Visitors to the Hundred of Ewyas Lacy cannot help but notice that geography and geology combine to make it a uniquely distinctive part of Herefordshire with a different pattern of agriculture to the rest of the county, and this was the case during the period covered by our inventories.

In the 18th century, Daniel Defoe gives an up-beat account of the 'diligent and laborious' Herefordians, in spite of their being 'so very remote'. Accounts given over many decades are almost unanimous in agreeing that the entire county lacked a good infrastructure of roads and navigable rivers and this was compounded in Ewyas Lacy by soaring hills to the west. This had an effect on the export and import of produce, from livestock to crops.

We are able to compare the nature of agriculture in Ewyas Lacy with that in the rest of the county from a number of contemporary accounts. Concerning the mid 17th century there is a detailed account taken by the Revd John Webb, and edited and completed by his son, from sources available at the outbreak of the Civil War. Then at the end of the 18th century there is John Clark's *General View of the Agriculture of the County of Hereford* (1794). This was drawn up for the Board of Agriculture with the object of suggesting improvements, and following that, John Duncumb's modestly entitled *Collections towards the History and Antiquities of the County of Hereford*. William Page wrote the only Victoria County volume in 1908. Of course, there are other accounts that help to fill in more of the detail such as the general coverage of the time between the Restoration and the end of the Napoleonic War by E.L. Jones, written in the 1960s. It is also useful to compare what was happening on farms just over the border in Monmouthshire as it would be odd if they were very different. Here we have an account by Frank Emery in *The Agrarian History of England and Wales*.[1] These accounts outline various problems which were compounded in respect to Ewyas Lacy by its relative isolation from the four major market towns of Herefordshire: Hereford, Ross-on-Wye, Leominster and Ledbury.

The Webbs' description of Herefordshire in the middle of the 17th century shows the difficulty of moving commodities along the Wye due to the weirs along its length that made the river navigable for only four months a year, and adds that the roads were rugged and almost impracticable for the transport of produce. Journeys were generally made on horseback or with pack animals, while heavy or bulky goods were transported by wain drawn by six oxen. The Webbs state that Hereford's commodities consisted of corn, butter and cheese, but that in general communities 'consumed their own produce, depended much upon themselves, and disliked change'. The rearing of sheep and horses was important to them, especially amongst people of rank such as Lord Scudamore of Holme Lacy and Sir Robert Harley of Brampton Bryan. Apples also, subsequent to improvement by Lord Scudamore, had, by the Restoration of the monarchy, become a popular export to London and Bristol.

Jones, writing of the 17th century and later, confirms the picture drawn by the Webbs, whilst admitting that poor communication with neighbouring counties stifled economic development. A wide range of surplus goods were produced, but all manufactured goods, lime and coal had to be imported irregularly up the Wye, or along bad roads, which pushed up prices. In 1831 David Smith had coal listed in his inventory, which may have meant that he was using it to burn lime, though there is no mention of the latter in any of the inventories. However, a lime kiln is noted under Craswall, in the field name survey for Ewyas Lacy.[2] Much earlier, in 1781, William Gwillim of Clodock had three loads of coal worth £3. As a postscript, at the very end of our period, in 1855, Elizabeth Jones of the Cayo in Llanveynoe made the munificent gift to the poor of Llanveynoe and Longtown and the National School, of £5 worth of coal twice yearly. Obviously regular quantities were coming in by that time, probably from Pandy railway station a few miles away.

By 1700 much of the agricultural surplus was marketed through Bristol, with London taking cattle brought along the road by drovers. Down the Wye went grain, cider and wool; the packhorse taking grain from Hereford market to Monmouth, whence it was often sent by Bristol merchants as far as Portugal. New schemes for improvement of transport links were put in place towards the end of the 18th century, by which time turnpike roads had been built, and a canal connected Hereford and Gloucester. Surplus goods could now go not only to the south of the county but also to the North and the Midlands.

It was said that the use of lime had become quite common, and that Herefordians were well supplied with rye, which was often mixed with wheat to produce something called muncorn used to make a rougher form of bread. There is a contradiction between the Webbs' account of lime being in general use in the 17th century and Clark's assertion that the coming of the canal meant that lime could now be conveyed to lime-deficient clays. Any mention of lime or coal appearing in the probate documents would help to clarify this.

By 1789 the principal markets for cider were still Bristol and London, but with the improved infrastructure in place the trade was beginning to shift to the midlands and the north. Cider was made in large quantities in Ewyas Lacy Hundred but whilst it was obviously drunk on the farms, was there sufficient surplus to export? Pigs were another notable export, Jones notes, with a growing trade for fattening at the London distilleries. This too needs further local exploration, as does the statement that, as Herefordshire was poorly supplied with dairies, butter and cheese was routinely brought in from elsewhere. Wool is rarely mentioned in the inventories because it was removed from the farm almost immediately, but there was a large export of this from the county where, at the end of the 18th century, farmers were cross-breeding the native Ryeland sheep in order to obtain a heavier carcass. Hereford cattle, on the other hand, were growing in popularity, and supplying beef for the increasing urban market.

What of crops? Much of Herefordshire was already enclosed by the 17th century, with the exception of the commons and land at very high altitudes. This should have been an aid to innovatory practice, but was it? It might be considered that Herefordshire was backward in the introduction of such new crops as turnips but there was a reason for this as they were not considered suitable for hilly lands, nor was it a crop generally grown in the west as sheep will tend to poach the land if fed on turnips in the fields in the winter. However turnips were being used as a supplementary feed for both sheep and cattle by the end of the 18th century, being noted in the Cornewall farm accounts from 1786 to 1799, as were swedes in 1801. Duncumb, however, was very disapproving in his comments in 1804, claiming that turnips were 'much neglected' and 'often sown without manure on poor and foul lands', and also claims that, unlike the eastern side of the country, there was no excess production of straw to turn into dung. Clover, being well suited to Herefordshire conditions, was adopted by the latter half of the 17th century. There is a reference to it in a tenancy agreement at Hay-on-Wye on the edge of the Hundred.

Jones suggests that the uplands were too wet for wheat, though Duncumb describes the surplus in the rest of the county which was exported to Bristol and beyond. Oats, he says, were mostly grown on the Welsh border.[3] Hops we need not consider, as Ewyas Lacy was not a hop-growing area.

Some Herefordshire landowners had long been in the van of improvements, beginning with Rowland Vaughan, who in 1610 published *His Booke – Most Improved and Long experienced Waterworks*. Later there was the symbiotic relationship between parson Beale and Lord Scudamore of Holme Lacy in producing top quality cider after the Civil War, when soldiers had acquired a taste for it.[4] There is no doubt that new ideas were growing and being widely disseminated. The Brecknockshire Agricultural Society was formed at

Looking across the Olchon Valley to the Cat's Back limb of the Black Mountains showing the comparative small size of fields and bracken covered flanks

47

Brecon in 1755, and the Herefordshire Agricultural Society in 1797. Emery mentions that in 1771, a Methodist settlement at Leominster was a source of improving innovations.[5] Flax and hemp were grown on a small scale in the county, encouraged by a bounty of £6,335 15s in 1796 to encourage its cultivation, but hemp can be seen in use in the Hundred much earlier.

All these statements can be explored in the context of the Ewyas Lacy inventories. While the rest of Herefordshire was considered prime agricultural territory in the 17th and 18th centuries, producing fine quality wool, cider, cattle and grain, Ewyas Lacy may not have been far behind, despite the drawbacks of relative isolation, poor communications, a lack of resident greater landowners to provide leadership, and the acknowledged poorer quality land, which could support fewer animals per acre than the rest of the county.[6]

Problems of accessibility and of non-resident landowners

So how much worse did Ewyas Lacy fare than the rest of the county in terms of accessibility? It is commonly thought that the area must have similar weather to that in Wales, i.e. wetter than the rest of Herefordshire, but in fact the Black Mountains provide some protection, much of the rain falling there. However, the run-off from the hills caused flooding of the roads on their eastern flank, something that Clarke considered a disgrace. He describes, sarcastically, the way in which landowners planned the turnpikes so that they benefited their own lands, sending the roads up a hill to 'oblige a friend or mortify an enemy'. It seems, though, that even with the coming of turnpikes, roads continued to be bad until

Looking across to the Black Mountains with the Cat's Back on the right, and the Darren on the left

the arrival of tarmacadam in the 19th century. When asked how friends reached remote farmhouses, deep in mud, in winter, the owners replied simply, 'We never expect them'.[7]

The lives of their descendants were to improve from the last quarter of the 18th century with the coming of a turnpike road to Pontrilas, Ewyas Harold and Clodock in 1772. On the border of the Hundred, at Pontrilas, the tramway that carried coal to Hereford from Wales was completed in 1829.[8] The railway from Hereford to Monmouth was under construction by 1845, but did not reach Hereford until 1855.

A knowledge of the topography of the area helps to understand the difficulties in the way of access to the rest of Herefordshire. To reach the Hundred from Hereford meant either coming from Ewyas Harold over the breath-takingly steep Bryn, or travelling on winding and narrow roads through Craswall or Michaelchurch Escley. These must have sometimes been impassable, especially in winter. Otherwise the only access was along a relatively flat road, often flooded in winter, from Abergavenny in Monmouthshire. The tendency, therefore, would be for goods from the centre and east of the Hundred, i.e. Clodock and Longtown, to go to Abergavenny market 11 miles away, and those from parishes or townships to the north, such as Craswall, to travel to Hay-on-Wye, and thence to Hereford, a distance of about 23 miles. In 1731, William Gilbert, a yeoman of Craswall had 'a fatt heifer sold at the Hay fair'.

The second difficulty experienced by farmers in Ewyas Lacy was lack of contact with the chief owners of land in the region. One of the main landowners, Lord Abergavenny, lived in Sussex and left his estates to be run by a bailiff, or steward, and the Jefferies family, the other lords of the manor, lived in Brecon. Some element of leadership was however given by resident landowners. We have already seen that several landowners in the county

Looking across Ewyas Lacy Hundred with the Black Mountains in the distance.
The Cat's Back is to the right of centre

with interests or farms in or near Ewyas Lacy were innovatory, beginning with Rowland Vaughan in the late 16th century and continuing in the following three centuries with Lord Scudamore, Lord Oxford and Lord Cornewall.

The farmers of Ewyas Lacy

The common idea that farming was entirely in the hands of the yeomen farmers turns out not to be entirely true when one looks at the inventories. There were at least six groups involved to some extent or another, including the local gentry, the yeomen, husbandmen and labourers, and also widows and tradesmen, who farmed a not insubstantial proportion of the land. The gentry, although owning large tracts of land, did not always farm it themselves but let it out to tenant farmers. There were exceptions to this, particularly at Llancillo where no fewer than six gentlemen farmed what must have been a substantial acreage. Three of them owned an unusually large number of oxen, suggesting that their landholding included a large amount under the plough. In 1719 Henry Powell of Llancillo owned seven oxen, four horses, sheep, pigs and poultry, valued at more than half the total of his inventory of £102 9s 4d; in addition one sixth of his investment lay in the value of his crops. It must be pointed out that these gentry farmed on the better land of the Hundred, well away from the Black Mountains.

The yeomen, besides generally owning the freehold of their land, also took on leaseholds from others, but in some cases their investment might be as minimal as that of any of the other groups, especially if they were nearing the end of their lives before the inventory was taken. Even the few husbandmen and labourers who appear had a tiny investment in livestock, like the labourer at Clodock who simply had a cow in calf, which he probably grazed on rented land (or maybe in return for his labour on someone else's land). A labourer at Michaelchurch Escley was unusual in that he owned a mare and colt together with a few sheep, but most of all because he had considerable financial backing in the shape of bonds worth £72, and his clothing was valued at £2, the average value of that of any gentleman.

The fact remains that, generally speaking, labourers were not owners of land but merely laboured on it for others. One or two 'Husbandmen' appear in most of the parishes who would have a very similar position in that they generally worked for others in order to earn a living. A touching picture emerges of one of them who died in Clodock in 1759, owning one ewe worth 5s and 'implements of husbandry', but also potatoes and a tobacco box (the only one to be mentioned in the inventories). Another husbandman who was well on his way to yeoman status died at Craswall in 1724 owning as much as many of the poorer

The sower depicted in stained glass in Canterbury Cathedral

yeomen. He had four cows, including one 'hip-shot' cow, 2 horses, 56 sheep and two pigs – one quarter of his total valuation of over £81, the equal of many another farmer. (The change of terminology from yeoman to 'farmer' began towards the end of the 18th century, no-one is quite sure why.)

The yeomen covered a wide spectrum from being worth as much as the gentry to as little as the husbandman, so it will be worth expanding a little on how the term originated and what it meant. The word yeoman emerged in about the 13th or 14th century and by the 15th century denoted a rank, or place, in rural society. As a freeman the yeoman owned a secure title to land which in time entitled him to a vote if he owned 40s worth of land, and by the 17th century, copyhold land, held from the manor, might also qualify. Lack of wealth, education or ancient family connections was the only difference between them and the gentry, just as lack of freehold land separated the husbandmen from the yeomen. The system was a fluid one in that the landless younger sons of a yeoman could become husbandmen and vice versa. No wonder that their contemporaries were sometimes in a quandary! Similarly sons of a yeoman might enter the ranks of the gentry in time by way of university, the law-courts or by military service.[9] Rather oddly to modern sensibilities, even the amount spent on clothing changed from class to class. Clothing for the gentry was generally valued at £2 or above, that for yeomen generally between £1 and £1 10s, and for classes below yeomen at under £1. Yeomen were also allowed to have a gun to shoot game on their own land.

Even in death they were divided, gentry usually being buried within the church and yeomen without. Gentry were expected to be generous at their funeral, sometimes providing for wine and biscuits. In the 17th century in Ewyas Lacy yeomen appear to have left around £10, often for cider and cake. The problem was that their generosity sometimes exceeded their ability to pay. James Nicholls, yeoman of Longtown in 1682, wanted the sum of £20 to be given to the poor of Longtown, but this together with other bequests exceeded the total value of his inventory. At least one of the beneficiaries was not paid at all.

There seem also to have been a high proportion of women running farms; in most cases probably after the deaths of husbands whilst waiting for children to be old enough to take over the farm. There were also cases where a woman had no sons, or did not remarry, or where spinsters inherited farms and were determined to hold onto the reins. In an analysis of the 1880 census it was found that female farmers formed a slightly higher proportion in western counties such as Herefordshire than in counties to the east.[10] This may have been because the average farm size was smaller and so easier to work and manage.

Size of Farms

Ewyas Lacy was pastoral country containing family run farms, with a preponderance of yeomen. There are some useful figures thrown up by the 1840s Tithe survey giving the size and type of land in four of the parishes or townships. Longtown was the largest with 6,104 acres, Craswall came next with 5,117, then Llanveynoe with 3,510 and lastly Walterstone with just over 1,241. The survey also gives a valuable picture of the region near the middle of the 19th century, just as the inventories are coming to an end. Of Craswall it says that the rotation of crops was fallow, wheat and oats with similar results for Llanveynoe and Walterstone, with the addition of barley at Longtown and clover at Walterstone. In each case

A typical farmyard between the mid 1800s and mid 1900s.
This is Quarrelly Farm in Newton; notice the pigs on the right of the photograph

the soil was noted as clay. The values given for the different types of land are illuminating, with the rental value of arable at Longtown being far and away the most valuable at 10s an acre as against 7s at Craswall and only 6s at Llanveynoe. Pasture at Llanveynoe, however, was worth more than that at Craswall, at 8s compared with 6s.[11]

The impression given is that, like the Welsh lands over the border, the Hundred was made up of small, mixed, family run farms of between 30 and 50 acres, but this turned out not to be the case in at least one parish. In 1861 at Llanveynoe, along one side of the Olchon, there were 31 farms of between 50 and 200 acres, which compare to an average size of farms in the entire Hundred of 58 acres in 1850.[12] These medium to large farms in Llanveynoe may have been a consequence of their proximity to mountain grazing, and the comparative barrenness of the soil.

Livestock

In order to ascertain the extent of involvement by the farmers of Ewyas Lacy in livestock and crop production a random sample was taken of approximately a third of the inventories; the information was then extracted and tabulated for each person. A certain demographic bias will be present as those inventoried had tended to be old or infirm at the time of death. (A table providing some analysis of stocking density between the 16th and 18th centuries is given in Appendix B.)

Cattle

Emery notes that the upland regions of Wales in the neighbouring Vale of Usk were mostly used for rearing store cattle rather than dairy herds, and this seems to also have been the case at Ewyas Lacy, though there were exceptions, as will be shown. The impression given is that the wetter uplands specialized more in cattle breeding and fattening.

It seems unlikely that live animals from Ewyas Lacy would be driven all the way to Hereford Michaelmas Fair when the beasts could be driven by the drovers to the closer market at Abergavenny (thence being taken on to Smithfield in London by the drovers), but there is also mention of the market at Hay being used. The only mention of a local drover is in the inventory of Jane Nicholls, widow of Longtown in 1683, in which 'money in the hands of James Nicholls the drovier' is listed, drovers often being entrusted with money to make payments to distant creditors. These drovers would normally buy their stock at the markets, but in the 18th century the coming of toll roads and the growth of enclosures, which reduced their access to wayside pastures, created difficulties for them.

The numbers of cattle that were slaughtered locally were linked with a seemingly abnormal number of tanners, twenty or more over the three centuries and across the parishes. Long journeys to market the 'finished' animals probably meant that it was more profitable to feed the growing industry in the manufacture of leather goods such as saddles, footwear and so on. Although there is not much sign of specialists producing the end product locally, there were several buildings called 'tanhouses' in the district. It would be easier, too, to export hides rather than beasts over bad roads.

It is clear from the inventories that beef and sheep production was mainly the province of substantial farmers as the cost of start-up was so high compared with other enterprises. The value of any livestock, especially cattle, would form a large part of the total value of

Hereford Cattle near Great Turnant in 2013

anyone's inventory. One example is that of James Nicholl, of Olchon in Llanveynoe, who died in 1731 with cattle worth £30 16s out of a total inventory value of £60 16s. In another case, in 1763, Samuel Watkins, gent of Clodock, had 'horned cattle' worth £114, compared with a total inventory value of £237 9s. In general, many of the farmers had more livestock than the Welsh farms over the border.

A subject of much interest to Herefordians is the origin of the Hereford breed. As we have seen, in the 1611 will of John Henry Maddock he referred to his 'Bull of twoe yeare olde coloured redd' and 'two heifers of twoe yeare olde the one coloured redd the other redd with white face'. Is this a very early mention of the breed that went on to colonise the Americas, and spread all over the world? The Hereford Cattle Society merely states on its website that the breed has been in existence for over 200 years, and its recorded sales only go back to 1723, by which time it was supplying best quality beef for a growing urban market. With a population increase from six million in the mid 18th century to nine million at the beginning of the 19th century, and again to almost 17 million by the 1851 census, it would be inconceivable that the farmers in Ewyas Lacy were not producing more meat to meet a growing demand.

Oxen

The use of oxen was far from becoming extinct in Ewyas Lacy, unlike on the eastern side of England where they had been almost entirely replaced by horses by the 16th century. At the end of the 18th century Page claims that half the ploughing in the county was still being done by oxen.[13] This was for practical reasons as well as those of tradition. They were slower but steadier than horses; beginning work at the age of three or four years old, they could be worked for another ten years before being fattened. They were used for plough land, beef and hide production and also transport in teams of four to six to a waincart. Their value actually increased by 7% overall from the mid 16th to the mid 18th century. There is some debate over whether the horse or the ox was the better draught animal. Page mentions a case of four oxen competing successfully on cost compared with three horses.[14] Oxen were steadier than horses and cost less to feed, but by the 20th century they had, in most cases, been replaced by horses.

Horses

The advantage that horses had over oxen was that they lived longer, and could be bred so as to potentially replace themselves several times during their lifetime. A horse's normal working life is about 21 years, comprising seven years training, seven years at peak capacity, and seven years of gradual decline. The statement by Tonkin that there appear to have been no horses in the 'Black Mountain area' during the latter half of the 17th century is puzzling. Virtually every inventory (except for those of the very old or very poor) mentioned a horse or two, understandably when it was the only mode of transport available to ordinary people. At Yetminster in Dorset, Thirsk notes that by the 17th century three-fifths of householders owned horses, and the demand for them gradually extended to yeomen and husbandmen. Welsh horses were much sought after and pastoral areas were also horse breeding areas.

The value of a horse varied considerably. Thirsk quotes prices for horses as ranging from £1 to £2 10s for mares in the first half of the 17th century, to £8 by the 1700s. Similarly, in the mid 17th century, a colt could fetch between £1 and £1 10s, and cart horses at the end of the 17th century between £6 and £7.[15] Prices at Ewyas Lacy seem fairly similar, though price would obviously vary according to the quality of the animal and the age, which is not always known. Mares were usually more valuable than horses, and more commonly kept because they were able to produce a foal on a regular basis. In the late 17th century in Ewyas Lacy a mare could be worth as much as £2 10s and a horse £1, rising to £10 for a mare and colt, and £5 to £7 for a horse by the early 19th century. Certainly, the horse or mare appeared to be an essential animal for anyone at Ewyas Lacy with business to transact, whether it was carrying farm goods to market or making visits of any kind. (The only mention of any kind of conveyance other than horses was a 'horse chaise' listed in the inventory of James Exton, gentleman of Michaelchurch Escley in 1774.) The only people without horses seemed to be the very old or the poor. In an illuminating letter from the agent, Mr Harris, to Lord Abergavenny in the 19th century, Harris writes that he considers his charge of £40 for the maintenance of a horse very reasonable noting that 'It is quite impossible to look after so scattered a property as his lordships in an efficient manner without keeping a horse', adding, with asperity, 'his Lordship I am sure would hardly wish me to do that out of £100 per annum'. One can only comment that the cost of the horse seems rather excessive compared with Mr Harris's own salary.[16]

Were horses actually being bred on a large scale in Ewyas Lacy? I think this unlikely during this period, except in one or two cases. There was one gentleman of Craswall, Thomas Watkins who, in 1666, owned 12 horses, but the usual number of horses on a farm ranged between one and four. Most widows had horses, or mares, as did tradesmen such as Walter Jenkins, a mason, who had one mare in 1691 worth £1 5s, but it is difficult to believe that the '1 old decayed horse' of Thomas Prosser, 'millard' (miller) was able to carry him very far in 1713; it was worth only 15s. On the other hand, the 'Bay Nag' belonging to Samuel Watkynes, gent, of Longtown was worth £6, even in 1676. In most parishes or townships in the initial sample of one-fifth of the total inventories mentioned earlier, more

Mares and colts in the Olchon Valley

than 50% of people owned a horse. In Llanveynoe 18 out of 23 owned a horse, followed in the ratings by Clodock and Longtown. It has to be borne in mind, too, that these lists were taken at a time when the deceased was probably old or ill, when they would be less likely to need a horse. Some of the horses listed were also old and 'decayed', illustrative of the farmer's fondness for his horses and desire to let them die on the farm.

In Craswall there is a field near Abbey Farm called Parc-y-meirch, meaning the large field of the horses, also translated by one Welsh speaker as 'The field of the wild white stallions'.[17] A startling entry in the inventory of David Myles, yeoman of Michaelchurch Escley in 1672, describes '4 mounten Mares', and three other mountain horses, worth just over £1 each. Were these the progenitors of the wild horses that still roam across the Black Mountains? As David Myles also kept other horses and mares, was this an attempt to cross-breed, and why is it that mountain horses are never mentioned after the early 18th century? There are three other mentions of these mountain horses, one in the 1572 will of Richard Weston, a yeoman of Michaelchurch Escley, where he leaves a bequest of six 'wild horses', another in the 1576 inventory of David ap Rees Madyein where they are called '4 wyld caples', and in the 1712 inventory of Nathaniel Morgan, yeoman, of Llancillo, who had '1 little mountaineer horse', worth £1.

In summary, then, as there were only five other people (one of them a widow, Mary Davies of Clodock in 1794) who had more than four horses or mares, this area cannot be considered to have been a horse-breeding region at this period, though it became so later, in the 19th century, for pit ponies for the Welsh mines.

Sheep
Given the importance of sheep farming at Ewyas Lacy in the 20th century, it was a surprise to find that in the period under review, relatively small flocks were being kept by farmers who

Sheep grazing in the Olchon Valley

seemed to concentrate more on cattle breeding. It is useful to bear in mind, however, that historians claim that sheep are consistently under-recorded in inventories, possibly because individually they were worth considerably less than cattle, or may have been difficult for the appraisers to count if they were away grazing.[18] Only very occasionally were large flocks listed and these, understandably, in parishes closest to the Black Mountains, where the farmers would have had grazing rights. At Craswall there were four farmers with large flocks of sheep, one of whom in 1768, John Symonds, had as many as 211 'of all sorts', while two farmers in Llanveynoe had almost a hundred sheep. Notably, at Walterstone, which was some distance from the Black Mountains, only a handful of sheep were listed in the sample inventories. Although the well known Herefordshire breed, the Ryeland, had a reputation for producing fine wool, it was not eventually viable because of its small size, and it was supplanted by sheep with a heavier carcass. However, there is no evidence of any particular breed of sheep being kept in the Hundred, except in the 1796 inventory of Phillip Gilbert of Walterstone where six 'Welsh ewes' are listed. In the 17th century at least, the sheep were housed at night throughout the year so were more prone to foot rot. This could have been the reason why local farmers preferred to keep cattle, which were less prone to disease in general. However it is interesting to note that towards the last half of the 18th century and beginning of the 19th there were one or two farmers in the Clodock and Longtown area who were beginning to keep larger flocks of a hundred or more. They were David Parry of Clodock, who in 1770 had 130 sheep, and, in Longtown in 1814, John Prichard, who had 100 sheep and lambs. This in itself is not conclusive of a change of heart or regime, of course. More evidence is required.[19]

Gathering the sheep off the Black Mountains in winter

Goats

Myles Hunt's bequests in the 16th century included some goats. Goats were certainly more prevalent in the 16th and 17th centuries than later, and by the early 18th century had virtually disappeared from the inventories. There were 12 examples in the 17th and only two in the 18th. Two of the 17th century examples of goat keeping were Johan Phillips, a widow of Llanveynoe with five goats and two kids in 1666, and John Symonds, of the same township, who had 12 goats in 1680. William James, a yeoman of 'Merryhurst' in St Margarets had six goats and a 'buckgoat' listed in his inventory of 1702. Thomas Mabe, a shoemaker of Michaelchurch Escley, owned four goats in 1743.

Pigs

The ownership of pigs seems to have been fairly evenly distributed across the three centuries under review. In the main, pigs seemed to be reared merely for home consumption, and more than half the villagers with inventories had at least one, possibly with piglets. It was sometimes difficult to tell what 'pigs of all sorts' meant as the appraiser could mean merely a sow with a litter of piglets. One husbandman of Walterstone in 1757, who could have been the prototype of Jack in the Beanstalk's father, had only 'a little cow', a hayrick, a cottage worth £1, two chaff beds and 'bacon', which hung in the first room the appraisers entered. As the inventory was taken on 9 February he had probably killed the pig in December and would not get another to fatten until the spring.

Most farms in Ewyas Lacy had one or two pigs, a second pig being a form of insurance. For instance in 1701, an aleseller, Thomas Price of Michaelchurch Escley, who in his will gave himself the grander title of victualler, had two pigs, and asked that his 'biggest' pig should be sold to pay his rent to his landlord.

However, there were exceptions where pigs were obviously being raised on a commercial scale. As the figures for pigs were studied an interesting pattern began to emerge. A figure of five pigs and upwards was taken as a minimum for production on a commercial scale and it was discovered that large-scale pig breeding was almost always done in conjunction with large-scale arable farming and the keeping of four or more oxen. Apart from one or two gentlemen, the pig breeders were yeoman farmers with comfortably furnished houses and a total inventory value above the norm. One or two examples will give a sense of the average type. In March 1683, James Watkins, yeoman, of Llanveynoe, had 12 pigs, a yoke of oxen, 4 bullocks, 9 cows, 11 cattle, horses and colts 'of all sorts', 23 acres of hard corn and 20 acres of Lent grain and an inventory worth over £115. John Powell, yeoman of Longtown had, in September 1736, 10 pigs, 4 Oxen, 6 cows, 1 bull, 10 'beasts' and 3 calves plus a harvest of 4 bushels of malt, 40 bushels of wheat, 80 bushels of barley, oats and peas. His inventory came to £113. In both cases their investment in livestock came to more than £63, more than half the value of their inventory.

Poultry

Poultry were quickly dismissed in the inventory, if mentioned at all, and were not worth much compared with the other livestock. Pigs, geese and other poultry could graze cheaply on the extensive commons, therefore would suit those smallholders with rights to the commons. One man who kept 24 geese in 1758 was Henry Morgan, an innkeeper of Craswall.

Bees

Bees are mentioned in a few inventories, chiefly in the 17th century, as they were then the only source of sugar before it began to come in from the New World. Thomas Gilbert, 'gent', of Llanveynoe owned six hives of bees in 1657 and John Shaw of Clodock had four hives in 1662, followed by Edmund Thomas, gent of Michaelchurch Escley in 1671 and Lewis James Williams in 1676 with two 'swarms' of bees. There was only two 'stalls' of bees in the mid 18th century in the inventory of John Lewis, yeoman of Longtown, apart from a mention of beeswax amongst the contents of Thomas Harris's shop in Longtown in 1786.

Dairy Production

Although Jones is fairly dismissive about Herefordshire dairies, saying they were competing with Cheshire cheese and Welsh butter coming via the Hereford to Gloucester canal and overland by the latter half of the 18th century, most farmers' wives must have been producing butter and cheese, some in large quantities. In his description of the Cecil's house, Alltyrynys in Walterstone, Duncumb repeats an account written in 1647 where the dairy is mentioned, saying 'there being many good cheeses at that time, arguing good pasture and plentiful kine'. Duncumb also claims that although Herefordshire was not dairy country butter was, in reality, going the other way, into Wales for winter use. This enterprise was ideal for the small producer, usually the housewife, as it gave a regular income and did not require much expenditure on equipment, though the inventories might suggest otherwise as these contain much evidence of utensils like pails, cheese presses, cheese wrings and vats.

However, dairying was labour-intensive compared with the other activities on the farm. Census returns show that larger farms had a dairymaid who would also make the cheese. The process was as follows: the cheese press had holes in the base lined with muslin and the curd was then pressed into it to extract the whey. The resulting hard cheese would then last a year. One gallon of milk produced 1lb of cheese, and effectively just over 1lb of cream produced 1lb of butter. The output of a cow in a dairy varied between 2.5 and 6cwt of cheese a year in the late 18th and mid 19th century, and a good cow could produce between 3.5 and 7lb per week in the butter making season.[20]

Butter is seldom mentioned in inventories as it would be unlikely to remain on the farm for long, going to market once a week. In only 13 cases is butter mentioned on its own, and curiously, of these, more than half were in the pre-1660 inventories. In the parish of Clodock, the widow Jayne Phillipps owned one 'loaf' of butter in 1633, in 1636 Alexander Lord owned 50 quarts of butter in addition to 100 cheeses, and David George, yeoman, had 15 'buckes' of butter at 9d a 'bucke'.[21] In the 1727 inventory of Abraham Pugh, a yeoman of Michaelchurch Escley, not only did he have 300 cheeses but his 'butter' was valued at £4, twice the amount given for the cheeses. At a combined value of £6 5s this went a considerable way towards paying his Michaelmas rent of £15 5s. To support this commercial production he had 11 cows and a bull, five heifers and six calves, 11 'Milch Trinds', one vat, one tub, two cheese coules, a cheese ring, four cheese vats and two pails.[22] At St Margarets in 1742, John Phillips, gent, had butter in the dairy together with cheese, and at Clodock in 1770, David Parry had no less than 12 stone of butter. In an inventory of 1857 for John Powell, there is the one mention of 'butter scales'.

Examples which mention cheese are too numerous to include individually, so only those with large amounts in their inventories were looked at in detail. The larger producers were clearly making cheese commercially, though one cannot be sure what type. The closest we can get to it is in the inventory of William Prichard of Michaelchurch Escley of 1663, which listed as '83 cheeses of several sorts', worth £4. Much of this would almost certainly have gone to the markets at Abergavenny and Hay and possibly even as far as Hereford. Even in the 20th century most farmers' wives would take their butter, cheese and eggs to the Tuesday market at Abergavenny on horseback, or by other conveyance, as they had doubtless done for centuries.

Apart from William Prichard and the already mentioned Abraham Pugh, another of the producers was a 'spinster' named Alice Williams John in 1663, of Michaelchurch Escley, who owned 'one half of the cheese' worth 15s at her death, obviously producing cheese on a small scale with someone else. Another major producer who was clearly selling on her produce in 1681 was Elinor Myles, a widow of Michaelchurch Escley. She had 30 new cheeses worth 10 shillings, but her husband, David Myles, before his death in 1672 had owned 124 cheeses and butter in his inventory worth £10. This could obviously be a prosperous business as both the Myles had clothing worth above the average for their time: that of David Myles was worth £3 10s, compared with the usual £2 for the gentry, and nine years later his wife's clothing was worth £1. For making cheese in large quantities it was usual to have between five and eight cows with associated calves. David Myles had seven cows with calves, besides two three-year-old heifers and one two-year old for later production. Elinor had five cows and two store calves. It is interesting to note that Elinor's inventory was dated 25 June, hence the 'new' cheeses; cheese was usually made in June when there was more casein in the grass. Close daily contact must have made many farmers and their wives quite attached to their cows. There is a delightful glimpse, in his 1802 inventory, of Walter Prichard's four cows, which were affectionately named Blossom, Daisy, Lovely and Cherry. (His horses were also given names.) His family at Llancillo were producing 'a quantity of cheese' worth 18s, and also had two butter baskets. David Parry, yeoman, of Clodock, had, at his death in 1770, 12 stone of butter and 2 cwts cheese from eight 'milk cows' worth £36, also nine heifers coming on as insurance.

The Parry family was the second largest producer in the Hundred, and their equipment included a 'Bake and Brewhouse' in which were probably kept the 'milk creans', six cheese vats, eight butter tubs, churning vessel, 'butter tack' and a kneading trough. The food for the farm was supplied from eight acres of wheat, 19 acres of oats, three acres of barley, two acres of peas and seven acres of clover. There was also £20 worth of hay in the barn and hayloft. In the same year one of the most comprehensive descriptions lies in the Newton inventory for Elizabeth Prosser, widow, with five cows in 1770, who had 12 cheeses at £1, a cheese press, 11 cheese vats, five milk vessels and a butter tub, as well as many other items too numerous to mention, except the unusual presence of 'butter prints'. She obviously took pride in her butter.

Unlike today, cows were not always brought indoors for milking, but might be milked out in the field, and we can catch a possible glimpse of this in the mention of four 'cow stools' and milking pails in the inventory of Joseph Beavan, husbandman, in 1721. He was a relatively poor man compared with the others but even he had six cows. Unlike the prosperous David Parry who had clothing worth £2, his was described as 'long wore', worth only £1 5s, and his total inventory came to nearly £42 in contrast to Parry's £234 19s 6d.

Cider Production

Whilst one cannot be sure that cider was produced commercially, it must have been drunk in vast quantities as there is plenty of evidence of cider making in the probate documents. Of course Herefordshire was cider making country par excellence in the 19th century, with more acreage under fruit than any other county. Much of Herefordshire's exports went to London where prices could be variable, at times of shortage in the 18th century, for instance, reaching as much as 100s per barrel. Cider was shipped to Bristol, too, and from there was exported further afield to the East and West Indies. However, there was a temporary decline during the Napoleonic Wars as farmers grubbed up their orchards to produce the more lucrative corn and meat – lucrative because Britain was unable to import from Europe, the supply routes having been cut off, and needed to rely on home-grown produce. Jones states that the profits of the Cornewall estates may have accelerated between 1783 and 1815 – that is, during the period of the Napoleonic Wars – and the war also had its effect on Ewyas Lacy farms.

The impression given is that most cider was for domestic use, though an inventory for a John Thomas in 1829, of Longtown, shows that he had enough fruit to make four hogsheads of cider; at 110 gallons each this is a lot of cider for purely home consumption. In the late 18th century a hogshead of cider was normally worth between 25 and 42s and the cost of producing it only 5s, so there was quite a profit to be made. At one guinea, the hogshead itself was almost as valuable as its contents.[23]

The yeoman farmers were the most likely to have hogsheads in their inventory as they had the responsibility of making enough alcohol to keep their workforce happy, but there is some evidence that they resented the encroachment of cider-making on the real business of the farm. Clarke tells the story of one farmworker who asks his master, 'what horse shall I take to drive cider mill?' The farmer replied, 'D...n the cider and the mill, too. You waste one half of your time in making cider, and the other half in drinking it.'[24] By the end of the 18th century drink composed a large part of the labourer's wages. In summer he would receive 6s per week and a gallon of drink, and in winter 5s and three quarts of drink. In the sample there were 14 inventories with one or more hogsheads, three of them for widows, presumably widows of farmers. One was a cooper who was likely to have such things for sale, another was a dyer who may have needed it for his trade, but the rest were either yeomen farmers or 'gents'. There was also a widow and four other farmers or yeomen with a cider mill, often listed with casks. One rich farmer, James Watkins, of Fair Oake in St Margarets, with an above average inventory worth £412 15s 6d in 1848, had £31 worth of casks alone. In 1769, the enterprising and wealthy farmer, David Parry of Clodock, was hiring out his eight hogsheads to other farmers.

We have already seen that cider was the accompaniment of funerals, in the documents of James Jones of Michaelchurch Escley, whose executrix was charged 12s for cake and 9s 6d for cider for his wake in 1759, and in another account of the same year and parish, that of Henry Estland, yeoman, which allows a total of £13 for cake, spice and cider.

Cider houses that were possibly illegal were to be found in out of the way places. In what became my study in a remote farmhouse, we were told of secret cider drinking in the past by the old man who had been born there 80 years before.

> Unspeakable carouses that shame the summer sky
> Take place in little houses that look towards the Wye
> And near the Radnor Border and the dark hills of Wales
> Beelzebub is warder and sorcery prevails.
> For in spite of church and chapel ungodly folks there be
> Who pluck the cider apple from the cider apple-tree
> And squeeze it in their presses until the juice runs out
> At various addresses that no one knows about.

No-one would suggest that orgies took place at that time but the farmhouse was sufficiently remote, and with no fewer than 12 gates dividing it from the road, it would have been difficult for the Excise men to get there in time to catch them drinking illicitly.[25]

In 1839 William Gilbert, yeoman, of Hunthouse, not only had cider but an entire array of brewing equipment to produce both beer and spirits. It is interesting to discover that of the 11 mentions of brewing materials in the probate documents, all but two occur in the 19th century. Hops are only mentioned once as part of a butt, and were not grown in Ewyas Lacy. Two of those brewing beer were gentlemen, John Price of The Moody in 1837 and Richard Watkins of the Upper Cwm in 1843, five others were called yeomen or farmers and there was one husbandman and one widow, Mary Probert, at a farm in Llanveynoe; a 15th-century longhouse called The Darren set half way up the Black Mountain.

Crops

For the poorer members of the population of the villages, bread, whether rye or wheaten, would be an essential part of their diet, together with cheese. The rotation of the crops in the county was described by Clarke as merely 'the custom of the parish', generally being the first year fallow, the second year wheat, and the third year peas or oats. Rotation in the nearby Golden Valley was the old system of wheat, then peas, then fallow, followed by wheat, barley and clover, which was then repeated. Where the soil was sandy, barley predominated. Barley was less evident in Ewyas Lacy, but peas, which are often mentioned, grow well in a clayey soil. Clarke's description does not mention oats which were widely grown in the Hundred, where wheat and rye were sown in autumn and barley and oats with other crops in spring. Lenten corn, so called because it was sown during Lent, is often mentioned in the inventories, as are peas and beans.

There has been some controversy in recent years over the optimistic figures given by Arthur Young in the late 18th century of the national estimate of 23 bushels of wheat per acre, an argument I am not about to enter. Sources are listed in a footnote for anyone anxious to follow the discussion for themselves. The figures given by Turner for average yields of wheat and barley for Herefordshire in 1800 are 20 bushels of wheat per acre, and 30 bushels of barley per acre.[26] For such a small region as the Hundred it is only possible to quote some of the figures gained from the inventories, and offer them as a small contribution to the central statistics. I must emphasize that in hazarding a guess at the size of any farm, only sown acreages will be used unless the size of the farm is that given by the Census. According to a tithe dispute in the early years of the 18th century Turnant Farm was described as having 140 acres under cultivation – 20 acres of wheat, 20 acres of muncorn, 20 acres of rye, 20 acres of barley, 40 acres of oats and 20 of peas, but these may be nominal figures as the values given for all the first four crops are suspiciously alike and inflated, at 40s per acre.[27]

Wheat

Bowden claims that grain prices declined by approximately 12% between the mid 17th century and the first half of the 18th, while livestock prices rose by almost 18%. This would doubly benefit the cattle breeder in that he could buy his feed cheaply and then get a better price for his finished product. The 1730s and 1740s brought particularly good harvests, but the 1790s brought bad harvests. The year 1799 was a particularly bad year in Herefordshire for grain production, both lenten corn and barley, because of heavy rain, making bread very expensive.[28]

'Hard' corn was the best corn and thus suitable for bread making, as Walter Price's inventory in August 1717 seems to imply, as he owned 20 acres of hard corn worth 5s an acre compared with his 30 acres of Lenten corn at Rowlestone worth less than half that at 1s 8d per acre. Another Walter Price of Rowlestone (probably his son) in April 1732, was getting 6s per acre for his 27 acres of Lenten grain – a considerable increase. Ten years later in June 1747, the 18 acres of Lenten grain of John Wall, husbandman, was worth 6s 8d an acre. The wheat went from a value of 12s 6d per acre when 'growing' in 1661, to 18s per acre in 1710, £1 5s an acre in 1770 and only £1 per acre in October 1794; the latter drop in price could merely indicate that the grain was of poor quality, or was, as it was still growing, an unknown quantity. All these figures are taken from Walterstone, Clodock or Craswall. Taking an overall view of wheat values across the Hundred, therefore, from the mid 17th to the early 19th century, there was a significant rise from 8s per acre in 1668 to 30s per acre in 1803. In particular, allowing for a poor crop because of weather conditions or the time of year that a crop was valued, there is from the middle of the 18th century a rapid escalation in the value of wheat, from 16s 8d in 1742 to £1 per acre in 1794 and half as much again in June 1803.

All accounts show that the end of the century was an especially hard time for the poor with the price of bread in orbit not only because of bad harvests, but because the Napoleonic Wars meant that grain could not be imported from the Continent. In December 1814, seven acres of wheat was valued at £2 an acre in Longtown. Prices per bushel (a bushel was usually equal to an 8 gallon measure, but varied with the locality) went from 2s in 1678 to 3s 8d in 1760, and 8s in 1829.

Barley, Oats and Rye

Clarke does not mention these three grains, but the first two were plentifully grown in the Hundred. A swift survey of the main arable farmers in the inventories reveals that wheat and oats were the dominant crops throughout the period under review, and were the most valuable. Unlike Norfolk, where oats were dwindling in importance over the 17th and 18th centuries, according to Overton, and used chiefly as fodder, oats remained favoured in the Hundred as they are a hardy crop that grows well in poor soil. Indeed, Duncumb writes that within Herefordshire they were mostly grown on the Welsh border. A profile of one farmer in Clodock will help to illustrate the local reliance on oats: William Pytt of Trelandon, a yeoman/gent on one of the largest farms in the region, was growing, on 22 August 1687, 14 acres of corn, 7 acres of barley and 3 acres of peas, but 22 acres had been allocated to oats. A similar picture is provided by David Parry, of the same parish, (who died intestate in June 1770). His inventory contained only 8 acres of wheat but 19 acres of oats. There seems however to be a greater emphasis on wheat towards the end of the 18th century, no doubt because wheat was fetching such a good price. In 1802, when wheat was fetching 9s per bushel, a bushel of oats would be worth only 3s 6d.

In wills rye was sometimes left as a donation to charity, but it receives few mentions in inventories. In fact the only place that seemed to grow it was Michaelchurch Escley, and even then it appears on only three occasions in the latter half of the 17th century. Was this due to some quality of the soil that obtained nowhere else in the Hundred? The cost of rye was approximately a third that of wheat.[29] Clearly, at this time it was a grain eaten by the poor. A widow of Llanveynoe, Catherine Ychan, left 30 bushels of rye to the poor of her parish in 1702 and Richard Phillip, also of Llanveynoe, left rye to the poor in 1704. After that it disappears from Ewyas Lacy as it seems to have done from the rest of the country.

Muncorn, a mixture of wheat and rye seeds, was another crop occasionally sown as a winter crop in September or October. There is an interesting pattern to observe here in that it is seen five times in the wills of the early half of the 17th century, and four times amongst the inventories up until 1715 and then also disappears. It was found only in four parishes: Michaelchurch Escley, Newton, St Margarets and Walterstone.

Clover, on the other hand, makes an appearance in the sample mainly from the latter half of the 18th century at Clodock, Craswall, and Longtown. The earliest appears at Longtown in 1730, as £5 worth grown by John Roberts, gent. The idea of growing it seems to have been slow to take root as more than 30 years later only 'a small quantity' can be found in the 1769 inventory of Lewis Watkins, of the same parish. From then on rather more enthusiastic growers make an appearance beginning with David Parry, yeoman, of Clodock in June a year later, who had no less than 7 acres of clover 'newly mowed and Damaged'. In 1781 William Gwillim, farmer, also of Clodock, was listed as having part of a clover rick in his inventory at Hunthouse. At Craswall, in October 1794, the widow Hannah Gilbert also had clover on her farm, as did another widow, Rachel Jones of Longtown in 1805 who was not only growing clover but also had a quantity of clover seed.

Peas were another fairly major crop produced by local farmers from early times and featured in several of the sample inventories, alongside the cereals. They first appear in the sample in 1666 in the inventory of Zachary Gilbert of Clodock. He had one acre of them worth 10s per acre and another six farmers followed him at Clodock over the next centuries. Peas seem, however, to have been soil sensitive as they were not grown in Llanveynoe and only on one farm in Craswall, and only a 'small parcel' at that. On the better land at Llancillo farmers appeared to concentrate on growing wheat, with some oats. At Longtown five farmers were growing peas. As might be expected on the often steep, poor land at Michaelchurch Escley, there is no evidence of peas being grown. Similarly, there were no peas at Newton, but out of 13 farms, four were growing them at Rowlestone. St Margarets also had four out of 13 farms growing peas. There was a much smaller sample to draw on at Walterstone and only one farm emerged here that grew peas, combined with other grains and pulses. Overall, the best land for them seems to have been in Clodock, followed by Longtown, and in growing them farmers partly had in mind the increased fertility which would result due to their fixing nitrogen in the soil.

As with all the other produce, over the centuries peas became more valuable, varying in price from the 10s per acre already mentioned to David Parry's two acres worth 16s per acre in 1770. There are no later mentions of growing them, only of harvesting them. In 1802 Anne Valentine, widow, had five bushels of peas worth 5s per bushel, but it is difficult to compare this with earlier prices as at this stage they were usually listed jointly with other produce such as barley.

Barley, although not grown in such large quantities as wheat or oats, was grown on most farms, especially in Clodock where out of a total of 37 farms, 14 were listed as having barley. However, there may have been more as so much is simply listed as 'corn and grain'. In the 17th century barley was worth 2s per bushel, or in one rare case given as 10s per acre, and in the 18th century it was worth between 10s and 15s per acre.

Other crops

Crops such as potatoes could give an indication of how well the region was adopting outside trends. During the time of poor grain prices in the 1790s many farmers turned to growing potatoes as an alternative. Introduced by Sir Walter Raleigh in the 16th century, they were at first regarded with suspicion, and then used as a source of flour rather than being eaten as a vegetable. There is evidence to show that a few farmers in Ewyas Lacy were already taking advantage of these during the last half of the 18th century as there are six mentions of potatoes in the inventories at this time, though some may have been hidden under the blanket phrase of 'Household provision'. The first are listed in 1759 amongst the goods of James Lewis, husbandman. David Parry, the go-ahead farmer, had some with his other 'garden stuff' when he died in 1769. In the same year Philip Parry of Craswall had potatoes in his inventory. In 1813 David Smith of Longtown had potatoes, as did John Prichard of the same parish a year later. Herefordshire is now one of the main potato producing areas in Britain.[30]

Hay fetched high prices in Hereford, evidence perhaps of the high level of livestock production. In 1740 hay, like wheat, reached record prices across the country, as the winter of 1739-40 was hard and spring was late in coming.[31] Farmers at Ewyas Lacy merely seem to have grown sufficient for the needs of their livestock. The most seen in the inventories was '2 ricks and 2 Mows', or three hay ricks. Otherwise, when mentioned at all, it would merely be recorded as 'hay in the barn', or 'hay and fodder'. The closest one can get to values is as follows: in July 1729 a 10 day 'math' of hay was worth 9s per day, in 1781 William Gwillim of the Hunthouse had 3 hay ricks worth £3 6s 8d per rick and in June 1807 James Jenkins of Trewerne had half a ton of hay worth £3 per ton. These figures were taken from Clodock, but at Longtown there are figures for July 1731 of one day math of 'ordinary hay' being worth '10s per day math [mowing]', one shilling more than that in Clodock in 1729. In June 1739 it is noted that John Penoyer of Michaelchurch Escley had 10 acres of hay at 10s per acre. In February 1790 James Prosser, farmer, owned 4 tons of hay at £1 10s per ton and in 1807 a ton of hay was worth £3 per ton, and by September 1829 John Thomas of The Lower House had 6 tons of hay worth £1 10s per ton. For the other parishes or townships the price of hay is not possible to calculate as it is either not mentioned or mixed with other items.

The use of manures or lime with which to improve the soil is difficult to ascertain with any certainty as lime is never mentioned. 'Dung' only appears occasionally, though it was meant to be included in inventories, so it can only be assumed obliquely from a frequent mention of dung wains or carts. A rare mention of dung as 'Dunge about the house' is in the inventory of John Harry of St Margarets, in 1662. It is assumed that this meant around the outside the house rather than in it!

Enclosure

Immigrants from other areas were attracted by the various ways of eking out a living from woods and waste land. One of the most extensive areas of waste or unused land (a total area of 20,000 acres in the county, of which half adjoined the Breconshire and Radnorshire borders) lay between the Golden Valley and the Black Mountains. This was a source of some concern to landowners as these areas, settled on by the landless poor, had a reputation for criminality. Clarke was highly critical of these wastes or commons, stating that if it were converted to meadow, arable or pasture it could be worth far more per acre, as much as 12s or 15s. In a statement that could have been made by many over the years, he considered that 'in this wealthy county, where there is so much work to be done and so few hands, comparatively, to perform it, there are few poor that do not deserve to be so'.[32] Of course he was not including the 'infant, the diseased, and the old' in these strictures.

Some feeling for the children of these folk was shown by Hugh Pugh, yeoman, of Newton in his will of 1707, in which he leaves enough money to set up a school, and stipulates that the children of the poor from the Maescoed commons, whilst not having free education, should pay less for it.

There was very little enclosure taking place in Herefordshire in the 19th century as there was scarcely any open field system. This did not mean, however, that there were no private agreements between landowners and their tenants to enclose waste land. Among the Abergavenny leases is one to John Lewis, a joiner of Clodock, where he is allowed to have one acre plus 'three acres of poor land' enclosed from the waste of Lower Maescoed. In 1664 Harry Jenkins of Craswall enclosed land out of Craswall common and in 1750 Lord Abergavenny allowed his tenant, William Davies of Craswall to enclose '3 acres or more' out of the forest waste adjoining his tenancy on 'Forrest Hene', and again in 1755.[33] And there may well have been others at a time of rapid population expansion.

A hatter might not own much land but use the waste in order to grow a little food; in 1712 Abraham George, hatter, was able to raise 'hard corn' and lent grain 'upon the lords wast' at Walterstone.

Wages

Information is hard to find on how much the Ewyas Lacy farmer paid his workforce, or even how many he employed, though some idea is given by the census returns. Out of a total of 2,677 farm servants in Herefordshire in 1851 the percentage of farm labourers under 20 years old was more than half, but this would include sons who were working for their fathers. In the 1861 census it was found that at Llanveynoe the larger farms of over 100 acres employed at least two servants.

Many farm labourers (in contrast to servants who were given permanent employment) were hired by the year at this period, and well into the 20th century, at the hiring fairs held up and down the country. A good many Ewyas Lacy farmers would have gone to the fair at Hay to hire their labourers.

Bowden notes that in the first half of the 17th century daily wages for agricultural labourers increased from 4d to 1s per day, but inflationary pressures soon left them worse off. However, during the first half of the 18th century matters improved with a 5% increase in money terms and 12% increase in real terms. During the 1730s and '40s a series of good harvests had the two-fold effect of on the one hand improving the labourers' standard of living but on the other, because the price of corn dropped, making the farmers suffer financially. In 1840 labourers' wages were only 10s 6d per week elsewhere in England.[34] It is difficult to discover from the inventories what the going rate was for wages in the Hundred as there are so many imponderables. Was the servant hired by the year, was he or she living in and therefore having food and lodging in addition? We do know what wages one workman was getting: the appraisers include in the inventory of one labourer, James Watkins of Rowlestone in 1796, that he was due 'one years wages' of £6 10s.[35]

Wills frequently mention bequests to farm servants, who were often held in high regard by their masters and mistresses, especially if they had worked form them for some years. William Price, a gentleman of Cayo farm, for instance, left money in 1817 to his servant, Elinor Powell, in recognition of 'faithful care ... during many years service'. It is sometimes difficult to tell how many of these 'servants' were actually employed to work on the farms, as the women could have been engaged in domestic work, or dairying, or possibly both. In 1814 a clear indication is given in the will of Margaret Gwillim, a spinster of Rowlestone, when she leaves, for one year, 'my servant in husbandry all my goods, chattels and moveable effects together with all the crops growing at the Wigga estate'. The farm passed after a year to members of the family but this was a generous bequest by any standards. Another very generous bequest was made in 1775 to one farm servant, William Preese, by his master, Thomas Prichard, yeoman of Newton, that on the death of his wife, Preese was to inherit the remainder of two leases and be residuary legatee, provided he continued to live with them for the rest of their lives. One is left to wonder what the exact relationship was between John Gwillim, yeoman, and his servant Hannah Jenkins and her three children when he left her money in trust for the clothing and education of her children in 1798. After Hannah's death his estate was to go to her eldest son John, with the household furniture divided between the other two children. A house and garden was to be provided for the mother and children in the meantime, together with a cow and a pig.

Conclusion

Despite the isolation, a generally happy picture of farming in the Hundred is evidenced, especially on the freehold farms with their greater independence from interference by the absent manorial landowners.

These yeoman farmers ruled their communities to a great extent and made up the bulk of the Hundred juries. Their cohesiveness is emphasised by a solemn gathering at Llanveynoe of the local jury in August 1825, after a little boy of 9 called William Gilbert was drowned in the Monnow, at Cwm Mill. The inquest into his death was convened by the coroner, William Pateshall, with a jury of 12 local men. They were George Anthony of Whitehouse Farm, John Farr of Great Cwm Farm, William Watkins of Lower Cwm Farm, Samuel Thomas, probably from Highfield, Thomas Powell of New House, James Price (two of them!), David Watkins, Jacob Davis, John Prosser, Daniel Davis and John Watkins. The first three were yeomen owning freehold farms of 100 acres or more and highly respected leaders of their communities, and of the other farmers and smallholders, only three were unable to sign their names.

Considering the problems they faced in terms of isolation, and poor quality land compared with much of the county, farmers coped remarkably well. True, they were busy and hardworking but many must have looked, at the end of the year, on barns full of grain, beast houses full of cattle, fields of sheep and yards noisy, and probably noisome, with poultry and pigs. There was plenty of waste land for the enterprising to take in, or use. Farming was always going to be subject to the vicissitudes of nature but prices were improving over time. Turnpike roads had arrived by the end of the 18th century, and these together with, in the 19th century, a railway within easy reach helped to move their produce to other parts of the country, or made it easier to buy in the equipment they needed. Rather than buying in produce like butter and cheese they were obviously exporting it in large quantities. The latter years of the 18th century and those at the beginning of the 19th brought prosperity to many farmers. These farmers were fortunate that they were not to see the years of depression that would come in the last half of the 19th century, when many were forced to leave their green valleys for North America.

6 TINKER, TAILOR ... HAMMERMAN

Some of the people represented by the population figures were tradesmen, an especially interesting group as they are an aid to understanding what were the chief products of the area and where trades were concentrated. Many were there in a supportive role to the main industry, agriculture, and they included blacksmiths, carpenters and joiners, coopers, masons, millers, shoemakers, shopkeepers and innkeepers, weavers, wheelwrights, and tanners – almost everyone necessary to sustain an independent community. One of the reasons why shops are rarely mentioned is because comparatively little was ready-made. If an object was required, it was either made at home, or made to order by the local weaver, blacksmith or other craftsman. For this reason there are no butchers, bakers or candlestick-makers among the will-makers. All these tasks would have been done at home. In living memory, when a pig needed killing over the winter, family and neighbours would do the job themselves, getting some part of the carcass back in return.

The most numerous amongst the tradesmen seem to have been the shoemakers and those who worked with wood, including carpenters, coopers, joiners and wheelwrights. There were 25 shoemakers over the 300 year period, and most of them, for obvious reasons, are found in the populous villages of Clodock, Longtown and Michaelchurch Escley. They were distributed fairly evenly over the centuries until there was a big spurt of tradesmen in general in the first half of the 19th century, as one might expect during a period when there was a large expansion of the population. Until the 18th century, there was a tendency for shoemakers to be known as corvisors, a name originating from the leather industry, which was located for centuries in Spanish Cordoba; they were called shoemakers or cordwainers after that. The Mabbe/Mabe family are a case in point. Foster Mabbe of Craswall was called a corvisor in 1697, but a descendant, Thomas Mabe of Michaelchurch Escley, was listed as a shoemaker in 1743. Most, if not all, the shoemakers (I will use this term from now on) were also involved in farming. Foster left his son Thomas a messuage and fairly substantial leasehold lands called 'The Abbey Lands' which had probably been part of Craswall Priory. The inter-relationships down the generations were not always harmonious, shown by the will of his son, Thomas, in 1730, in which most of the £46 total value was owed him by his eldest son, another Foster, including £17 rent. The Church courts took an interest in this family, on a subject that will be discussed later – see chapter 11. Other shoemakers were William Watkins of Michaelchurch Escley, who died in 1762 leaving shoes, leather and shoe-making equipment, and David Smith of Longtown, who died in 1813. David Smith did not leave a will, but his inventory is an especially interesting one. Whilst his investment in his trade was small (only £2 in leather), the rest of his inventory was worth £185, a not insubstantial amount for the time, and mostly in agricultural goods including 'Money due on the Books at the time of his disease [decease] – £78 9s 7d'. That he was both shopkeeper and farmer is confirmed by the fact that his inventory was appraised by the Longtown shopkeeper, Thomas Harris (of whom we shall hear more), and a farmer, John Price.

There is evidence of various trades connected with furniture-making in Ewyas Lacy, including that of turner, of which there were at least seven working across most of the parishes at various times. It is instructive to note that most of them were active from the mid to late 17th century and throughout the 18th century, a symptom of the expansion of ownership of more, and more sophisticated, furniture. There was Richard Beavan of St Margarets who died in 1679, Harry Prosser, a yeoman of Craswall in 1703, Walter Watkins, a contemporary of the same parish in 1708, John Watkins of Longtown in 1715, Evan Lloyd of Clodock in 1719, and, possibly a son or grandson of the earlier Prosser, Henry Prosser, 'the elder' of Craswall in 1750, followed by James Davies of the same parish in 1764. Of carpenters, there was John David of Newton in 1678, Thomas Eustance of St Margarets in 1725 and James Wood of Clodock in 1765, John Prichard of 'Gwin Mattock' in Longtown in 1814, and James Cook of Longtown in 1826. A George Watkins, carpenter of Michaelchurch Escley is mentioned in a National Archives will of 1857.

There were also those called joiners; a joiner was a superior kind of carpenter, and it would seem that they were in short supply. They included Matthew Lewis of Rowlestone in 1748, a William James of Newton who is mentioned in a will of 1668, and two listed in Lord Abergavenny's leases for lives. One was a John Lewis of Clodock in 1755, and another Thomas Lewis of Newton in 1733. However, in his review of probate inventories, Tom Arkell considers that, of this group of tradesmen, carpenters were likely to be under-represented as their tools and materials, often provided by their customers, were worth so little.[1] An interesting development in the first half of the 19th century is the appearance of no fewer than four wheelwrights, located in Clodock, Llanveynoe, Newton and Michaelchurch.

Masons, 23 in number, were understandably one of the largest groups for whom we have wills and inventories. There would have been plenty of work for them in maintaining and building the stone farmhouses, outbuildings, mills and churches of the district. Within Ewyas Lacy they were concentrated in the more populous places such as Clodock and Longtown, and active during two main periods, the first half of both the 18th and 19th centuries, which seems to indicate a fair amount of either new building, or rebuilding at this time; perhaps in two waves, the first of new buildings in the early 18th century, and the second a hundred years later when re-building became necessary. In the Olchon Valley, across the yard from Brass Knoll Farm, is a substantial barn, built around 1700;[2] and half a mile away is an example of a rebuild at Olchon Mill in Llanveynoe, in the early 19th century. The names of the owner, J. Price, and the masons, William Gilbert and S.J. Prosser, are proudly displayed on the massive barn next to the mill, together with the date, 1816. Underlying the rebuilding, of course, was the growing prosperity of farmers because of increasing returns from the land during the Napoleonic Wars.

There were also three tilers, Richard Harry of Clodock in 1589, John Beavan of St Margarets in 1721 and William Parry of Michaelchurch Escley in 1790. There was one tile-dresser, Philip Seabourne, in St Margarets in 1807 (and no thatchers, naturally in an area rich in stone which was then used as a roof covering).

Weavers, clothworkers and dyers form another comparatively strong group of 22 men, though it is interesting to note that they are most in evidence in the early 18th century. The largest number (four of each), are to be found in Clodock and Michaelchurch Escley, with another three each for Craswall and Llanveynoe. There was also a flax dresser at Newton in 1819, but, as was seen in the last chapter, very little flax appears in the inventories though in 1665 there is a 'little platt of flax' listed with three acres of barley and two of corn in the inventory of a gentleman, Symont Jones of Rowlestone and 'flax and hemp' in David Smith the shoemaker's Longtown inventory, six years before the death of the flax dresser at Newton. The weavers seem to make a come-back in the early 19th century, as the population grew, but they tend to emerge elsewhere, in Newton, St Margarets, and Walterstone, with only one now at Michaelchurch Escley. Spinners are frustratingly difficult to identify, as many of them were females and not, in the main, defined by their occupation. I will say more about this in the chapter on clothing and household linen (chapter 9).

Blacksmiths could be expected to be the backbone of any agricultural community, and Ewyas Lacy is no exception, with 18 of them. They follow a similar pattern to the clothworkers in that there were a small cluster in the early 18th century, and even more during the agricultural prosperity of the first half of the 19th century. Eleven of these were shared between Craswall and St Margarets. It might be expected that they would be found along major routes, but this does not seem to have been the case. That they were not always successful is shown by the pathetic will of Edward Griffiths, 'smith' of Walterstone who, in 1681, left clothes worth only 2s and a total inventory worth £6 12s 6d. Later on there were several blacksmiths who were more prosperous, for instance owning their own freehold

Forest Mill in Craswall

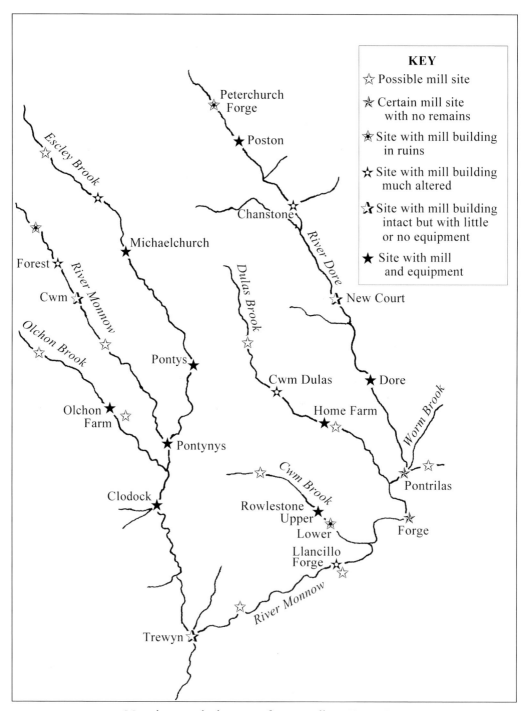

KEY

☆ Possible mill site

✳ Certain mill site
    with no remains

★ Site with mill building
    in ruins

☆ Site with mill building
    much altered

⭐ Site with mill building
    intact but with little
    or no equipment

★ Site with mill
    and equipment

Peterchurch
Forge

Poston

Escley Brook

Chanstone

River Dore

Michaelchurch

Dulas Brook

Forest

River Monnow

Cwm

New Court

Olchon Brook

Pontys

Cwm Dulas

Dore

Worm Brook

Home Farm

Olchon
Farm

Pontynys

Pontrilas

Cwm Brook

Clodock

Rowlestone
Upper

Forge

Lower

Llancillo
Forge

River Monnow

Trewyn

*Map showing the location of watermills in Ewyas Lacy
(redrawn from* Watermills of the Monnow and Trothy
by S.D. Coates and D.G. Tucker)

blacksmith's shop, like Robert Francis of Michaelchurch Escley in 1803, or Samuel Jones, who died in 1856 owning several properties: The Upper House, Howell's Land, and The Neave. In addition, he left his son Elijah 'Two Cottages Known By the Names of The Three Horseshoes and the Forest Gate with the Blacksmiths Shop, with the Orchard Gardens' together with his shop tools. In return he expected Elijah to pay off the £100 mortgage, and to bury him in 'a Decent and becoming Manner ...'.

Where are the millers? Mills are known variously as corn or grist mills for milling grain, or tuck or fulling mills used in cloth making. These two uses were interchangeable according to necessity. There is no record of paper mills in this area. With plentiful water supplies from the Olchon, Escley, Monnow and Dulas it can be expected that there would be many water mills in the region. There were at least three or four known to be at Craswall, two, and possibly a third, in Llanveynoe, one in Clodock, one in Longtown and two at Rowlestone.[3] A search through the probate documents reveals that one of these was owned or tenanted by George Wall of Rowlestone in 1829. This may have been the one mentioned earlier in the will of James Price, a yeoman of Rowlestone in 1735, or in the will of William Wall, yeoman of the same parish in 1781. The latter mentions it together with a house and garden 'in Pudding Street', a rare mention of a street name in the documents, which could be a clue to its whereabouts. There is also an oblique reference to a miller in the will of Catherine Gunter in 1746, who leaves her cottage lying to the north of Walterstone churchyard to William, son of William Phillip, miller, but of course we cannot be sure that the miller himself lived in Walterstone. There were two mills at Michaelchurch Escley and another one on the road to Ewyas Harold, known as Cwm Dulas Mill. A will for John Gwillim, yeoman of Longtown in 1797, leaves in trust to his cousin and his brother a water grist mill tenanted by Robert Gwillim of Wain Herbert in Newton. Twenty years before, in 1776, John Jenkins, of Trewern was owner of 'a water corn mill called Olchon's Mill' in

'Olchon's Mill'

Clodock Mill, also known as Lower Mill

Inside the recently restored Clodock Mill

Llanveynoe. Lower Mill at Clodock, also known as Clodock Mill, still exists on the banks of the Monnow and has been skillfully renovated to produce flour once again. Also on the Monnow, but in Longtown, is Pontynys mill which also ground corn and was operated by the Miles family during the second half of the 19th century. Is this the same as an earlier one in Longtown, left by Thomas Prichard, gent of Longtown, in 1738 to his nephew, John Prichard, tenanted by Job Williams and 'Shusan Morries' and known as 'William Eustance mill'? Coates and Tucker also mention a mill at Pontys, on the Escley River near Longtown. The miller in Craswall in 1713 was a man called Thomas Prosser. In 1840 Michaelchurch Mill was owned by James Farr, and the miller in 1855 was James Jones who was also a shopkeeper. There are earlier examples of people who owned mills but let them out to others – William Rogers of Craswall had a mill adjoining his messuage in 1671 which was paying a yearly rent of £8, while David Nicholls, yeoman of the same parish in 1728, owned water corn and tuck mills. Even earlier still, in 1582, there was Griffith Harrie, gent who owned Tric Hay and a mill with half an acre in Clodock. He would have leased this out to a tenant.

Water wheels were also used for iron-working. Amongst the Llancillo probate documents for 1663 the name of Giles Griffith, 'hammerman', appears. A careful man he made his will in 1659, but did not die until 1663. Though his inventory was worth only £8 3s 4d he owned substantial farming assets including four oxen. The iron-working forge on the river

Michaelchurch Mill

Aaron Farr, wheelwright at Bryn Cottage, Longtown in the late 1880s

Monnow has already been mentioned in connection with the Scudamores of Kentchurch, who owned it but leased it out to the Foleys, major iron-masters in the region (see chapter 3). It appears to have operated from at least the 17th century until the beginning of the 19th. That the forge at Llancillo was a substantial one is shown by the fact that much of the site was still visible in the 1970s. Fortunately we have details of some of the output of this forge over the years 1677/8 and 1725-1731 when it reached 150 tons and 120 tons respectively. Pig iron was obtained from other places such as the Forest of Dean and St Weonards and converted into bars of wrought iron by hammering, using water-powered hammers. It was then sent to Monmouth and shipped to Bristol.[4]

Another group relying on a good water supply were the tanners, a particularly interesting group and the sixth most dominant one after shoemakers, carpenters, masons, clothworkers and blacksmiths. Because of the nature of their work, which others were reluctant to undertake, they had the field, literally, to themselves. As a result they made good profits and several were quickly able to climb the social ladder. It has been claimed that the leather industry has been overlooked by historians, although, apart from cloth-making and perhaps building, it was a trade that employed more people than any other.[5]

In the past, using traditional methods, tanning had been an odorous and dirty trade kept to the outskirts of settlements. The skins of animals would come to the tannery after being cured with salt, and would have to be washed and scoured to remove any residue of flesh. They were then generally soaked in urine to make it easier for the hairs to be scraped off. They would then be beaten, or kneaded, in a solution of dung for two or three hours before being placed in vats containing oak bark and kept there for some weeks.[6]

Aaron Farr at Sunny Bank Farm, Longtown in the early 1900s. Arthur Griffiths, the owner of the cart, was a prosperous farmer of Olchon House Farm, Llanveynoe

The Tanhouse, Clodock.
The original tannery was probably somewhere behind the house, close to the river Monnow

It seems unlikely that the tanners described here actually did the work themselves; their social rise was too rapid for that. They probably employed labourers to carry out the menial tasks whilst they managed the business. At least half of the 16 men in the sources seem to have been concentrated in two places, Newton and St Margarets, probably because it was best for such a notoriously smelly industry to be concentrated in as few places as possible! The other parishes had one or two tanneries each during the 250 years under scrutiny, with the exception of Llanveynoe, Llancillo and Rowlestone. In the case of Llanveynoe its distance from main roads down the narrow valley of the Olchon would have made it difficult to get the product to market. There was one period during the 17th century when the trade seemed to be particularly active, and even hinges were made of leather, for iron was expensive. Governments, always alert to any profitable industry that can be taxed, imposed a tax on leather in the late 17th century. On one occasion, in 1697, his Herefordshire constituents threatened to pull down MP Paul Foley's house at Stoke Edith because they thought he was responsible for the tax.[7]

Understandably, tanners tended to remain a small group, inter-marrying with other tanners. The Jennings family were the most prominent tanners in the area from at least the early 17th century, inter-marrying with the Prossers and Prices, but by the mid 18th century they had made their pile and become gentlemen. The first Jennings to come to light is Thomas, a tanner of Newton, who, as some indication of his wealth, had his will proved at the Prerogative Court of Canterbury in 1620. He had four sons, Rowland, Thomas, John and Charles, and two daughters, Margaret and Johan. Three of the sons – Rowland,

Thomas and John – were to inherit the tannery, the other, Charles, had already made his own way in the world, though his son, Thomas, was to inherit family land at Poston and eventually Merry Hurst. One of the daughters, Margaret, was already married but there was provision made for Johan, who had a legacy of £140 as a dowry (a large amount for the time). The devil was in the detail; a codicil states that the executors had, since the writing of the will, been advised that if she decided to marry a man of insufficient means 'to match her portion' then the sum could be reduced to whatever they thought suitable to 'his estate and means'.

We see the family again in 1661, when the first son Rowland, still living in Newton, made his will. Although called a tanner, there is nothing in his inventory to indicate that he was anything but a substantial farmer by this date. The family were still formidably wealthy, having probably made money from supplying the army during the Civil War with leather buff coats, the body armour of the day, and also boots. Rowland had no children of his own, so his money was passed on to his brothers or their children. Johan his sister was still alive and had been unable to match a man with her portion, poor girl. However, the brothers were obviously very fond of her and she continued to be well looked after in monetary terms, getting Merry Hurst in St Margarets for her lifetime.

Rowland's brother, Thomas, was still in the tanning business and died a year later in 1662, leaving 'Oaken Barke' in his inventory. He was also phenomenally wealthy with land in various parishes including the 'mansion house called Myle Hunts house' in Clodock. There seems to have been a tendency in the family to have daughters at this date as he had only daughters, Constance and Margaret, and thus they pass out of sight, as do all the women in the family. Brother John was left a close and arable land called 'Cort Melyn' in Longtown and it was to go on John's death to his eldest son Rowland.

At the time of Rowland's will in 1661 one of his nephews, Thomas Jennings of Newhouse, was already calling himself a gentleman, and he inherited further property from his uncle Rowland. At the time of his death in 1686 Thomas owned not only Newhouse but other property at St Margarets and Bacton. His wife, Elizabeth, was also to inherit all his leasehold property at Snodhill. There are no surviving wills for the other brother, John, though there is a will for two Charles Jennings in 1671, both of them tanners of St Margarets and dying within a few months of each other. The Charles Jennings known as 'the younger' was possibly the son of John, and he left leather and raw hides and 'One Barke Mill in ye tanhouse' in his inventory.[8]

With growing wealth came obligations to the community. In 1643 Charles Jennings was involved with Lewis Gilbert's charity as a trustee, then, in 1683, Rowland Jennings and three others conveyed five closes in Longtown, measuring 18 acres, to the charity in trust for the poor in Longtown and Llanveynoe. This local charity, already mentioned in chapter 4, has survived until the present day.[9] By the end of the 17th century there are so many Jennings offspring called Charles, Thomas and Rowland, obviously a family name they clung to, that it becomes difficult to differentiate between them. However, they turn up again in the early and mid 18th century, now firmly established as gentlemen, with no mention of tanning either in wills or inventories. Rowland Jennings the younger, of The Wayne, had died in 1742 without leaving a will, so his death was probably unexpected, and he left four orphan children called Mary, Elizabeth, Catherine and John. Their grandfather died six years later, leaving the entire estate to them in equal shares. By this time everything was invested in property. One of these Rowlands, it is not clear which, but listed as one of the 'principal inhabitants of Clodock', became confident enough to challenge the Church in the form of the local vicar, which is a story reserved for another chapter (see chapter 11).[10] After this there are no more Jennings, or, indeed many other tanners listed, save for William Prosser of St Margarets in 1758 and William Jones of Clodock in 1816. There is still a farmhouse called Tanhouse lying close to the Monnow, between Clodock and Longtown, a Tanhouse Farm in Craswall, another at St Margarets and the remains of the name tanhouse in St Margarets at 'Tanhouse Wood'.

Shopkeepers are few, for the reasons already given, i.e. that people tended to be self-sufficient, only buying luxury goods or those they could not make themselves. In the eleven listed there are mercers, small shopkeepers, victuallers and innkeepers. Mercers did not specialize but sold a wide range of goods, and among the actual shopkeepers are two mercers during the 18th century, Charles Hunt and his son-in-law, Thomas Harris, both of Longtown. The Harris family provide a remarkable record of three generations of service to Longtown as shopkeepers, and for even longer, as the Revd Llewellyn (at the turn of the 20th century) mentions the benefaction of the lychgate by a Miss Maud Harris, of Gilbertstone, granddaughter of 'a very excellent churchwarden ... the late Henry Harris, Esq'. Henry Harris, the grandson of Thomas Harris, appears as a Clodock shopkeeper in a will for David Smith, cordwainer in 1813. Another three, more minor, shopkeepers are to be found around the first half of the 19th century, and scattered between Clodock, Newton and Michaelchurch. One is mentioned in Sible Pritchard's will of 1822 as Mr Jones of Maescoed and the other is James Jones of Michaelchurch Escley, who was both shopkeeper and miller in 1855. Sometimes a shrewd guess as to the trade a man or woman followed has to be made, as in the case of Alexander Lord of Clodock in 1636. There is no will but his inventory lists large numbers of candlesticks, brass kettles, sheets and coverlets, far more than would be needed by an ordinary family, and in addition there is a list of 36 creditors.

The difference between an inn and a simple alehouse was that inns offered accommodation as well as drink. From the 15th century onwards ale (made from malted barley) became beer with the addition of hops which not only gave it a bitter flavour but helped to preserve it.[11] At least three innkeepers are active in the early 18th century: Thomas Jenkins of Clodock, who died in 1715, David Evans of Walterstone, who died in 1729 and William Gilbert of Llanveynoe, who is singled out in the will of Thomas Parry, a labourer of Rowlestone in 1737. Another name for them was 'victualler' and Thomas Price was called a victualler at his death at Michaelchurch Escley in 1701. Sible Pritchard again leaves money to Elizabeth Parry of Longtown, 'victualler' in 1822. I was surprised at first to find that there were so few records of innkeepers, as there were at least seven pubs in Longtown, and seven in Michaelchurch during the 19th century, however it seems clear that not only were most of the pubs simple beer houses that came and went, but that some of the 'innkeepers' pursued another trade by which they were better known. The many pubs of Ewyas Lacy are well documented in a recent book by John Eisel and Frank Bennett, which notes that some pubs might be named after the main occupation of the owner as is probably the case with

The Crown, Longtown

the Carpenters Arms at Walterstone. In one case, the owner, or tenant, of the Black Lion at Clodock, behind the Crown, had no fewer than four trades.[12]

A meeting of the Turnpike Trust was held in 1782 at the Crown in Longtown, when the inn was owned by Samuel Jones. By the early 19th century it was being run by Thomas Hybart, an incomer with connections elsewhere in Ross on Wye, Hereford and Ludlow. One of the witnesses of his will in 1834 was the vicar of Longtown, John Rogers. Thomas Hybart's wife, Elizabeth, continued to run the inn for a few years as she appears six years later in the tithe awards of 1840.[13] It was quite common for widows to run pubs or alehouses taken over from their husbands when they died, although they are referred to solely as 'widow', rather than innkeeper. Margaret Beavan of Michaelchurch Escley, who died in 1727 is probably one such case. Though listed as 'widow', her inventory lists £30 'for goods in the shop' and £20 for 'desperate debts due by shop book'.

Another notable figure during the 19th century was Thomas Penry, the innkeeper and owner of the New Inn, formerly the place where the Court Leet of the manor was held, and which continues to be a centre of activity in the village as an outdoor education centre. It has been possible to provide a more rounded image of him than with most of the Ewyas Lacy innkeepers. The family seemed to be of long standing in the district (an ancestor, another Thomas Penry, acted as surrogate for the church courts in the 17th century), and both Thomas and his father were active as innkeepers over a combined period of at least half a century. At the centre of the village of Longtown, for over 50 years the New Inn and

Thomas seemed to be at the heart of almost every occasion or celebration during the first half of the 19th century.[14] It is easy to imagine the convivial evenings, the glowing faces of the farmers, waited on by the landlord's five young, and doubtless pretty, daughters. Apart from farmers' clubs, the inn was also the place where auctions were held, including the sale of oaks from Brass Knoll in 1813.[15] The first we see of Thomas in the records is when he and his father both witness a will for Mary Cheese, a widow of Longtown in 1806. In 1822 he appears on his own as a 'victualler' when his daughter Mary is left £10 by Mrs Sible Pritchard, lately of Brooks Farm, and when a child dies in tragic circumstances in 1828 he appears as a juror on the coroner's list. From then on he was active in various ways until his death in 1856, aged 75. As one might expect of such an efficient and well-respected businessman, his will was written seven years earlier in 1849 and had as co-executor the vicar of the parish, the Revd Charles Probert. Penry owned two other properties besides the New Inn – the Little Wain and Penpwllsond – together with leasehold land called 'Castle land', which were all to be sold to pay off a mortgage and the surplus invested with the rent to go to his wife Margaret. He had five daughters, Ann, Mary (the beneficiary of the bequest mentioned earlier), Sarah, Margaret and Elizabeth, one of whom, Anne, seems to have pre-deceased him. He and his wife, Margaret also had a son Henry, and he left bequests to his three granddaughters and a grandson. A meticulously fair-minded man, he left the profits from the sale of all his property, after his wife's death and all the bequests had been paid out, to the family on a 'share and share alike basis' (one of the last Ewyas Lacy probate documents probated by Brecon).

Something of what happened to the family can be found amongst the gravestones in Clodock churchyard, and they also give a clue as to why Thomas wrote his will so early Perhaps after all it was prompted by another factor, besides his efficiency. It seems that in most cases where wills were concerned people drifted on until it became obvious that they were dying and writing a will became essential. There are, however, cases where a trigger occurs much earlier, perhaps when a wife or close relation dies. In Penry's case it was perhaps the death of another son, Thomas, the Inland Revenue Officer for Longtown, who had died aged only 24 a few months earlier, in July 1849, two months after his baby son, also called Thomas. In 1860, Margaret died in her 73rd year, after another loss in the family when the 3-year-old daughter of her son Henry died. Infant mortality was high then.

I have mentioned that in the case of both Hybart and Penry their wills were witnessed by the vicar of the time. The connection between inns and the Church was long and close. The chances are pretty high that any public house sited next to a medieval church will have its origins in a church house in which ale was brewed and sold to raise funds for the church. Some of these church houses combined a house for the priest and the 'church ales'. Not all the church houses became public houses as many were turned into schools especially at the coming of the Interregnum, when the Puritans took control, as they had long regarded them with disapproval. In Ewyas Lacy, however, there was the New Inn not far from the chapel near the castle, while the Carpenters Arms is next to Walterstone church and the Cornewall Arms next to Clodock church. The Sun Inn, an alehouse in Longtown, had the advantage of being not only next to the church but also where the sheep and cattle fairs were held in the 19th century and earlier.

The Carpenters Arms, Walterstone

James Davis, cooper, was also the innkeeper of the Royal Oake Inn, Newton, in 1845; he had no inventory but his will was endorsed as being a healthy £300. Coopers, seven in total, though comparatively small in number, make up for it in interest. Four of them lived in Newton, two in Clodock and one in Craswall. Judging by the ones who left wills or inventories, they appear to have been well off. Enterprising, too, as they sometimes had an alternative sideline, usually farming and often other jobs besides. John Watkins of Longtown had the lease of Longtown Castle in 1692, and several acres of land from the lords of Abergavenny, which he presumably farmed. Robert Shaw of Craswall died in 1674 possessed of 'All maner of tooles belonging to his handy Crafft' but he also owned 18 cows and four bullocks, so might be considered a small-time farmer. We have already met two others of their number, Thomas Williams and his son, also called Thomas, as they were called to the death bed of David Price, in 1745 (see chapter 2). In 1799, James Thomas, cooper, also of Newton, owned the freehold of two sizeable properties, only one of which has been identifiable as 'the Rock' in St Margarets, and was also a farmer. Thomas Thomas, cooper of Newton, who was almost certainly the nephew and heir of James Thomas, owned several properties, at least two in Newton, one in St Margarets, and leasehold lands in Craswall into the bargain in 1816.

In summary, it seems that not only was the community self-sufficient, providing most of the things that people needed in the way of food and farming equipment, but there was clearly some surplus. Many at that time never needed to move from their villages, except to go to market. The tradesmen also demonstrate the two periods of economic growth in

Ewyas Lacy, the first beginning in the early 18th century, and a second of greater extent in the early 19th century. In quite a startling fashion, some of the tradesmen, such as the Jennings and Harris families also illustrate the rapid social mobility possible for the hardworking and determined among them.

7 Women, Wives and Widows

What was the relationship between men and women in the Hundred of Ewyas Lacy? First, it is important to look at the role of women elsewhere to set out the parameters within which they lived. Women who made wills tended to be at the middle to top end of the social scale; at Ewyas Lacy we are looking at a quite restricted group. In the sample of post-Restoration probate documents, out of 106 Craswall wills only 20 were those of women, of whom 12 were widows, five were 'spinsters', two were of unspecified status, and one was listed as 'maiden'. Research across the country reveals that this was somewhat higher than in other regions in England and Wales, where about 15% of wills or inventories belonged to women.[1]

When looking at the pre-Restoration documents the average proportion of women's wills seems to be even higher. For Clodock and Newton combined, the result was 16 women's wills from a total of 80, in other words one fifth. In other parishes the proportion was greater still. In Michaelchurch Escley, for instance, 22 out of 47 probate documents were those of women. In Llancillo, which had more gentlemen to the square mile than elsewhere in the Hundred, out of 71 probate documents 20 of them were for women.

Women's wills can often be amongst the most interesting as they tend to give more detailed descriptions of their houses and possessions. This is understandable as they were less concerned with farming activities, their attention generally focused on home and children. Very often this was the only part of an estate that they could feel was their own.

Literacy

In the diocese of Norwich in the 1630s only 12% of women will-makers could sign their names, compared with 56% of men, though being able to sign one's name did not necessarily mean that one was able to read and write. Research has shown that by the 16th century less than 10% of women were literate, but this increased through the 17th century until by the 1720s as many as 25% were literate. This statistic varied across the regions: in London almost half the women were literate towards the end of the 17th century, compared with between 7 and 14% in other areas.[2]

There can be no question that women were immensely disadvantaged during the three centuries covered by the Ewyas Lacy probate papers. Not only were they generally given no education at all, or at best one that was vastly inferior to that of their brothers, but their lives were not under their own control but entirely controlled by the male members of the family. Legally they seemed little better than slaves.

Despite this, records from the mid 18th century seem to suggest that between a sixth and a fifth of all property was owned by women.[3] They tended to be widows, or heiresses who had inherited property from their parents, and even this property could be at risk on marriage. In the 17th century, despite the odds against her, the heiress Lady Anne Clifford successfully fought her husband and the rest of society to preserve her inheritance, but she was exceptional. In a case of a husband's possible ruin, a loyal wife would often be prepared to sacrifice her own fortune to protect his reputation, or be blackmailed into doing so. There will be an example of this within the Scudamore family later in this chapter.

The coming of the Civil War broke many traditions. Women were given the freedom by some sects (such as Baptists and Quakers) both to preach and to organize. However, when women protested to Parliament during the Commonwealth that they had 'an equal share with the men', they were told 'to go home and wash the dishes'.[4] On both sides of the conflict, whilst husbands were away, brave wives had protected their homes against attack. Lady Brilliana Harley of Brampton Bryan was one such example in Herefordshire.

The relaxed morals of the Restoration opened very different avenues for women. Charles II encouraged women to take to the stage for the first time in roles that gave them considerable freedom not only to act as men but to criticize them from the stage. Nell Gwyn, one of several of Charles' mistresses given pensions and titles, was an example of the new tough-minded, powerful breed of women. There are also examples of women who fought for their country as soldiers and sailors, disguised as men; one of them, Christian Davies, was given a pension and a place at the Royal Hospital, Chelsea.[5]

In the 17th century, Aphra Behn, a former spy turned author and playwright, was the first woman to make a living from her writing and was buried in Westminster Abbey. Another well-known writer was Margaret Cavendish, Duchess of Newcastle, the first woman to write on scientific subjects and be made a member of the Royal Society. One of the most outstanding women of her time was Celia Fiennes, a single woman who travelled alone through the length and breadth of England at the end of the 17th century recording in detail what she found.

But women had few careers open to them, other than marriage, and in the 18th century the opportunities actually became fewer. When it came to earning a living, doors formerly open to them were rapidly closing, literally. In response to what was considered the licentiousness of the previous age, London theatres were reduced to two in the early 18th century. Craft Guilds would not accept women and careers once open to them such as hairdressing and midwifery were taken over by men. When Samuel Johnson's mother was pregnant with him she engaged a male midwife.[6] If reasonably well-educated, women could, however, become governesses, described by one of Jane Austen's characters as being little better than being in the slave trade, or set up a school for girls like Mrs Goddard in *Emma*. At the lower end of the socio-economic scale they could become domestic servants or prostitutes.[7]

It is immediately obvious that the women who were successful were often women of leisure; either because they were single or widowed or because they had a houseful of servants so that they could concentrate their energies on things other than the care of husband and children.

Education

The key to all this was education. Girls were overlooked when grammar schools were set up for boys in the 16th century after the Dissolution of the monasteries. Before the Reformation the daughters of the rich might be sent to a convent where the range of learning was very limited as girls might learn to read but not to write.[8] The dictionary definition of illiterate is 'unable to read'.

In 1804 William Gilbert, yeoman of Michaelchurch Escley, who was himself literate, enjoined his heir to give the younger children 'Education (that is to say) to read and write'. In the 17th century people could often read even if they were unable to sign their names. Beside the vicar, or the lord of the manor if one was resident, at least one person in every village could read and write, which meant that they were often called on to write wills for people. It is easy to spot which these men were in every generation in Ewyas Lacy.

Little was done for girls until towards the end of the 17th century when funding was supplied by charitable gifts, often by women themselves. Education for the daughters of the aristocracy and gentry in the 17th century was often good, as they were educated privately by tutors.

In clergy families, especially where the father was also a schoolmaster, girls would be taught by their father. Mothers, if literate, would supervise the education of their children; such women included Damaris Masham, the friend of John Locke, who educated her children in between publishing works of theology, and the mother of Charles and John Wesley. Dr Johnson's mother, Sarah, not only taught him to read and write but helped to train his prodigious memory. In country districts dame schools were sometimes run by poor widows who could teach reading at least, and possibly a skill of some sort.[9] By the late 18th century girls schools were covering more academic subjects such as arithmetic, grammar, French and geography.

It was generally accepted that all the gentry and many of the yeomen would be able to read and write. In Ewyas Lacy, almost invariably, the gentlemen signed their wills and it probably followed that they would be anxious for their daughters to be literate also. Generally speaking women, when witnessing a will, could only make their mark throughout the 16th, 17th and 18th centuries, with change only taking place in the 19th century. However, in one exceptional case, in 1635, three women's signatures appear on the will of Elizabeth Rees, widow of Michaelchurch Escley. Elizabeth Rees herself signs with an assured flourish reminiscent of the hand of Queen Elizabeth, in whose era she was undoubtedly born, and the other two witnesses' signatures are no less confident. Mary Gilbert of Llanveynoe signed her will, though shakily, in 1830.

It is not possible to know where Ewyas Lacy families sent their daughters to be educated, but there are occasional instances of women being able to sign documents, and in one case writing her own will, so they must have been getting some education from somewhere. In 1707, Hugh Pugh of Newton, who had a study in his house, left provision for a schoolmaster, with the children to pay one penny a week, but we do not know whether this included girls. Oliver Maddocks, Esq., of Clodock left a charity to establish a Sunday school in 1716 and this probably taught girls and boys to read in order to enable them to read the Bible. The Gilberts, a gentry family of Craswall, were probably better educated than most, and Thomas Gilbert's will of 1654 was signed by two women as witnesses. Thomas Price, a gentleman, was named in Lawrence Read's will of 1726 as the tutor and guardian of his children, John and Mary, who were both minors. Lawrence Read was a yeoman but there was equal concern for education on the part of both yeomen and gentlemen. In 1794 Hannah Gilbert, a widow of Craswall, left trustees all her goods and money 'for the Maintenance Clothing Washing and schooling [of her three children] ... until they come to Help themselves'. In 1844 there is a direct reference to the education of a girl when Thomas Poole of Walterstone left £80 in the hands of his trustees for the maintenance and education of his only child, Emma.

Ownership of books was not confined to men. Morgan Thomas of Clodock specifically mentioned in his will of 1740 that his favourite daughter Elizabeth was to have a particular theological volume of his, although his other books were simply divided amongst his other children. Other directions in wills give instruction that books were to be shared out amongst all the children, not just the boys. The 1763 will of Samuel Watkins, gent, of Clodock is an example of this.

Spinsters

The importance of the father as 'head of the household' in the early 17th century and later was emphasized by a system which applied in Wales and also in the Marches, whereby girls were commonly given the appellation 'ferch', or 'daughter of', even after they were married, and into widowhood. It worked like this. A Cicley David of Clodock married a Thomas but on widowhood reverted to being Cicley ferch David. Her daughter Elizabeth married Howell Jeffrey and when she became a widow in her turn she became Elizabeth ferch Thomas. This particular instance appears in 1636. The watershed for this custom appears to be the Interregnum as it does not seem to occur after that – not in legal documents at any rate, though I suspect that it continued in speech long after.

As far as young girls were concerned, they were dealt with fairly in Ewyas Lacy as the Welsh system of inheritance seems to have applied. Bequests in wills were generally careful not to differentiate between boys and girls, who received legacies in equal proportion. However girls, on marriage, were more tightly controlled than men. Wills often stipulate that they must only marry with the consent of parents or parent. The 1582 will of a leading member of the community, Griffith Harrie of Clodock, stipulates that his illegitimate daughters, Elinor and Jane, must follow the advice of the executors over their marriages. Otherwise, the bequest of £30 on marriage would be distributed amongst his sons, none of whom were directed in similar fashion. This was not simply because the girls were illegitimate, as the same proviso also applied to his niece Gwenllian. In 1622 the daughters of Richard Parry, gent, of Longtown had to have the permission of their mother before 'they dispose of themselves in marriage'.

In fact, women were sometimes in a better position financially and possibly in other ways too if they were not married, provided that they had some other alternative open to them. There is evidence that there were more single women in adult society in the late 16th and early 17th century than at any time since.[10] Few of them could be as fortunate as Blanche Parry of Newcourt, who wielded considerable authority at Court during the time of Queen Elizabeth, and after whom many Ewyas Lacy girls seem to have been named in the succeeding century.[11]

On a much smaller scale, Jane Prise, a spinster of Craswall in 1656 had considerable freedom to run her own farm with its horses and cattle. One woman, Ann Price, was a shepherd who was named by Harry Phillip Harry of Craswall in his will of 1625. Winifryd Phillips, spinster of Clodock, who left a nuncupative will in 1684, mentions her nurse, Elizabeth Phillips, and three other women as beneficiaries. One example of firm control by women lies in the will of another Anne Price, spinster of Clodock in 1771, who, whilst leaving her parents £20 each, ties the bequests to the discretion of her executrix, Helena Jones, to administer it in small amounts as she thinks fit. One of the witnesses was another woman, Joan Prosser.

Mary Watkins, another spinster from the same parish in 1828, left a large sum of money and displayed a level of gentility by her ownership of six silver spoons and sugar tongs. She was of some standing, too, as her will was proved by the Prerogative Court of Canterbury. Freehold property generally tended to be left to sons but in 1835 Susannah Williams, spinster of Craswall, left her Craswall property called The Tump, which had been left her by her grandfather, to her parents. She was able to sign her will.

The most striking example, but, it is hoped, hardly representative of the independent single women of the 18th century, was Constant Tomlins of Clodock. She, in passing, also gives a fascinating picture of the pastimes enjoyed by some of the people living in Ewyas Lacy at the time. In her will of 1766, which she proudly claims 'I have writ with my own Hand', she leaves everything to her tenant at Bulva, Thomas Jones, provided that out of the profits he pays her niece Elizabeth one guinea a year and several other legacies to members of her family. After his decease the farm was to go to Thomas Evans at the Bryn. As added security, she asks two other men to be trustees and adds an assured signature. Unfortunately, her single state seems to have left her with a poor view of humanity as she also takes the opportunity to inveigh against her neighbours in a way no careful attorney would have allowed. Thomas Evans was instructed to entertain her five old servants when they came for their legacies which she says is to encourage them to be respectful to their masters and mistresses.

She went on to criticize the drinking, smoking and drunkenness of Ewyas Lacy, adding idleness and slander to the list, and ending up with 'Cursing Swearing & Lewd debauched conversation being used so much amongst all Ages'. In an attempt to alleviate this she left money for 14 sermons to be preached in Lent in the hope that they would 'work a reformation on the Hearers'. The next two sermons on Easter Monday and Tuesday were to tell the congregation that they should abstain from drinking on Easter Day and the 'so vile Revelings [as] are contrived on tusday or munday Cockfiting or such Like as all sorts of vice is practised which is a Greife to all well disposed Christians to see it'. She ends by saying that she prays God 'it may have the effect I desires'. However, she was not without charity. She left a total of £15 p.a. to the poor of Longtown, Ewyas Harold and Rowlestone.

Wives

According to the custom of the manor in 1566 the wife had claim to a third of the holding for her life, known as 'dower', when her husband died. The will of Lewis Gilbert of

Llanveynoe mentions in 1686 that his lands 'were settled and assured by dower'. However, this was not much use to those without land. A list of freeholders in the Leicester papers held at Longleat mentions that Myles Hunt had through his wife Alice a right to 21 Welsh acres in Longtown (84 English acres).[12] When he died a few years later in 1574, he left Alice 13 cows, stating that eight are already 'uppon her londes called Bulva', which implies that she had an unalienable right to these lands. Freehold or copyhold land could be held by the husband and the rents received by him, but he could not sell the land without her consent.[13] Of course this bland statement probably hides many cases where the wife could be 'persuaded' against her will.

Until the Married Women's Property Act came into force in 1870 (with further amendments in 1874, 1882 and 1907) everything a woman could lay claim to became the property of her husband on marriage, a system called coverture. In 1758, Henry Morgan's appraisers even went to the extent of including his wife's clothing in his inventory. However, women at the higher end of the social scale were usually protected by marriage settlements which were entered into on their behalf by their families before marriage. Dower was, by the late 17th century, superseded by jointure (provision for a widow made at the time of the marriage settlement), which was intended to protect the woman from an improvident husband, ensuring that any property she owned before marriage would be kept for her support and that of the children of the marriage. In addition a 'portion' could be paid to the groom which helped to maintain the couple with an rental income from land, an annuity which would rightfully become the widow's.

Examples of these settlements are found in most of the parishes and townships across Ewyas Lacy, and were made occasionally even by husbandmen, even though this would have been a time-consuming and expensive process. Gentry families like the Gilberts and Prices of Michaelchurch and Craswall agreed a marriage settlement on the marriage of Jane Price to John Gilbert in 1659-60. In 1669, the gentry family of Elizabeth Parry drew up a marriage settlement for her which paid £50 to the groom, John Rogers, plus some parcels of land in Clodock, as her portion. Watkin Powell of Craswall, a husbandman, mentions a marriage settlement in his will of 1750. In 1711, Thomas Smyth, yeoman, invokes his marriage settlement dated November 1673. Eleanor Smith, 'wife', of a yeoman in 1813, was able to cite her marriage settlement of August 1782 which gave her the right to dispose of half the household goods, money, live and dead stock and the property called Pentwine in Michaelchurch Escley. Mary Lewis, widow, mentions a marriage settlement in her will of 1729. She had obviously lent her nephew £60 against it and he was now due to repay it.

There were some husbands who stooped to blackmail to sidestep the arrangement. A blatant example is that of George Watkins the elder of Walterstone, yeoman, who left an equal division between his wife and son in 1750, subject to a proviso that if his wife tried to invoke her marriage settlement then his son would have everything.

Divorce was almost impossible as it required an Act of Parliament. It was not until the end of our period, in 1857, that the Divorce Act made it possible for middle-class people to get a divorce. If the wife wanted to escape an impossible marriage she could take nothing with her, not even the children. Even at the last she could not make a will without the permission of her husband, as she could not claim ownership of anything, unless it was the things brought to the marriage – and sometimes not even that, as everything depended on her husband's generosity.

Hannah Williams of Newton Cottage, Newton had, as late as the mid 19th century, to ask permission from her husband and wrote 'This will is made with the full consent and approbation of my beloved husband Richard Williams ... and has given unto me the same power over the part or parts which I shall insert in this my will being my own property ...'. These wills made by 'wives' are rare. Another earlier one, already quoted, is that of Eleanor Smith.

Apart from being immensely important to the social well-being of the family, not least in the running of the household and the production and rearing of children, wives also contributed to the household's income in the making of cheese and butter and the raising of poultry, as well as in other tasks on the farm like helping with the harvest. Not to mention the provision of linen and woollen goods to the household, and any goods that the woman brought to the marriage.

Many women were understandably extremely anxious and fearful about pregnancy and childbirth. There were no, or few, painkillers and Caesarian sections were not successful until the 19th century. Once they survived the hazard of childbirth they could live longer than men.[14] This fear of childbirth emerges occasionally in the documents, for instance when Thomas Gregg, a yeoman of Newton in 1632, leaves a bequest to his three daughters 'and to the burden which my wife is now in child if please god should give her a safe deliverance'. Edward Perkins, gent, of Michaelchurch Escley in 1736 states in his will 'if it should happen that Mary [his daughter] now wife of Thomas Williams should Depart this life at or upon her Delivery of a Child she is now Pregnant, and the sayd child should dye' then the property is to go to another daughter. If Mary died but the child survived, Thomas Williams, his father, would receive the bequest that was left to his mother, Mary.

Losing children in infancy was another hazard that women faced, with all the misery that that involved. Many were fated to bear children for 20 or more years of the marriage only to lose at least half of them before they reached adulthood – and it was not uncommon for only two to reach that status. Mortality figures were rather worse for boys, as whilst one-third of female children were dead by the age of five the figure was two-fifths for boys. Infectious disease was the main culprit in the first few years, a figure that was highest in the first half of the 18th century and worst in London and the big cities, for obvious reasons.[15] Accidents were responsible for many deaths in childhood, especially amongst adventurous boys. We have only to look in the coroner's records for two sad 19th-century examples in Ewyas Lacy. The first occurred on 20 August 1825 when 9-year-old William Gilbert, who was playing beside the Monnow at Comb Mill with his 7-year-old sister, Anne, 'accidentally and by misfortune' fell into the river and was drowned. Another drowning happened in Llanveynoe three years later, when 4-year-old Horatio Pembridge 'fell into a certain well situate in a certain yard' and was discovered by his grandmother, in whose house he was staying.[16]

Wives could also be abandoned by their husbands during their lives and without money they could be left destitute, especially if there were children involved. These were some of the people most likely to end up in the workhouse. Any wife who managed to stay independent, say by running a small business, knew that at any time her husband could return, take the profits and abscond again.

More often than not husbands left their property to their wives only on condition that they did not marry again. Griffith Harrie in 1582 stipulates in his will that his wife, Margery, was to have use and occupation of a tenement left to his son Marcus until he reached the age of 21 'provided she keep herself chaste and sole'. She was left Bury Barn under the same conditions, with the addition that it was to be used for the upbringing of those of her children whose father was the testator. She was also left enough livestock for a small farm. All the rest of his goods, cattle and household stuff were bequeathed to the five younger children. Nevertheless, his wife could have the use of them until the children reached the age of discretion (21) as long as she remained unmarried. Her well-being then, in later years, was almost entirely dependent on her children. From the man's point of view there were practical reasons for this, but it could be hard on the widow if she was left very little money or none at all.

Widowhood could be made even more hurtful by the bequest to her of only one shilling or the second best bed. One of the most striking of such bequests was that of John Jones of Craswall, who, in 1797, left his 'beloved wife' a messuage plus £6 p.a. if she remained unmarried after his death, or only 1s if she had the temerity to marry again. This was in spite of Jones having asked for the considerable amount of £30 to be spent on his funeral. As startling was the statement in a will of 1748, when Matthew Lewis, joiner of Rowlestone, left his wife's own goods, including her clothes and rings, to her as long as she did not remarry, and that of William Exton, yeoman of Craswall who, in 1711, left everything to his daughter, Sarah, except the household stuff which his wife, Elinor, brought with her and which he bequeathed to her. She was also to have a room in the house and a piece of the garden.

In 1815, the will of Philip Jones of 'Pontanas' states that if his wife married again she would get only £10, but that his heiress daughter Eleanor was to give her £20 if she remained a widow. Another widow, that of Henry Watkin, the tanner of Rowlestone in 1627, was allowed to remain in the house until Michaelmas, or if she left earlier she was to have the second best flitch of bacon, the second best side of beef, two bushels of muncorn and three bushels of oats. Rather like putting an old horse out to grass.

There is one other occasion when the voice of a woman can be heard. In 1785, 20 years after Constant Tomlins wrote her diatribe on the residents of Ewyas Lacy, Sarah Scudamore, the wife of the owner of property in Llancillo, Rowlestone and Kentchurch is a sad example of how helpless even a strong-minded and well-educated woman could be in the hands of a profligate husband.

On marriage to John Scudamore, Sarah brought a large estate in Lincolnshire to the family, but by the late 18th century this, together with other property in London, had to be sold to pay vast debts. Poor Sarah had to leave home for a while and take shelter at Rudhall, near Ross on Wye, to escape the scandal. Her son was arrested for debt and had to take up lodgings in Carey Street, London, a by-word for debtors. To add to her worry she was overborne by her husband in the choice of trustees to manage the estates and did not entirely trust the agent, Mr Bird, who seemed to her to be 'her husband's creature'. On 23 February 1785 she wrote to the agent that she feared that the Lincolnshire estate was not worth more than £16,000 and the London and Essex estate perhaps £4,000, a total of £20,000. 'The family estate after such a dismemberment will still be encumbered with debts of £11,000 exclusive of the younger children's fortune, eight thousand more'.

In July, still sheltering at Rudhall away from her family, she wrote that her husband had returned to Hereford 'at last' and before he went over to Kentchurch, 'I partly acquainted him with my sentiments ... vizt that unless I could be assur'd beforehand of the safety of my situation when there – both present and future ... I would keep away rather than go home now and be obligd to quit it again'. She added as a postscript that she could not stay at Rudhall much longer.

The following month, still at Rudhall, Sarah wrote that the one thing giving her most concern was that Sir George Cornewall and Mr Walwyn were not to be trustees 'as more unexceptional men, in every respect, cannot be found. As to making the miserable state of our affairs more publick by their being appointed that is a vague idea ... since the very advertising the larger part of our property, to be sold, implies clearly, there are large debts incurr'd which must be paid, as ought by every honest Man, ... so that can reflect no disgrace ... but, alas, our affairs have long been scandalously publick'. To add to her misery, she had been forced to leave behind her dog, 'my affectionate and trusty companion Flush ... Alex says if he has her with the other dogs, she will get the mange. Mr Roberts cannot take charge of her, neither can I take her to Rudhall, poor dear!'[17]

In spite of the scandal, the core of the Kentchurch estate was saved, and as the family retained their position as MPs for Hereford for the next two generations their reputation does not appear to have been irretrievably damaged.

Whilst there is no doubt that women were under considerable constraints within marriage, the picture that emerges in practice is generally positive – that of husband and wife working in harmony, with the husband considerate of his wife on his deathbed. The words often used in the man's will 'my Beloved wife' were usually not just a matter of form.

It is greatly to the credit of many of these husbands that they did not abuse the power that they had over their wives but obviously loved them and cared what would happen to them if they were left widows. Evan Parry, labourer of Clodock in 1710, left his wife Joan half his money and 'the keeping and using of all my stuff in her lifetime during she be unmarried ... I doe give to my wife £5 to bestowe to her owne pleasure'. In 1719, William Lewis, a feltmaker of Michaelchurch Escley, left his wife, Jane, virtually everything – a messuage, 'household stuff' and £100 – unconditionally. William James, yeoman, left his son his property in 1721, on condition he provided his mother, Elizabeth, with the necessities 'fitting and becoming a Woman of her Degree and Quality', or if she disapproved of 'her Entertainment' and went elsewhere she should have £2 out of the property. Thomas Mabe, a shoemaker of Michaelchurch, was a decent man who, in 1743, asked his son to pay his widow, Izabel, 20s p.a. even if she remarried. William Prichard, gent, of Clodock left his wife everything in 1772 and more or less encouraged her to remarry. One man, a labourer of St Margaret's, made the best provision he could think of by leaving his cottage to his best friend on condition that he co-habited with his widow. One wonders what his wife had to say about that!

Some men left annuities to their wives. The amount seems to have increased over the years from £2 in 1721 in the will of William James of Llanveynoe, to the 1779 will of David Prichard, a yeoman of Michaelchurch Escley, who left all his household furniture to his wife Susanna, plus an annuity of £8 out of an estate 'lately purchased'. James Mayberry/ Maybury, yeoman of the same parish in 1811, left his wife to be taken care of by his son James 'or if not he is to pay her £12 p.a.'.

Widows

The curious thing was that the vast majority of the executors of wills who attended the ecclesiastical courts were women; men seemed willing to trust women to deal with the arduous work involved in sorting out the estate after their death. It has been estimated that across England and Wales three-quarters of those applying for probate were women, either daughters or widows of the deceased.[18] Conversely, there seems to have been some prejudice against women acting as an appraiser, as on the inventory of David Samuel, a labourer of Llanveynoe, his wife Jane signs as an appraiser but the signature is crossed out.

A quarter of all widows were left in debt by their husbands; many more were left with a drastically reduced estate.[19] These are the women who disappear from view and are seldom heard of again. Debts had first claim on an estate, which often left the widow with nothing after the necessary goods had been sold. The following two cases, out of many across the centuries, illustrate this. In 1637 Joane Prees, the widow and administrator of the estate of Thomas Lewis Prees of Craswall, presented her account to the ecclesiastical court at Brecon. The total value of the inventory had been £74 14s. After paying off her husband's debts, owed all over the parish, of £76 plus the £2 cost of probate, she adds, sorrowfully, 'So as this accomptant hath nothing remaining in her hands but hath discharged more than she hath re[eived] and is in supplicate - £3 9s'. The second sad case was that of the widow of mason Abednego Price of St Margarets. In 1857 she was left in such penury that, according to the vicar, she could not afford the probate charge and had to take service in London. On the other hand, one has to be careful not to judge a widow's circumstances too quickly. Anne Dukes, a widow of Longtown, seemed on first appearance very poor with possessions worth only £8 13s in her inventory dated 1815, but she had £220 laid out or invested.

Defined by their husband's occupation in life, they continued to be 'widow of' even after his death, whether or not they had a business of their own. There was the case of Margaret Beavan of Michaelchurch Escley in 1727, who is called 'widow' on her probate documents in spite of the fact that, in her inventory, she had a value of £30 in 'goods lying in the shop' and desperate debts 'due by shop book'.

It was clearly not, on a financial level, in the interest of the better-off women to marry again, whilst a poor widow was less marriageable, especially if she had a brood of children. The majority of women who made wills were therefore widows who had gained their independence on the death of their husbands.

There were ways in which women – including widows and spinsters – could make a living for themselves. One such way was to put money out in loans and there were a number of women who did this very successfully in Ewyas Lacy, apart from Anne Dukes noted above. Olive Button, widow of Clodock (and related to the Scudamore family) was

A photograph of a dairy class in 1924,
taken at the time of a ploughing match held at Old Court

clearly lending money out at interest in 1631. Out of a total inventory value of £81 8s 10d, more than £65 was being lent out at interest. What is more, she cunningly ensured that one debtor cleared his debt to her by leaving a legacy to his wife if he paid up. In the early 17th century Cecily ferch David, a widow of Clodock, kept much of her money out on loan receiving interest. This was a sensible and generally safe way of using capital, if protected by bond or 'specialtie', which was used by many women.

But perhaps the main income was to be made by spinning and weaving cloth. Throughout our period there were widows making a living out of cloth, though there is greater evidence of this in the earlier years. Henry Watkin, a tanner of Rowlestone left his wife, in 1628, 'half of the hemp already dressed that now layeth in the loft'. In 1666 Joane Phillips of Llanveynoe left flax and hemp in her inventory, and in 1739 Mary Jones, a widow of Craswall, had two old wheels, two pairs of cards and 1s 6d worth of wool in her inventory. Hannah Gilbert, widow of the same parish in 1794, had two spinning wheels and 13 shillings worth of flax. There were many others and these are mentioned in chapter 9 (on clothing and household linen).

Widows could act quite confidently on their own, running farms, alehouses, inns and mills. In 1594 one widow, Jane Prithergh of St Margarets left a very clear will and was manifestly accustomed to running a substantial farm. Unlike some widows whose clothing and household effects take prominence in their wills, in her will the livestock took first place. Another determined widow, who appeared before the manorial court in 1829, was Elizabeth Parry of Clodock, who claimed a right to pasture her sheep and cattle on lands adjoining Longtown Castle in 1829. Her livestock were distrained by the keeper of the Pound.[20]

Elizabeth Watkins, a rich widow of Newton in 1712, probably ran an inn, judging by the number of malt bottles and drinking vessels she left, and was also a competent businesswoman with her own seat in the chapel, silver plate and books. Ann Powell was a well connected widow of Clodock. In 1810 she left hundreds of pounds to her relations, and the balance to the parish priest – £1 for preaching four sermons a year, three in Clodock and one in the chapel at Longtown, all the money to be raised from her Garngalled estate. The sting in the tail was that if the minister 'misses or fails to deliver any of the above sermons he is not to be paid'.

The experience of being a widow in financial terms varied greatly, yet even the blind widow of John Prees of Pontrylas Mill had a little money to leave in 1666, including 10s to 'Elizabeth Morgan, my guide'.

A few widows appear to have been left very comfortably off. Helena Delahay of Alltyrynys in Walterstone was able to leave a silver tankard and a 'great silver salte' with other silver and a 'hamper of London pewter' in 1650. In 1780 there was Sarah James, a widow of Rowlestone who owned a gold ring, another ring and a snuff box. This is one of the rare cases when small luxuries and jewellery are listed. Another widow who had been doing very nicely in 1805 was Rachel Jones of Clodock. Despite the fact that she could not sign her name to the will, she not only left several cottages on Lower Maescoed and numerous bequests, but had employed two servants.

However there were many cases where it is obvious that life was a struggle. Jane David, widow of Longtown in 1685, had listed in her inventory 'a decayed low bedstead', rough hurden sheets, clothes worth 6s 8d, and only one 'broken pewter dish'. One 'pauper,' Walter Watkins, yeoman of Longtown in 1708, could only leave his wife a lease of a piece of poor land at Lower Maescoed Common and his children one shilling each.

Looking at a number of inventories, it is easy to see the level of poverty or otherwise from the value of the clothing listed. There were many widows who had clothing valued at only a few shillings. Mary Prichard, widow of Craswall in 1679, had clothing worth only 4s. Jane Price, widow of Michaelchurch in 1723 had clothing worth only 5s.

However, there can be little doubt that those left worst off were the spinsters, with the added drawback of having no children to take an interest in their welfare or look after them in old age. There must have been many single women who died in poverty, like Winifryd Phillip in 1684, who left a sad little inventory with not much more in it than two pairs of sheets and a frying pan worth 4d. Almost the entire value of her inventory was in money owed to her.

Another example from the 19th century was that of the 'pauper' spinster, Anne Lewis, who died near Clodock church aged 85 of 'Gradual decay of Nature'.

Conclusion

An attempt has been made in this chapter to place the mostly silent women of Ewyas Lacy in the context of their time. Common to all in the 16th and early 17th century was the complete control men had over women legally, the lack of education for any woman save the wealthiest, and the contempt shown by men to any woman who stepped out of line. In the 16th century it was considered indecent for women to appear on the stage but by the 17th century this prohibition was breached. Other barriers were gradually removed, for example by Aphra Behn and other women writers by the end of the 17th century, and increasingly so during the 18th century, when women not only appeared on the stage but were becoming playwrights.

Quite dramatic changes were taking place by the 19th century, but three things still had to change. Women had to gain the same educational opportunities as men, the ability to be financially independent and the support of the law. Women were beginning to come into their own, including writers like Jane Austen, Mrs Gaskell and the Bronte sisters. Literature became thronged by women writers, although many of them only broke through the barrier by giving themselves men's names at first. George Eliot is one example, and the Bronte sisters also had male pseudonyms. One of the first women of the 19th century to keep herself and her family by her writing was Fanny Trollope, mother of Anthony. No doubt partly inspired by his mother's example, Anthony Trollope explored the prohibition against women becoming heirs in his book *Cousin Henry*, published in 1879. This story focused on the indecision of a country squire who wanted to leave his estate to his niece but was deterred by the probable loss of the family name.

Many women were writing poetry or hymns that were to become widely known, including Mrs Alexander's 'All things bright and beautiful', and Mrs Gurney's 'O Perfect Love', which was to become such a favourite at weddings. Many people do not realise that it was a woman, Adelaide Anne Procter, who wrote 'The Lost Chord' and assume that it was Sir Arthur Sullivan, who only put the poem to music.

Women were becoming more vociferous in support of their independence, aided by a campaign in the Press, concerned at the number of cases of men who were running through their wives' fortunes and leaving them destitute.[21] There was growing concern on the part of fathers, too; worried for their daughters' financial security and the safety of the family property, they attempted through their wills to ensure that the property handed on was under their daughters' control. The will of David Gwillim 'the older' of Hunthouse, made in 1832, shows that he was concerned to protect his three daughters, one of whom was married to an obvious 'ne'er-do-well'. She, Ann, wife of David Watkins, farmer, was to enjoy the interest only of the money left her and not subject to her husband's control, 'his debts, contracts or engagements'. John Rogers, vicar of Clodock showed a sad lack of faith in humankind, or was perhaps simply worldly-wise, and protected his daughters' legacies in 1836 from control by their husbands by including in his will the statement that '... the husbands are to have no claim, demand, or control over these legacies'. He left two cottages to his daughter Jane, and to safeguard her property his instructions were that if she permitted her husband to live in either of the cottages, they were both to be placed by the executors in a trust for her children when they reach adulthood.

There were similar statements to this effect in, for example, the 1855 will of George Hughes, yeoman of Craswall, who he left his 'two beloved' daughters, Caroline Lewis and Catherine Lessimore jointly his two farms called Fern Furrow and The Old Shop in St Margarets. They were to hold them 'as their private property, independent of their present and any future husbands'.

Women were often careful to do the same for their beneficiaries. Mary Symonds, widow of Craswall, a year later in 1856, left her estate to her niece, Mary Jones, stating that this was to be 'for her own and separate use independent of any future husband'. Mary Jones as 'widow' subsequently administered the estate and gave her address as the Three Horse Shoes, Craswall.[22]

As for education of women, the provision of schools throughout this period and until the mid 19th century was pretty much on an ad hoc basis, and dependent upon the Church or charities as there were no established Grammar schools in Ewyas Lacy. While there was an endowed school in one or two of the parishes, which probably merely offered to teach pupils to read, we cannot be sure that girls were even allowed to attend. It is difficult to identify any schools during the 18th century, unless they were mentioned in wills, but by the mid 19th century there was a school for both girls and boys in almost every parish or township. Until then, most schools taught enough to enable children to read, with the aim of their being able to read the Bible. Evidence from the wills seems to suggest that by the end of the 18th century many men and some women could sign their names. In 1867, at Longtown, there was not only a National school[23] for boys and girls, supported by a small endowment, subscription and the children's pennies, but also a Baptist school. In the smaller parishes or townships, children would have been close enough to have walked to the neighbouring school. Llanveynoe, for instance, was only two miles across the fields from Longtown. The commodious school here was built just below the castle and could take 110 pupils; it has now been converted into attractive housing, as there is a larger modern school nearby.

It has been possible to see only subtle changes taking place in the position of women in society over the period covered by the probate papers. It is clear that there was a growing realisation that women had more to offer than homemaking skills and that they were quite capable of running their own affairs, but by the end of the 19th century women were still submissive to their husbands. They had to wait another 30 years or so before they could expect, as a matter of course, to earn their own living or be eligible for a university degree; but at least opportunities were increasing and were now bolstered by legal support.

8 THE HOUSES OF EWYAS LACY

It appears to be a natural impulse to enjoy looking at other people's homes and lifestyles, as membership of organizations like the National Trust confirms, but it is more difficult to explore houses below the country house level. This is where wills and especially inventories come into their own as to some extent they enable us to recreate the home lives of people lower down the social scale.

A guide to the houses surviving from the 15th century onwards in Ewyas Lacy is given in the Sites and Monuments register for Herefordshire (SMR) which shows that the area has a total of 97 such farmhouses. An earlier inspection by The Royal Commission on Historical Monuments had covered Ewyas Lacy in the late 1920s, and other evaluations of houses that followed have been incorporated in the SMR. At Craswall there are only nine farmhouses listed on the SMR, scattered amongst barrows, barns, the church and the ruins of Craswall Priory. Llancillo has seven buildings listed, of which only two are farmhouses whilst Rowlestone has only four such

Bridge Farm, Michaelchurch Escley

99

Moody Farm in Longtown, rebuilt in the 1900s

Lower House Farm, Michaelchurch Escley

farmhouses. Eleven buildings are listed for Walterstone, of which one is Alltyrynys Hotel and two are surviving farmhouses. Longtown and Clodock combined have 25 farmhouses listed, Michaelchurch Escley no fewer than 31 and Newton, in contrast, only eight. St Margarets has six. Thus, Michaelchurch Escley has the highest number of surviving old farmhouses. Why should this be? It is no more isolated than the rest and the soil does not seem to be particularly fertile. There is, however, ample evidence to suggest that in the 18th and 19th centuries it was a busy commercial centre on the main road that led from Longtown to Hay.

When considering the numbers, one is struck by the fact that although a few farmhouses remain from the 15th and 16th centuries, the majority of the historic houses in Ewyas Lacy were built in the 17th century and extended in the 18th. This seems to tie in with the theory that towards the end of the 16th century there was a massive expansion of building, something W.G. Hoskins called 'The Great Rebuilding', an event which Jim and Muriel Tonkin discovered continued well into the 18th century in the Welsh border counties.[1]

Of course, these are the survivors; there must have been many others that were entirely rebuilt on earlier sites or fell into decay. Some were marked as 'derelict' even in the time of the Royal Commission in the 1920s. Wern Farm in Llanveynoe is one such. Sited at the foot of a steep slope on the east side of the Olchon river, it can scarcely be seen today under its mantle of ivy. Moody Farm in Longtown was rebuilt on its old site during the last century.

Abbey Farm, Craswall

Coed Porth, St Margarets

The comparative size of houses in the last half of the 17th century can roughly be gauged from one of the first taxes imposed by the incoming Restoration government in the early 1660s. The hearth or 'chimney' tax was extremely thorough, all parishes having to be checked twice yearly and households charged 2s per hearth on each occasion. As chimneys

Dukes Farm, Craswall, the core of which is a 15th-century cruck house

were easy to spot even from a distance, it was considered an easy way to collect money from the majority of people. Houses with only one chimney were exempt, meaning that many of the poor didn't have to pay the tax. The immense value for the historian of the hearth tax is that it gives us a glimpse not only of the large, medium and small houses in the area but also of their occupants at the time, and Ewyas Lacy is particularly fortunate to have a complete set of returns for all the parishes.

A recent study of Cambridgeshire houses suggests that a house with one hearth would have had two rooms, one with two hearths four, three would equal five, four would equal seven and so on, but even this seemed to be influenced by geographical factors, as it was felt by one writer, oddly, that people living in rural areas had fewer heated rooms.[2] Only two people in Ewyas Lacy are shown as having substantial houses with eight hearths. David Phillipp's house at Longtown is listed among the returns, and so is that of John Delahay, who had inherited Alltyrynys through marriage with the Cecils. Several people lived in large houses with three or four chimneys, including Gronow Prichard, who lived at Rowlestone in a house with four chimneys. This may have been the house called Vedw subsequently lived in by his descendants.

Craswall had 44 chargeable hearths and 30 non-chargeable (houses belonging to people who were too poor to pay the tax), Llancillo and Rowlestone combined had 37 chargeable houses and only 16 non-chargeable, and Llanveynoe had 43 and 33 respectively. Longtown and Clodock combined had the largest number, at 82 chargeable and 73 non-chargeable. Michaelchurch Escley had 53 of the first and only 24 of the second (the second lowest number, after Llancillo and Rowlestone, perhaps indicating an especially industrious and prosperous community). Newton had only 46 families able to pay the tax, and many more, at 57, exempt. Walterstone paid on 48 houses, with 30 escaping the tax.

All the surviving houses have features in common such as walls of the local sandstone, flagged floors and stone or wooden mullioned windows. A common feature is the possession of plank and muntin oak screens, or partitions, chamfered ceiling beams, cross passages going from the front to the rear of the house and winding stone staircases. More unusual is the presence of the cruck beams found in the earliest 15th- or 16th-century houses. There are at least two of these in Llanveynoe, at Great Turnant and Darren Farm, and at least three cruck-framed 16th-century houses surviving at Michaelchurch Escley – the King's Arms, Pikes Farm and Tyn-y-gwynt.[3]

Although Jim Tonkin maintained that Ewyas Lacy had the distinction of having the smallest houses in the county, there are some large mansions remaining, notably Alltyrynys in Walterstone. The core of the house dates from the 16th century, and it was remodelled in the 17th or early 18th century. Michaelchurch Court, in Michaelchurch Escley, is possibly part medieval but basically of the 16th and 17th centuries, with changes made in the mid 19th century during the ownership of the Trafford family. Other interesting survivals of large houses are Olchon Court in Llanveynoe, and Great Turnant, both on the lower slopes of the Black Mountains. Great Turnant shares the distinction together with Trewerne in Longtown of having ancient links with Llanthony Priory, which took from them the Great Tithes of corn and hay. One of Jim Tonkin's favourite houses, Brass Knoll, lies about a mile from Great Turnant, and is sheltered by the Black Mountains at its back; it is an

Vedw farmhouse, Rowlestone

almost unchanged 16th-century building of which only part survives. Vedw farmhouse at Rowlestone is a later substantial 18th-century rebuilding of an earlier 17th-century house.

Smaller examples of simpler yeoman houses include Darren Farm, also known as Black Darren, situated just above the 1,000 foot contour of the Black Mountains, Darren meaning 'rocky hillside'. Unlike Brass Knoll farmhouse, which was built for a gentry family, the Gilberts, with all the extra detail that this entailed, Darren Farm was a genuine longhouse built in the 15th century, with living accommodation at the upper end and the byre and drainage at the lower end, where people and their cattle shared a common entrance. Other houses, nowadays called cottages, would have been small farmhouses as many of the earlier dwellings of the poor would have been too insubstantial to have survived. There is proof of this in the 19th century census returns, which list the existence of many more houses than survive today.

Many, if not all, of the houses in Ewyas Lacy were built of stone; the many buildings, walls and stiles that survive from earlier centuries are testimony to the quality and strength of the red sandstone used here. There were plentiful supplies of stone and roofing slates available in the district, particularly in Craswall, and their value to the landowner was recognised by their generally being excluded from tenancy agreements. Elsewhere in the Hundred, the number of places called Quarrelly or Quarries is evidence of other quarries. A Quarries Green occurs in Walterstone and Quarrelly Farm in Newton. There are records of stone being extracted for road mending from 'Moody Quarry' and other quarries at Trewern and Wayne in the early 19th century.[4] But these would have been more of a commercial concern.

Many of the houses would have been built of stone dug out of the owner's land, and for ambitious projects there was a plentiful supply of stonemasons across every century and parish. No fewer than 22 are listed in the probate documents. Oak was also plentiful, and was used in the plank and muntin screens dividing up the rooms, or to frame the wattle and daub panels that can be found as stud walls within stone houses.

The windows of houses were small, with mullions of oak or stone which were unglazed, or filled with horn or parchment until the 17th century, as until then glass was expensive and used only in very grand houses. Initially, shutters to the inside kept out the cold at night, then later, fillets of glass were inserted between the mullions. In the better quality houses floors were of flagstones; of beaten earth in the rest. Rugs and carpets were used as coverings for beds and tables rather than floors. During the 17th century, halls were ceiled over with wide oak planks supported by sometimes massive joists, which were chamfered and stopped at either end as a decorative feature.

Another innovation in the 17th century was the removal of the central fireplace to a side wall which not only removed the smoke from the rest of the house but had the added advantage of providing a smoke chamber to preserve meat, and in some larger houses a corn drying or malting chamber with a floor of pierced tiles.

Disposal of sewage was very basic, as the flushing lavatory was only invented in Elizabethan times and took many years to come into general use. Chamber pots would be used at night, and these appear from time to time in the inventories, made of china or, in one case, pewter. Occasionally, in the better quality houses there might be a garderobe, or chute, either within the walls or attached to the outside of the house, whence the refuse descended. This was a method commonly used in the medieval great house or castle and there are the remains of one at 12th-century Longtown Castle. Along the valley below the castle there is one house which is unique in the district in having the remains of one of these: Brass Knoll. Here a simple but cunning disposal system operated. A particularly large flat stone lay at the base of the garderobe onto which the 'night soil' descended. Periodically

Brass Knoll farmhouse in the 1920s, with members of the Watkins family.
The ghost of the garderobe chute can be seen on the gable wall

a dam was made in a stream higher up the yard which was then turned into the yard to flush the ordure away and down the meadow into the river Olchon at the bottom. This would also have dealt with accumulations of dung from livestock in the yard, and have the extra advantage of fertilising the fields at the same time. At Yellow House Farm further on down the lane an even simpler system operated, though its health and hygiene implications do not bear thinking about. Here the outhouse or privy was sited over a stream where ducks dabbled and laid their eggs, which were then almost certainly taken to market.

The privy built over a stream at Yellow House Farm

Rooms and their contents

The common perception of old houses is that they are small, dark, and with low ceilings, but the better quality houses tended to have plenty of windows (though generally small) and high ceilings. On the rare occasions when rooms are individually identified in inventories, one can gain a very sharp sensation of being with the appraisers as they walk from room to room. One of the best examples is the 1671 inventory of Edmund Thomas, gent of Michaelchurch Escley. There is an unusual early mention of a 'dyneing roome'; also a study, a nursery, a 'green chamber', the 'maides Chamber' (probably in the sense of 'young girl' rather than a servant maid), a 'Copt' loft (where the hops were kept, a rare mention of both hops and a cock-loft), besides a store house, pantry and cellar.[5]

When individual rooms are not mentioned in the inventories, it is sometimes possible to make a guess at the number in a house. Studies have shown that by the end of the 17th century the majority of houses up and down the country consisted of four or five rooms, though this could vary from county to county.[6] Some places are better than others at listing the number of rooms, unlike Ewyas Lacy where they are mostly tantalizingly absent. In Kent, for example, a much larger proportion of named rooms appear in inventories, 87% by 1720-49, against only 20% in Cornwall. In some counties, if not most, it is possible that the average number of rooms doubled from the early 17th century to the mid 18th century, a change brought about in part by the ceiling over of the Hall to make upstairs chambers.[7] Also, of course, houses grew in size over the centuries as the use of rooms became more specialized and people required more privacy than that provided by the medieval open Hall house.

Looking at the inventories with named rooms, it is easy to see how many have been left unchanged over the centuries. Assuming that rooms were noted in the order in which the inventory is taken, it is sometimes possible to follow the appraisers round. They would have entered the house by the cross passage which went from the front to the back of the house, then entered the hall which might have, in the larger houses, a buttery or one or two other rooms leading off to the side. The chambers, or bedrooms, would be above these rooms. However, the chambers were not just used for sleeping in. They could also be used as a parlour as many had large fireplaces and plenty of seating space as well as the main bed; and they were also handy for storage. Numerous inventories mention grain being stored in the house, to protect it from the predations of rats and other vermin.

There is a tendency in the probate documents to describe in detail only the houses of the better off, and not always even those. There are a total of 49 houses with rooms identified throughout Ewyas Lacy Hundred against a total of 277 inventories in the sample, or approximately one fifth of the total. Jim Tonkin had similar difficulties in his work on 178 houses at Ewyas Lacy, where he found only eight with named rooms.

Tonkin says that both the two-roomed and three-roomed ground-floor plan were common in Herefordshire in the 17th and 18th centuries. The two-roomed plan was made up of a hall-kitchen and an un-heated parlour; the three-roomed plan of a hall, parlour and buttery, or a hall, parlour and kitchen with cellar.[8] Many of the Ewyas Lacy houses followed this pattern, with the addition of chambers above the ground-floor rooms. The appraisers of William Price, yeoman of Craswall in 1778, vaguely mention the 'ground floor' and 'above stairs'. At Llanveynoe only one inventory out of 33, that of Edward Price, mentions the number of rooms, and then only in the vaguest terms. At Rowlestone only three houses have named rooms out of 26. One was the house of Milburne Prichard, gent, listed in 1756 as having nine rooms, including two rooms over the Hall, a room over the parlour, a 'new room', old and new kitchens, and a 'Day House'; there were also two cellars, a dairy and garret. This suggests a large, old house which had been recently extended. Another Prichard gentleman, possibly his grandson, is the second 'Mr' John Prichard, listed 35 years later as having eight rooms consisting of great and little parlour, a hall, a kitchen, and four rooms above (excluding dairy, cellar and garrets). The Prichards' house at Vedw still stands and is listed as late 17th-century and 'extensively remodelled during the 18th century'. A farmhouse now, the clue to its former grandeur lies in the presence of a coach house a stone's throw from the house.

The other house in Rowlestone with named rooms mentioned, in 1747, was that of a husbandman, John Wall, with a house only slightly smaller than the other two, containing five rooms: a hall, parlour, kitchen and buttery and an 'outer room', with a room above stairs. This would have been a sizeable house for a husbandman. Of course, if there had been little or nothing in the rooms for the appraisers to include in the inventory then they would not have mentioned the room at all, which makes these sizes little more than approximate. The presence of halls and butteries indicates that all three houses were medieval or sub-medieval in structure. In 1802 Walter Prichard, yeoman, of Llancillo, had six rooms with the interesting addition of a 'Coal' room, indicating the advent of coal supplies to the area by the 19th century.

In 1664 the house in the Michaelchurch Escley hearth tax lists that has the largest number of chimneys might be Michaelchurch Court, currently the grandest house in

Olchon Court dates back to the 15th century

the parish. This listed building is a part survival from the early 17th century, though considerably altered by the Traffords in the mid 19th century. It is still possible to walk through the porch, cross stone-flagged floors, past plank and muntin screens, and see both panelling and early 17th-century painted decoration.[9]

Also listed is 15th-century Olchon Court, one of the oldest houses in Llanveynoe, and reputed to be a hide-out of the Lollard Sir John Oldcastle, since extended and altered in the 17th century. It still has its cross passage and mullioned windows, four downstairs rooms and four bedrooms.

Another exceptional house that survives in the Olchon Valley, though only a wing remains, is Brass Knoll farmhouse, home of John Gilbert and his wife Judith and their three daughters in the late 17th century. It is still possible to walk through the heavy oak front door into the cross passage and on uneven flagstone floors through one massive oak door after another, each with a different opening mechanism, pass under heavy chamfered beams with pyramid stops and the original hooks for bacon, see window openings with diamond mullions of the time, heavy oak lintels over fireplaces, as well as plank and muntin partitions, clearly marked with numbering by carpenters who were alive when William Shakespeare was a boy. The hall with its large fireplace was the main kitchen and off this to the left were two unheated service rooms, one of which would have been a dairy, or buttery. On the right at the top of the winding oak-capped stone staircase, lit by a small square window overlooking the river valley below, is the room where the garderobe was situated. On the left is a large chamber, well lit by three deep set casement windows, with room for a four-poster bed and space to entertain in. Here was another big fireplace, and hidden behind the wattle and daub wall to the right of it was a narrow passage leading nowhere, only discovered when renovation work was being done to the house in the early 21st century. There is a large attic above where

*The staircase
at Brass Knoll*

servants must have slept. Sadly, the Gilberts' inventory does not survive, but they are listed in the hearth tax return of 1664 as having two chimneys, and a year later three, with two blocked up, so that tax was due for only one. At the time that Brass Knoll was built during the last quarter of the 16th century, this was a perfectly adequate house for a prosperous family (bearing in mind that there was a wing to the right of the cross passage, which was replaced in Victorian times).

With growing prosperity as prices rose for the producer during the 17th century, houses were extended to meet the greater need for specialization and privacy. Already we have seen in the grander houses, like Michaelchurch Court, the increasing use of a parlour, a dining room, a nursery and a study, and the ideas behind some of these would gradually filter down the ranks of the gentry and to the better-off farmer. The parlour would now be fitted out for entertaining with round tables and possibly pictures on the walls, and with more comfortable chairs than the old benches or stools.

Michaelchurch Court

There are some houses which we are unable to link to the listed buildings register but which give quite clear descriptions of their rooms in inventories. In 1743, a shoemaker of Michaelchurch, Thomas Mabe, is described as having a surprisingly substantial house containing hall, dairy, buttery and two chambers, though simply furnished. A husbandman's cottage, that of William Price of Walterstone, is described as including clothes and bacon under 'Goods in the first room', then 'In the Two Little rooms on ye righthand ye Housedoore a Chies [cheese] ring and other goods'. He owned one 'upper room' in which were '2 Chaff Beds & other Goods' worth 15s. The cottage was worth £1. This clearly would have been typical of the kind of house listed in the hearth tax returns as being of only one chimney and probably not charged.

Also unidentifiable but giving interesting detail of rooms is what might be considered a typical mid-18th-century gentleman's house in St Margarets consisting of eight rooms and a cellar in the 1742 inventory of John Phillips. He also had a brewhouse. One of his chambers was called the 'White chamber'.

There were several occasions when rooms were distinguished in this way, probably in an effort to make it easier to identify the furniture within them. In his case it was where the linen was kept, but it might also have simply meant the colour of the walls. In 1803, at Great Turnant in Llanveynoe, the 'White Chamber' was left to an unmarried son, for as long as he remained unmarried. It was not unusual for individuals to be protected by being left parts of a house in this way. Thus James Nichols, gentleman of Llanveynoe, left Little Turnant to his wife, but stipulated that his widowed daughter should be allowed to live there with her. In 1668 Rees Phillip Harry of Craswall, yeoman, left his daughter Sible 'to enjoy the upper chamber or loft over the lower chamber ... during her liefe for herself only'. In 1711 William Exton, yeoman of Craswall, left 'one chamber over the Parlour' to his wife and daughter, whilst the 1772 will of John George, yeoman of Clodock, left a room in his house at Bilbo to his wife. This was commonly done to ensure that the widow was not pushed out of the house by the next generation, which could happen if her daughter-in-law disliked her, or she was a step-mother. This was one of the reasons for having chambers large enough for more than sleeping in, as at Brass Knoll.

As we saw in the last chapter, provision was often made for wives if the son was the heir. In 1721 William James, yeoman of Llanveynoe, left his son, Phillip, all his property on condition that he provided his mother, Elizabeth 'with the necessities fitting and becoming a Woman of her Degree and Quality'. One of the oddest legacies, in the same year, was that of David Jenkins, labourer of St Margarets, who offered his cottage and four acres of land to his best friend, John Beavan on condition that he provided for the testator's wife, Catherine 'necessary meat, drink, apparel, washing and wringing ... [and] cohabitation with him in the said cottage'. In addition he was to allow her a chamber and cellar for her own use, together with a fire, and the permission to keep a cow, winter and summer, for her own use. In the event of this tempting offer being turned down, then Catherine would inherit everything and John Beavan would merely get what remained of the lease on her death. Sadly, we shall never know the conclusion to this story.

Thanks to the efficiency of some appraisers we are sometimes allowed a glimpse of what was in each room, the contents being as it were fixed in aspic. One April in 1796 the appraisers of the freeholder Jane Jenkins of Craswall, who had died a few days before, began in the yard where they listed all the livestock, then entered the house via the kitchen, where they noted a table, a dresser and one old settle, numerous kitchen utensils, two old chairs, earthenware dishes and plates, and beef and bacon. They then went through the brewing kitchen, where they found brewing vats and casks, old cheese presses and benches, to the dairy. Jane must have produced butter and cheese in quantity, for this contained a churn, seven milk pails, seven cheese vats, six butter boukes (a container, or basket for holding butter) and a small quantity of cheese. From the cellar, which had a saltstone and three benches, they climbed to a room over the brewing kitchen and found a feather bed, bedstead and bedclothes and two spinning wheels among other 'lumber'. In another room over the kitchen were two feather beds, bedsteads and bedclothes and, oddly, 'a few hoops', an old coffer and some oats. Finally they came to two more chambers, one of which contained 'One Feather Bed, Bedstead, Curtain and Bed Cloathes', a chest, three boxes and an old bench, and the other room the same, minus the curtain but plus a 'Wardrope'.

Contents ... or Household Stuff and Trumperies
The 16th and 17th centuries were an age of wood, leather, brass and pewter, and this is reflected in the probate documents of Ewyas Lacy, with subtle changes in the 18th and 19th centuries as outside influences and the Industrial Revolution intruded.

One of the reasons why shops are rarely mentioned in the earlier years is because comparatively few items were shop-bought. If an object was required, it was either made at home, or made to order by the local weaver, blacksmith or other craftsman. It would seem that there was no shortage of people who were able to knock up any piece of furniture required, from a chair to something more complicated. Numbers of tradesmen increased in the early 18th century, and again in the early 19th, but was there an associated increase in the number and complexity of pieces being used by households? As one would expect, a recent study found that furniture became more diverse and increased in quantity and sophistication from 1675.[10]

Not all inventories provided the same level of detail, especially where furniture and equipment was concerned. Quite clearly in this farming district the most important, and valuable, items were the livestock, and it was common for the household goods to be merely listed as 'Household stuff' or, in extremis, 'trumperies'. Another reason for missing items might be that as a purpose of the inventory was to enable the executors to sell goods to pay off creditors, whatever was considered unsaleable was not included; it also seems accepted that anything bequeathed could be removed beforehand.[11]

Standards
It is to be expected that an accumulation of goods would take place over time, merely through inheritance alone, but a peculiarity of this district is the occasional mention of 'Standards'. These were items of furniture not bequeathed to individuals but intended to stay with the house. The first example occurs in the will of Job Powell in 1725 of Newton, where he mentions six 'standers in my hous'. These were three bedsteads and three tableboards with associated benches. Five other examples are to be found among the wills. In the 1728

will of David Nicholls from Craswall, he required his bedstead to remain in his dwelling. John James, yeoman of Craswall, bequeathed 'ancient standarts in my dwelling house', and in 1731 Phillip Beavan of Newton also asked that his bedstead remain. In 1766 Noah Jenkins of Clodock added a cupboard to a table and bedstead; and in 1770 another man of the same parish, Samuel Jenkins, intriguingly listed a cider mill, rummer and rope. Most of these examples referred to essential items such as sleeping and eating equipment rather than luxury goods. The one thing all these men had in common was that they were yeomen. Is this significant? Was the practice due to a desire to ensure that the house in question always remained habitable, or a sentimental attachment to the objects in question, or merely that the item had been built *in situ* and would be awkward to move? It will probably remain a mystery, as 'Standard' does not appear in probate collections elsewhere in the country.

Beds

The most essential item was obviously a bed of some sort, and there are several kinds of these, often listed separately as 'bed', and 'bedstead'. By 'bed' was meant the mattress, as distinct from the solid base that supported it, and they were sometimes described as of feather or flock, or simply as 'bed with appurtenances'. 'Flock' beds used the waste from wool, and there were also 'mucke' or 'chaff' beds, probably filled with chopped hay or straw. The bedsteads could sometimes be listed as 'low', which were probably beds for children or servants, or a kind of truckle bed that went under other beds. Only on one occasion were beds described specifically as being for children, in the inventory of Joseph Beavan, husbandman of Newton, who, having mentioned 'two best feather beds', added 'two ordinary beds ... for the use of the children'. Clearly, beds were considered precious enough to be handed down from generation to generation as they are often mentioned in bequests. For instance, in 1662 William Price of Llanveynoe left his daughter two feather beds 'which I had from my mother'. In a rare mention of colour, Matthew Lewis, a joiner of Rowlestone, left his two daughters 'a feather blue bed' and a 'red feather bed' in 1748.

The more expensive and elaborate four-poster bedsteads, usually with feather mattresses, were confined to the gentry or richer yeomen households. One yeoman of Longtown, Thomas Lewis, owned a four-poster and a half tester (a half canopy as against a full canopy over the bed), together with a 'press beed' in 1765, which at £1 was worth the same as the four-poster. This was a bed in a cupboard of the type that may still be seen in Scottish crofting museums. The half tester was worth only 3s. William Price of Llanveynoe left two tester beds in 1662. Mr Harris, the Longtown shopkeeper, left a 'Table Bedstead' as well as other beds and bedsteads in 1786. There seems little connection between the inventories and the wills in this respect. None of these testers or four-posters appear in the wills of the person concerned, though there are three further testers mentioned in the wills, for instance in that of Elizabeth Rees Harry, widow of Craswall, in 1669. Items listed in a bequest were probably removed before the inventory was taken.

The tester, or ceiled four-poster, was usually surrounded by curtains, but not many of these are mentioned as they were generally included as a group of items simply listed as 'appurtenances'. Only two sets of these curtains are mentioned in the wills: Gwenllian Gilbert, widow of Craswall bequeathed her bed in the parlour, with the appurtenances 'except the curtains', in 1689, and almost a hundred years later, in the will of Samuel

Jenkins, yeoman of Clodock, they are called the 'best set', so he must have had more than one. The inventories mention a set of 'green curtains' amongst the bedding of William Pytt of Trelandon, gent of Clodock, in 1687. A notable item in the 1702 inventory of William James, yeoman of St Margarets, is the mention of two beds on one bedstead, 'the outside of curtains'. The lack of curtains in any other context implies that curtains at windows were not common, shutters being used instead.

Tables

Beds did not change very much over time, but the development of the table is an interesting feature of the inventories. Again, most, if not all, inventories listed tables, in the second half of the 17th century usually described as tableboards (or a trestle table), mentioned with benches or forms. One mention in 1662 refers to 'two tableboords with frames and benches', value 13s (Jane Rees, of Clodock). This undoubtedly uncomfortable arrangement was gradually replaced by square and round tables and chairs. In the first half of the 18th century the two types existed alongside each other, the tableboards now often described as tables 'with frames' or 'long tables'. One of the earliest and fullest descriptions is in the 1664 will of James Lucas, yeoman of Longtown, where he left 'one square tableboord ... with fower posts now lyinge in my kitchen and fitted to make a frame for the said table ...'

17th-century tables and benches

to his 'loving friend' Rowland Jennings. By the 1740s people often owned square, round and long tables. Blanch Roberts, widow of Clodock in 1743, owned one round, one square and 'two Long tables old ones'. In 1742 another Rowland Jennings, gent, of the Wayne in Clodock, owned 'one long table' in the Hall, plus 'one Round table and two side Tables'. This is a rare mention of a side table and indicates a certain level of sophistication in accordance with his gentry status as it was the forerunner of the sideboard, initially without cupboards or drawers, simply used to serve food from.

Where tables were kept was not often mentioned, but when it was, they were found in the kitchen or hall in the earlier years. By the second half of the 18th century they were also found elsewhere, the smaller tables being used for more intimate dining, or to serve the new beverages such as tea and coffee in the parlour. John Lewis, yeoman of Longtown in 1760, had 'a Little Table' in a 'Small Closet'; John Symonds, yeoman/smith, also of Longtown, was the owner of two tables in 'the new Parlour' in 1761; and the cooper, James Thomas of Newton had a square table in a chamber, in addition to another elsewhere, in 1799. (This would seem a large investment in tables for an inventory with a total value of only £17 15s). By the early 19th century the use for the table was quite specific in the will of John Morgan, yeoman of Walterstone, who he mentions his 'round Tea Table'.

Chairs

Chairs began to be listed from the second half of the 17th century, sometimes alongside tableboards, benches and stools. Two examples from Clodock are in the 1680 inventory of William Lewis, which notes a combination of all four, as does, slightly earlier (in 1672) that of Lewis Powell of Trewerne, yeoman. Earlier still was the mention of three chairs in the inventory of a well-off Clodock tanner, Thomas Jennings in 1662. Their number and variety increased as time went by. In 1742 Rowland Jennings, the possessor of the side table, also owned a dozen chairs. It is difficult to find out what most of these chairs were like, but occasional details emerge, such as the ostentatious 'carved wainscot chair' owned by the wealthy William James, yeoman of St Margarets, in 1702; a 'twig' chair owned in 1706 by Rowland Prichard, gent of Rowlestone, or the ten 'seggin chairs', possibly made of sedge or rush, in the 1727 inventory of Margaret Beavan, widow/shopkeeper of Michaelchurch Escley. These must have been similar to the 'straw' chair owned by a widow, Sarah James of Rowlestone, 53 years later; while in 1857 an 'easy armchair' is mentioned in the will of Samuel Griffiths of Olchon House, in Llanveynoe. Another form of seating was the settle, which seemed popular from at least 1702 onwards, though it had been noted some time earlier in other parts of the country.[12] One of these appears in the 1702 inventory of William James at St Margarets, another in the inventory of Rowland Prichard, already mentioned as owning the twig chair, in 1706. A widow, Elizabeth Watkins of Newton owned one in 1712. Then there is a cluster of them appearing from the middle years of the 18th century, starting in 1732 with Thomas Jackson, innholder of Longtown and continuing to 1805 with Rachel Jones, widow of Longtown.

In spite of the lack of comfortable upholstered furniture in the early period, few cushions are listed, and there appear to have been none in most of the parishes or townships. It is notable, though, that in the parishes of Llanveynoe, Michaelchurch Escley, Newton and

St Margarets, where cushions were recorded, they all occurred in the late 17th century and very early 18th century. Presumably this was because they were superseded by more comfortable seating. There were only six people with cushions, four of them women. The earliest of the women was Johan Jenkins, widow, of Michaelchurch Escley in 1673 with two; followed by Mary Parry, spinster, of Llanveynoe, in 1679, with '3 stool cusins'; Elinor Myles, widow, of Michaelchurch Escley; and finally Elizabeth Watkins, a rich widow of Newton with 'Silk Cushions' in 1712; she had an inventory value of £497, the highest by far amongst the women and clearly with tastes that matched. A carpenter, John David, had 'two Cushions' with two chairs and small stools. As the value of his inventory was only £11 5s 11d, perhaps these were all for resale. William James of St Margarets turns up again as possibly the only man to enjoy the comfort of two such items in 1702.

Storage
Essential for storage purposes and appearing in one form or another in most inventories were chests, coffers, chests of drawers, dressers and presses. A good point is made in *The Material Culture of Consumption*[13] that the proliferation of storage furniture was caused in part because of the growing number of items that needed to be found space by the end of the 17th century. A 'catch 22' situation.

The chest, or coffer, which was supplemented at a later date by a chest of drawers, was never included as a 'standard' because it was intended to be more mobile. Virtually every will or inventory lists one or more chests. The most evocative mention of their use has already been mentioned – as a storage place for linen (an early form of 'bottom drawer', which girls still aspired to centuries later), but it could also be used as a secure place for jewellery kept under lock and key. Coffers were more likely to be the receptacle for small items as they were generally smaller than chests.

Chests of Drawers
According to other surveys of furnishings, the chest of drawers first appears in inventories around the middle of the 17th century. In Essex it appeared in the last quarter of the 17th century, and in the bustling cloth-making town of Uffculme, in Devon, by 1690.[14] Fewer than 1% owned them in the early 17th century, but by the mid 18th century almost 60% of people in Kent owned them, compared to only 14% in Cornwall.[15] Rather surprisingly, in his survey of 3,000 inventories of Herefordshire covering the period from 1660 to 1760, including 178 for Ewyas Lacy, Tonkin found chests of drawers mentioned only three times and presses only nine times.[16] At Ewyas Lacy the sample, admittedly continuing into the 19th century, produced 14, with the earliest chest of drawers in the 1702 inventory of William James, yeoman (always a leader of fashion, as we have seen). His was swiftly followed by that of Rowland Prichard, gent of Rowlestone in 1706, and it is possible that this one was passed down the family as in 1756 one appears in the inventory of Milburne Prichard, gent, of Vedw in the same parish and there was another 35 years later in the inventory of John Prichard, gent, (almost certainly a descendant) also of Rowlestone.

As one might expect, these items of furniture were generally kept in the bedroom chamber and the value is rarely listed on its own. Thomas Howe, gent, has one noted in

1739 as an 'old chest of drawers' in the 'Lower Chamber', valued at £1. There were only two parishes where they were not found in the sample: Craswall and Walterstone.

Dressers and Presses

Other storage items used were dressers and press cupboards. In his survey of Essex inventories Francis Steer notes the former as having first appeared in 1727. The first one at Ewyas Lacy appears in the Longtown inn of Thomas Jackson, gent, in 1732 (worth 5 shillings together with a settle), but it took a little while for them to catch on generally and then chiefly in the homes of the better off. The next one appears at Tir Jaynoe, the Clodock home of Rowland Jennings, gent, in 1742, where it is recorded in the hall and is followed in the list by the 16 pewter dishes and two dozen plates which were no doubt displayed upon it. After this the remaining dressers listed occur in the last 30 years of the 18th century and, where their location is mentioned, they appear in the kitchen. This seems to indicate the growing importance of the kitchen over the hall as a cooking arena, and the usual description of them as 'Dresser and shelves' denotes their use as a place to 'dress' the dish and have a place for plates above. There are only three parishes without ownership of a dresser in the sample – Llancillo, Michaelchurch and St Margarets – and in the remaining seven there are a total of eight. Most were separately valued, at between 5s in the earlier years and reducing to 1 or 2s towards the end of the 18th century.

There were two kinds of presses, one a form of dresser used for serving food and the other an early form of wardrobe mainly used for the hanging of clothes, or the storage of linen. At Ewyas Lacy presses seem to have been mainly of the latter kind, called a 'Hanging Press'. The earliest occurs in 1662, owned by William Price of Llanveynoe, who also owned a desk. The next one is to be found in Craswall in 1667, and there are 11 others. Quite an expensive piece of furniture, it is listed in the inventory of Elizabeth Prosser, widow of Newton as being worth one guinea. Presses continued to be used until the 19th century, though by 1796 the press was called a 'wardrobe' in the effects of Jane Jenkins of Craswall.

Dressing Tables, Desks and Bureaux

Only one dressing table was mentioned, that of David Parry, yeoman of Clodock in 1770, in the chamber above the kitchen. It was listed with a group of items, so the value is not known, but he was comfortably off and could afford such a luxury with a total inventory value of £234 19s 6d.

Desks are rather more numerous. There were one or two in every parish in the sample except four – Craswall, Michaelchurch Escley, Newton and Walterstone. As might be expected, they were mainly confined to the gentry and better-off yeomanry. Llanveynoe had the distinction of having the first in 1662, in the inventory of William Price, swiftly followed by another Llanveynoe gentleman, Howell Ychan in 1668. There are no individual values given. There are three listed for Longtown yeomen scattered from 1678, 1762 and 1798. Again, no values are given. At Clodock, William Pytt, yeoman of Trelandon, had a desk listed with three coffers at 10s. A widow in the same parish, Blanch Roberts, owned one in 1743. William James, yeoman, of St Margarets crops up again as one of the first to own one, which turns up for some initially inexplicable reason 'in the maid's Chamber' in 1702, until one remembers that this could have been his daughter's bedroom. Two gentlemen of Rowlestone owned desks for which no values are given, one in 1706 and one in 1756. In their case it is possible that they were elderly widowers who had handed over the housekeeping to the younger generation as their total values were very low, £41 1s 6d and £19 5s 6d respectively. Even so there seems a disparity between the sophistication of the desk and the low value of the inventory. Only one inventory gave a value for a desk as 5s – and that was at Llancillo in the early years of the 18th century in the inventory of Walter Prichard, yeoman. Out of a total of 11 desks mentioned, all save three were in the effects of yeomen (and one widow), with total inventory values of from £9 to £290 19s 4d. I have not included Thomas Harris, mercer of Longtown in this list as his desk was noted as 'a Bereau'. With his corner cupboard it was valued at £2; the corner cupboard, another storage unit, being the only one in the inventories. Clodock is credited with having 'one old skrutoe' (worth 5s), which almost certainly means an escritoire, and was found in the goods of John Maddocks, gent, in 1746.

Looking Glasses, Pictures and Clocks
Some of these might be considered luxury items, owned by the gentry or the better off. For example, in the late 17th century only the rich were likely to own looking glasses.[17] At Ewyas Lacy the six listed appear only in the last quarter of the 18th and in the early years of the 19th century. Of these, which were never called mirrors, three were found in the homes of those with total inventory values of about £200 or more. A small looking glass was valued at 6d in 1776, with 5s for two by the end of the century.

Pictures also seemed to be luxury goods, and predictably they only appear amongst the goods of three men: two gents and one rich yeoman. Almost inevitably William James, yeoman, was the first to own any pictures. Two are listed as being in the best chamber in 1702. The two gentlemen were both Prichards who lived at the Vedw in Rowlestone, and died 80 years apart. Presumably, one inherited the pictures from the other. The first was Rowland Prichard, gent in 1706, who owned 'Nine pictures', the same number owned by 'Mr' John Prichard, gent in 1791. He had '6 small pictures' in the 'Little Parlour', and '3 Pictures in the Room over the Parlour'. Sadly, no individual values are given, though his total inventory came to over £400.

There is an intriguing link between two later Prichards of Vedw. In the 1756 inventory of Milburne Prichard is a line which states 'In the staires Leading to Garret and the above Rooms a Clock'. More than 30 years later a line in John's inventory gives a frisson of excitement. The appraisers have simply written 'Staircase. Clock and Case'. Was it the same clock? We will never know, but what is clear is that a clock was standing there, probably in exactly the same position, after a generation of Prichards had gone by. At six guineas the clock was the most valuable in the inventories. A clock of this sort would have been a luxury item in the mid 18th century, particularly in such a remote district; they were generally valued at between £1 and £3.

The Vedw clock would, of course, have been what is generally known today as a long-case or grandfather clock, and was called a 'clock and case'. The case was introduced in about 1660 to house the heavier eight day clock, with the pendulum introduced later to improve time-keeping. The cases were initially made of oak, then, as fashions changed, walnut and mahogany. Dial painted clocks were introduced in about 1770.

From a search of Longtown Historical Society's website, seven clocks were named 'clock and case', one in the inventory of Thomas Harris was listed as a 'clock & a Larrum' and the rest simply 'a clock' or an old clock'. Only one was called an '8 day clock', in the will of John Parry, mason of Longtown, and he leaves it to his daughter, together with his pictures, in 1845.

None of these clocks appear in Ewyas Lacy documents before the 18th century, although in 1702 one is called 'an old clock', so, presumably dates from the previous century. Out of a total of 43 mentioned in wills and inventories across the ten parishes, only eight are listed in the first half of the 18th century, almost all of them owned by the gentry, and one in the ownership of a prosperous tanner. In documents in which their whereabouts is mentioned, one was in the hall in the first half of the century, one in the parlour in 1742, the Prichards' two on the stairs and almost all the remaining six in the kitchen towards the end of the 18th and beginning of the 19th century. This confirms the trend that articles in the house were becoming increasingly centred on the kitchen and less on the hall.

There was another kind of timekeeper in use – the watch – but only three turned up in the wills or inventories, one in 1794, one in 1803 and one in 1845.

Silver Plate, Musical Instruments and Jewellery
The two Prichards appear again as owning silver plate or a musical instrument. Silver plate was mentioned in only three inventories, including that of the already mentioned Rowland Prichard, gent, in 1706, in which silver plate is valued at £5, and that of Elizabeth Watkins, widow of Newton in 1712, in which the plate is valued with a mixture of books and rings at £9 10s. It is no surprise to find that in 1650 Helena Delahay, a rich widow of Alltyrynys, left the most valuable collection of silver. Her son John was to have her 'silver tankard and great silver salte', and her daughter Elizabeth Parry was left two silver porringers and spoons. These three people were at the top end of the social scale, though Prichard had a total inventory value of only £41 1s 6d.

As already mentioned, for a region on the borders of Wales with such a reputation for music, it seems strange that only one musical instrument was recorded in the wills of this time: a violin owned by John Prichard of Rowlestone in 1791, and kept in the 'Little Parlour'. This question will be discussed further in chapter 10.

Books
Books have already been mentioned amongst Elizabeth Watkins' goods, and there seem to have been plenty of them elsewhere. It is interesting to note that ownership of books was not necessarily linked to wealth. Of the 18 owners in the sample, only nine had inventories valued at more than £100 and six had less than £50. However, possession of books does seem to be linked to the 18th and 19th centuries only, and they were found in all the parishes with the exception of Craswall, Llancillo and Walterstone. Clodock, the most central of the parishes, had the lion's share of seven listings, followed by St Margarets with four. Longtown and Newton came next with two each and Llanveynoe, Michaelchurch

Escley and Rowlestone took up the rear with one mention each. As might be expected, the vicar of Clodock and curate of Rowlestone had the most valuable collection of books. The Revd 'Mr' John Walters, curate of Rowlestone had 'Books and Manuscripts' worth £2 2s (out of a total inventory of £3 5s), in 1744, and the Revd Phillip Price of Clodock had his tantalisingly unnamed 'Books', worth £2, in 1787. One of the most endearing records notes that Delahay Symonds of Llanveynoe in 1795 owned a 'small Number of small Books and a paire of spectagls'.

Rarely is the location of the books mentioned. Of the five occasions when they are, it was as 'old Books in the Lower Chamber', 'Some old Books' found in the kitchen, or 'Books' upstairs and 'Some old books' in the kitchen. One has the impression that they were not valued very highly by their appraisers, or not considered important enough to describe individually. Even an august body like the National Trust has sometimes assumed that there was no library in a country house because there is an absence of books in the inventory.[18] Of course it would have been tedious to list every book by name if there was a large collection and the tendency was to simply use a cover-all description such as the phrases mentioned above. Another reason for omitting a library would be that shelves were a fixture therefore not required to be mentioned by law. For these reasons it is difficult to assess how many or what kind of books were in circulation.

However, as they are more likely to be identified by their owners in their wills, we do have an idea of the titles of a handful of these books, most of those named being Bibles or religious in some way, though an interest in history is shown by Noah Ychan of Llanveynoe, who died young in 1679 owning 'Severall Prynted Bookes of Divinity & Hystory'. Samuel Watkins, gent, of Clodock left in 1763 a large Bible and other books to be distributed among all his children. In 1770 Samuel Jenkins, yeoman, also of Clodock, left his manservant, Lewis Jenkins, all his books save two Bibles and a Prayer Book. In the same parish Morgan Thomas, gent, in 1740, had 'Books of all Sorts' valued at £1 10s in his inventory, which his will identifies a little further when he divides his books between his three children, and names *Isaac Ambrose*, a book of divinity, which he left to his favourite daughter, Elizabeth. Isaac Ambrose was a 17th-century nonconformist Divine whose writings were considered to be on the scale of John Bunyan's *Pilgrim's Progress*. This is interesting for the light it throws on the hold that nonconformity had on this area. Thirty-four years later Elias George, farmer of Llanveynoe, left £3 to the Baptist church meeting in Olchon towards the purchase of two volumes of 'John Bunyan'. There were also books for sale. Shopkeeper Thomas Harris had amongst his stock 'a small parcel of books', value 2s, and a 'Horning book', or primer, mixed with other goods.

Law books were mentioned on two occasions, the first in the will of John Davies, yeoman, of Michaelchurch Escley in 1695, and the second in the 1749 will of the Earl of Abergavenny's steward, Job Gilbert, gentleman of Craswall, in which he left his 'law books' to his two sons. Other parishes elsewhere, such as Uffculme in Devon, are able to give considerably more information on books; as many as 16 Bibles and 2 Prayer Books were mentioned in 32 inventories, the first in 1610.[19]

Either the tide of literature available in the 18th and 19th centuries had not reached this remote corner, or anything other than a religious tome was not considered to be worth mentioning. In any case, only the gentry or the prosperous farmer or tradesman would have the leisure, or the ability, to read the works of Defoe, Fielding or Richardson, the plays of Charles Dibdin, or the poetry of Pope, Thomson and Gray. By the end of the 17th century the children of the gentry were becoming familiar with *Aesop's Fables*, *Don Quixote* and nursery rhymes such as Jack and Jill, and in the next century *Robinson Crusoe* and *Gulliver's Travels*. Jane Austen describes how in quite small households at the end of the 18th century and the beginning of the 19th there was a craze for performing plays, and also tells us how the yeoman farmer in *Emma* would read aloud to the family and had read *The Vicar of Wakefield*.

Kitchenware: Posnets, Porringers and Patty Pans

People of this period probably had more fireplace equipment than we do today, when all our cooking processes take place neatly within the oven and on the hob. Logs had to be laid on the hearth onto something that would hold them firm such as andirons or andogs. Above these hung chimney crooks from bars inside the chimney breast, from which pots could be suspended. By the beginning of the 18th century an item seen less and less was the cauldron in which it was possible to cook a complete meal. One has the idea that this item was central to the hearth and seen in the average home, but this does not appear to

A typical collection of goods that would have been gathered around
a 17th-century farmhouse or cottage fireplace

A jack

have been the case in Ewyas Lacy. Only seven cauldrons are left in the wills, five of those in the 17th century, and only two were noted in the 17th-century inventories.

A brandis, often mentioned in inventories, was a three-legged stand which supported the pots over the fire. A spit, or broche, was commonly used to hold the meat in front of the fire, with a dripping pan below to catch the fat dripping off the meat. In order to turn the meat, a laborious task generally done by hand, an invention called a jack, a complex pulley system operated next to the fire, was introduced in the early 17th century. In large country mansions elsewhere in the county they were operated by clockwork, by a fan in the chimney or by terriers who worked on a treadmill inside the mechanism. The idea was slow to be adopted in some areas and does not appear in Ewyas Lacy until the first quarter of the 18th century – not too surprising as a jack must have been expensive to install and was the ultimate in kitchen equipment at the time. Thomas Harris, the well-to-do shopkeeper, owned a jack in 1786, as did another shopkeeper, Margaret Beavan, widow of Michaelchurch Escley, as early as 1727. Otherwise, it appears in only four gentry households, the first of these being the Vaughans of Llancillo, who handed it on to the next generation in 1723. A jack also crops up in the kitchen of Rowland Jennings of Clodock in 1742, and that of James Exton of Michaelchurch Escley in 1774. In the Prichard family of Vedw in Rowlestone, a jack appears only at the end of the 18th century.

The Prichards of Vedw were usually in the van of improvements. Milburne Prichard had a new kitchen installed in 1756 and the later Prichard, John, installed the jack there, as we know from the evidence of his inventory. Milburne Prichard's new kitchen held an interesting collection of furniture. As well as brass and pewter, it contained an old chest, old vessels, three old cupboards and old bedsteads, seeming to suggest that he hadn't yet got around to using the kitchen for cooking in. As the hall was mentioned only in passing perhaps the cooking was still being done there. Thirty-five years later, in 1791, the kitchen was full of the kind of kitchen equipment that would have been fairly common in well to do households by the end of the 18th century, including a fire shovel, tongs, no fewer than three spits, a sway (a bar swung out of the fireplace on which to hang pots), two dripping pans, an ironing box, a cleaver, a pair of cob irons, bellows, three iron pots, a small brass kettle and the jack.

Ancillary equipment, also listed in the inventory, consisted of the flat irons kept near the fire and ready for use, one iron candlestick, and lanthorns ready for going out on a winter's night. John was probably eating in the kitchen by then as he had his dresser there, together with 'earthen ware', four trenchers and several chairs. In some inventories there was a salt box kept beside the fire in order to keep the salt dry, and in 1758 we find the first rolling pin – noted in the inventory of Henry Morgan of Craswall.

Twenty years earlier, Elizabeth Prosser, widow of Newton had an even more lavishly furnished kitchen than the Prichards. As well as having a sway, she had further refinements in the shape of a brass mortar, spoon and skimmer, a colander, three porringers, patty pans, more spoons and a frying pan. In addition, she owned a considerable quantity of dishes including seven pewter dishes, 14 plates and 24 trenchers. This was more than the normal domestic requirement which seems to suggest that she may have been keeping an inn. Her two brass candlesticks were also kept in the kitchen.

There were all kinds of candlesticks in the probate documents and the numbers mentioned in almost every inventory are testimony to the importance of lighting. However, there would have been an attempt to economise on candles by the simple mechanism of rising only when it was light and going to bed soon after sunset. Metal rushlights, probably used in some households, consisted of a bowl filled with fat from which a wick protruded. Many of the inventories contain at least one candlestick, usually of brass, pewter, iron or tin, but there may have been others of lesser value, like the rushlights, included amongst the treen and 'trumperies' listed in the inventories, as not all the inventories mention candlesticks. Amongst the ones that do are the inventories of a clothworker, shoemaker, a carpenter and a shopkeeper, who would often have needed to work late. Thomas Harris, the local shopkeeper, had on sale in 1786 both beeswax and tallow and a candle mould and press.

Only one candlestick would be necessary for a family of four. The children would be seen off to bed by candlelight and then the parents would follow. In at least one old farmhouse the ghostly remains of candlelight flares on the wall of the chamber are evidence that candles were used there on many occasions. For one thing, babies do not time their arrivals to be within the hours of daylight.

Candlesticks were generally to be found in the kitchen, as were items such as warming pans, which were mentioned seven times in the probate documents. One of the most detailed wills as far as kitchenware is concerned is that of Elizabeth Watkins, widow of Newton in 1712. It must have been an exhausting business deciding who was to inherit what amongst the dozens of candlesticks, patty pans, skimmers, brass kettles and chamber pots (two, one of earthenware and one of pewter), and a warming pan. In contrast, another widow, Jane Jenkins of Craswall, who died at the end of the 18th century, has a rather dull will with all the detail given in her inventory, which again lists a warming pan amongst kitchen utensils that include andirons and tongs, brass kettles, skillets and the usual paraphernalia. Both Elizabeth and Jane were clearly well off so theirs cannot be used as examples of the average 18th-century kitchen; Jane also had 'smoothing irons' and 'One Dutch Oven', the latter a fairly new innovation introduced in the early 18th century; it was a cast-iron cooking pot with a tight-fitting lid onto which hot ashes were piled, and it was quickly superseded by the range. Many of the three-legged items which gave stability on the uneven surface of the hearth were not necessary once the range had arrived to take the place of the open fire. There is no clue as to its arrival date in Ewyas Lacy as ranges would have been considered fixtures and therefore were not included in an inventory.

It seems there was little reduction in the quantity of kitchen utensils needed from the 16th century onwards, although in 1586 John Cattallas, a tanner of Michaelchurch Escley, had merely a pot, two pans, a posnet (a three-legged saucepan), an iron broche and two candlesticks. Almost a hundred years later, Jane Gunter, a widow of Llanveynoe, had an inventory in 1675 which probably lists the minimum number of items that would have been essential: three pewter dishes, one saucer, one pewter candlestick, four brass kettles (open pots, not kettles as we know them today), two skillets and two brass pots. Salt cellars are not often mentioned, but when they are, most appear in the 17th century and were usually owned by the better-off in Ewyas Lacy, like Elinor Miles, a widow of Michaelchurch Escley who died in 1681 owning five brass pots, one brass pan, three cauldrons, one posnet, ten pewter dishes, two pewter candlesticks, a frying pan, a gridiron (a grill with a long handle), tongs, 20 pewter spoons, two dozen trenchers (wooden platters) and a salt cellar. Was she running an inn or an orphanage? Spoons are often mentioned, sometimes of silver, but more commonly of pewter. Forks and other flatware are never mentioned unless they were the 'flesh' forks used to handle meat hot from the fire. A knife would probably have been considered a personal possession, and forks, which were beginning to be used in the early 17th century, were not generally adopted until later in the century.[20]

During the 18th century one major change taking place was the reduction in the use of wooden or treen vessels as earthenware took its place for eating from and for display. In 1796 Jane Jenkins was still using the now old fashioned pewter and wooden plates, but long before that, in 1712, Elizabeth Watkins was proudly mentioning her 'best earthen blew ware and half a dozen red earthenware', in her will. These were probably the 'Delft ware' made in England from the 16th century and beginning to be generally used by the end of the 17th century, so she was probably well in advance of her neighbours. Implements made of horn were still being used in the kitchen of Thomas Smyth, yeoman, of Michaelchurch Escley in 1711.

Hanging somewhere nearby in many kitchens of this era would have been flitches of bacon or hams being cured. In her cellar Jane Jenkins had a saltstone and three benches, doubtless used for the salting of the pig after it had been killed and brought into the house. There it would have been thoroughly salted over a matter of weeks, and then the ham would have been covered in muslin against the flies and the flitches hung from a hook. Smoking chambers beside the fire would have been used to cure the hams or they might be hung in the chimney. Provided they had a pig or two, the people of Ewyas Lacy never needed to be short of meat; when a pig was killed, the chitterlings were shared out amongst the family and neighbours, and later it provided other things such as brawn, sausages and black puddings. Any fat from the intestines or stomach was rendered down to be used to make candles. There was very little of the pig that could not be used.[21] Possession of a cow meant that it was possible to be self-sufficient in butter and cheese. Fish was plentiful in the many rivers and streams of the Hundred, though mention of fishing gear is absent from the documents.

Details of the kinds and variety of foodstuffs are difficult to discover as often food is merely listed in the inventories as 'Household Provision' or 'victuals', but probably partly because it was possible to preserve it, the most common item was a flitch or two of bacon. In the sample of 40 Clodock inventories, eight list 'household provision' of which seven mention bacon, one 'meat' and two beef. In the second half of the 18th century, butter and cheese are also listed, together with potatoes.

Bacon was a valuable commodity even to the extent of occasionally being left in wills. In 1715 William Morgan left 'two of my best flitches of bacon' to his cousin James Morgan, and John George of Bilbo in Clodock left the 'meat in the house' to his wife Anne in 1772. It is interesting to see how the value of these flitches increased over time. David Thomas, yeoman, had two small flitches of bacon worth 5s in 1669. In 1748 Rowland Jennings, gent, owned three flitches worth 15s. By 1769, one and a half flitches owned by Phillip Parry, yeoman, were worth as much as £3 11s 6d, though one has to bear in mind that the size of the joint might vary. In a 16th-century inventory is a mention of brawn and suet. Neither mutton nor lamb is ever mentioned, although it must have been part of the diet, but, of course, it could not be preserved.

There was usually cheese and butter in the house, and two loaves of bread were mentioned in the inventory of James Lewis, husbandman of Clodock in 1759. Bread-making would have been done in a bread oven incorporated into the structure of most if not all farmhouses, and farmers' wives might have done the baking of loaves for those lacking the facility, or there might have been a communal bake-house nearby. Equipment for making bread is sometimes mentioned. A dough trind is listed in the effects of a poor widow of Michaelchurch Escley called Catherine Davis in 1743, and Anne Valentine of Rowlestone owned a kneading trough in 1802.

As we have seen, before the advent of sugar from the West Indies in the mid 17th century, hives of bees are commonly mentioned, either left as bequests in wills or listed in inventories. John Shaw of Clodock had hives of bees worth 8s in 1662, and Gwenllian Gilbert left a hive of bees to her granddaughter, Mary, in 1689. However, bees are rarely mentioned during the 18th century.

The local shop stocked anything unlikely to be produced at home. Amongst a fascinating list of 1786 that includes 'Coffee Teas', 'Tobacco & Snuff' are items such as the 'Loaf and Powder Shugars', and 'Sugar Candy and Treakle', 'Nutmegs and Spices', 'Currans Raisins & Rice'.

Most farmers and cottagers would have kept a few head of poultry, so there were often hens and cockerels to be culled, not to mention eggs constantly available, and geese were kept on the commons. There is a sad reference to 27 geese that would have been ready in time for the Michaelmas feast on 29 September in the inventory of Lawrence Read, yeoman, who died during that month in 1726, and another in the inventory of Elizabeth Thomas, widow, who died at the end of August leaving 16 geese worth 10s. It would not be surprising for a number of households to start in the spring with a goose and a gander resulting in offspring ready to fatten in time for Michaelmas.

Then there were the crops that would have been grown for household consumption, even in the gardens of the poorest people. Peas, for instance, must have been plentiful as they were grown commercially in the area. Fruit would have been readily available too, in a county renowned for its apples. Drinks in the form of cider or beer would have been plentiful and very necessary at a time when water might have carried disease. The inventories and wills show evidence of coffee and tea drinking from the mid 18th century.

Evidence for the food eaten by the poor is lacking, but a comment by Arthur Young in the last quarter of the 18th century suggests that poor people ate mainly bread and cheese, with meat only on Sundays. This view is to some extent supported by the daily diet of Abbeydore workhouse (which was the workhouse for this district) in the mid 19th century, which consisted of 6-7 ounces of bread, 1½ pints of gruel for breakfast, 5 ounces of meat and 1lb of potatoes on Sundays and Thursdays. On Mondays, Wednesdays and Saturdays there would be 1½ pints of soup with ½lb of potatoes. This diet was 'enlivened' on Tuesdays and Fridays, when the inmates had nothing but suet or rice pudding. Supper was broth, with potatoes three times a week and bread and cheese on the other four nights. A humane touch was added for the benefit of those over 60 in the shape of 1 ounce of tea, 5 ounces of butter and 7 ounces of sugar weekly instead of the gruel. This seems pretty grim fare to us today, but it may have been an improvement on the hand to mouth existence of many of the poor at a time of agricultural depression.[22]

By the end of the 18th century, there would have been much that would be familiar to us today, such as the 'toster' and copper tea kettle mentioned in 1780, the scissors, hourglass and mouse traps, coffees and teas on sale in the local shop of Thomas Harris, and the coffee pot owned by the cooper of Newton in 1799.

Meal Times

Among the middle classes in the 18th century, midday dinner was the substantial main meal of the day. By the end of the century, however, breakfast became a more solid meal, though not accompanied by tea or coffee, but cocoa or chocolate. This breakfast was generally taken at about 10 o'clock. The hour for dinner was also changing from midday to about 5 o'clock, followed by a small snack later in the evening. Subsequently, as the dinner hour moved towards seven or later it became necessary to have another light meal, which became afternoon tea.[23]

Conclusion

Intense scrutiny of wills and inventories leaves little doubt that the contents of a house not only increased over the period under review, but were also of much greater diversity. Tables in particular not only increased in number, but changed from the simple 17th-century oak trestle table which could be assembled by any householder to a variety of shapes made from a range of woods. Furniture also became more sophisticated and comfortable. Chairs morphed from the simple bench of the 1660s to the 'easy arm chair' into which no doubt Samuel Griffiths gratefully sank at the end of a working day, in his Llanveynoe farmhouse in 1857. Another yeoman farmer of Llanveynoe to die in the same year, John Powell, had in his inventory three beds and bedsteads (one with hangings), bedding, one chest, four boxes, two spinning wheels, four tables, one dresser and shelves (and a quantity of pewter to go on it), one cupboard, nine chairs, a clock and a looking glass, besides other smaller items.

In contrast, almost two hundred years earlier, in 1671, another yeoman of Craswall, John Jenkins, had in his inventory only one feather bed and bolster, one flock bed, one chest and four coffers, three chairs and one tableboard 'with the frame under it'. His furniture was all basic stuff relating to sleeping, eating and storage, with the beds being the most comfortable of all the items.

Nowhere is there any mention of cutlery, apart from the occasional spoon, although sets of knives and forks were being made by the 1660s. They may have ended up amongst the 'Trumperies' in the inventory.[24]

9   CLOTHING AND HOUSEHOLD LINEN

Details of clothing are few and far between in most collections of inventories and Ewyas Lacy is no different, with very few clothes mentioned in either wills or inventories, and most of these in early 17th-century wills.[1] Luckily, there is a set of probate documents among the Ewyas Lacy collection which enable us to see the range of goods available to the people of the Hundred over the mid to late 18th century, especially in Longtown, the commercial heart of the district.

Ewyas Lacy parishes or townships which in my lifetime supported a full complement of shops produced only two shopkeepers from the probate records. There are four possible reasons for this, apart from the point already made that in the early years most goods would have been made at home or locally to order. One reason might be that there were shopkeepers who were existing at too low an economic level for it to be worth making a will, another that the shops were too short-lived to remain on the radar. A third reason was that shop-keeping may well have been combined with some other occupation, for example in 1788 Henry Morgan, whose occupation was not given, seemed to be combining shop-keeping with running an inn; his inventory contained more goods than one would expect an innkeeper to have. There was also John Jones of Michaelchurch Escley, who was a 'shopkeeper and miller' in 1855. Lastly, there were many who eked out a living by running a shop, but whose primary designation would be as a widow. One of these was Margaret Beavan of Michaelchurch Escley, a widow, who, in 1727, left 'goods lying in the shop'. Her inventory value was not inconsiderable at £122 9s 4d.

Thomas Harris was a mercer[2] of Bryn Rhewy, on a steep hill overlooking Longtown, and his inventory of 1786 gives a wealth of information. Thomas had taken over the business from his father-in-law, Charles Hunt, who had died in 1747. It is difficult to imagine his customers coming to anything like a shop at his house, which was well outside the villages of Longtown and Clodock, up a steep and narrow lane. One can only assume that he brought the goods to his customers, or, more likely, also had a shop in the village, or a stall at the village market.

One wonders whether local people were aware of the romance that lay behind the contents of Thomas Harris's stock. Amongst the shelves piled high with bolts of 'Irish Cloth' there were 'remnants of Russian Duck and Drab', Fustian (named originally after a Cairo suburb), Turkey Cotton, 'Camlett' from the East, and remnants of 'Doulas' or Dowlas (a coarse linen popular in the 16th and 17th century), originally from France. Adding an exotic note was the 'swanskin', and whalebone stays.

The inventory of Thomas Harris's stock in 1786

80 yards of Irish Cloth at 2/3	9	0	0
80 yard ditto at 1/6	6	0	0
80 yards at 1/-	4	0	0
Remnants of Clear Lawns		10	0
Remnants of Muslins	1	10	0
Remnants of Long Lawn	1	4	0
Best Lace		18	0
Remnants of Coarse Lace		10	0
Box of Ribbands	3	0	0
Silk Handkerchiefs	4	10	0
Silk Muslin Do	2	0	0
Stamp Cotton Do	2	0	0
Check ditto	2	0	0
Printed Cottons	4	0	0
Printed Linens		15	0
Remnants & ea [etc?] of Checks	5	0	0
Remnants of Stript Linens		8	0
Remnants of Bed Ticking	1	8	0
Remnants of Russia Duck & Drab	2	6	0
7 Remnants of Doulas	6	10	0
2 Remnants of Sheeting	1	10	0
4 Remnants of Draper		15	0
1 Remnant of Masella		10	0
1 Remnant of Tinken		5	0
2 Remnants of Brown Sheeting	1	5	0
3 Remnants of Hempen Russia		14	0
3 Remnants of Cheese Cloth		14	0
2 Remnants of Hempen Cloth & Hessings	1	10	0
2 Remnants of Pocketting		10	6
Incles [?] & Cheese filletting		5	0
Buckram & Canvas		12	0
Threads Coarse & fine		10	0
Silk & Twist & Ticking		15	0
White and Coloured Tapes		4	0
Laces of different sorts		4	0
3 Remnants of Broad Cloth [fine, plain black hardwearing cloth weaved 2 yards wide with a short nap, used for men's outer clothing]	1	1	0
3 Remnants of Coarse Serge		17	0
3 Remnants of Coloured Serge		12	0
2 Remnants of Court/ or Coarse Cloth		10	0
2 Remnants of Flanel	1	2	0
2 Do of Blew Linsey [an inferior, loosely woven, coarse cloth made from a mixture of wool and flax, originally from Lindsey, Suffolk]		7	0

Item			
Worsted Stockings	1	10	0
1 Shelf of Mancoes[?]	5	0	0
1 Shelf of Shalloons [a loosely woven woollen cloth often used for linings]	4	0	0
2 Shelf of Tammys [a fine worsted cloth of good quality, with a highly glazed finish, originally made in Tamworth, Staffordshire]	4	0	0
1 Shef of Stript Camlets [a fine light linen made from a combination of wool, silk and hair and especially from the wool of angora goats. Frequently used for hangings, upholstery and women's clothing]	5	0	0
Remnant of Crapes [crepes] for Shrouding	4	0	0
4 Remnants of Corderoy & Fustian [a coarse fabric made from a mixture of cotton and linen, with a silky finish, used for furnishings and heavy clothes]	5	0	0
2 Remnants of Turkey Cotton	1	0	0
2 Remnants of Curtain Stuff		5	0
2 Remnants of Lasting [?] and Shades	1	0	0
4 Small Shelfs of Twist and Metal Buitons	1	5	0
3 Remnants of Velvaret	2	10	0
2 Remnants of Mourning Crape [A light cloth, thin worsted stuff, made in Norfolk, sometimes used for woollen shrouds (compulsory after 1678); also for clothes of the clergy]		10	0
Ferreting [stout cotton or silk tape used for garters, often decorated] Quality Binding and Gartering		10	0
One Shelf of Stays	2	10	0
5 Remnants of Swanskin	1	5	0
1 small drawer of Shirt Buttons		1	0
2 Boxes of hats	3	0	0
5 Remnants of Silk	5	10	0
Sheets & Table Linen & Worsted Caps & Mitts	3	5	0
Knives & Large Buckles	1	5	0
Schisors & Small Buckes [Buckles?]		5	0
3 Small Looking & Hour Glass		1	0
Snuff Boxes Pencils Horning Book & Rule		2	6
A small Parcel of Books		2	0
Mouse traps Locks & Rings		10	0
Curry Cwmb Wire Awl Blades & Afts		2	6
CandleSticks Brushes Stirups & Packthread		5	0
Cord Twine Hemp & Packthread	1	0	0
Paper Pitch & Radle	1	0	0
Hops Whetstone & Black Lamb	2	0	0
Saltad Linseed & Train oils		6	0
Salt & Glue	1	5	0
Nails of all sorts	2	0	0
Gunpowder Shot & Choke		10	0
Childrens Shoes & Patterns		7	6
Thongs Rat Traps & Bees Wax		2	0
Files & Inges [Hinges?]		3	0

Coffins Trimmings & Flints	1	10	0
Tins Noodles [needles] Nails Paser & Nitting Needles		4	0
Flour & Stone Brimstone & Saltpetre		5	0
Several Sorts of Drugs	1	10	0
Blue & Starch		10	0
Mortars & Thimbles		1	6
Coffee Teas etc.	2	0	0
Tobacco & Snuff	3	0	0
Loaf & Powder Shugars	2	10	0
Currans Raisins & Rice	1	0	0
Sugar Candy & Treakle	1	5	0
Nutmegs & Spices		15	0
Scales & Weight		3	0
Candles and Soap	2	5	0
Coffee & Pepper Milll		1	0
Stock of Tallow in Hand	5	0	0

It is a startlingly expensive collection for such a rural and, one might have assumed, unsophisticated population. He did not stock ready-made clothes. Clothes would either be made at home, or by the tailors of the district, though there are surprisingly few of these, only one appearing in surviving inventories for any of the parishes, and three amongst the wills of this time. Either suits were being made at home, or tailors did not have sufficient worldly goods to justify making a will. The busy housewife could buy everything she needed from Thomas Harris in the way of sheets and table linen, 'worsted caps and Mitts' and shoes for the children, worsted stockings for the family, and hats. (The only ready-made shoes likely to be available were for children, as adults would have had theirs made by the many shoemakers.) Harris also kept an entire shelf of stays so they were obviously much in demand locally. Apart from the wide choice of cloth, best and coarse lace, sheets and table linen, there was much to help home production, including knitting needles, cord twine, threads 'coarse and fine' and packthread, flat irons, scissors and buckles, shirt and metal buttons, as well as 'Ferretting Quality Binding and Gartering'.[3] Thomas did not forget the needs of his customers at the ends of their lives, either. His inventory lists crepes for shrouding, and mourning crepe, as well as coffin trimmings.

The total value of his shop goods amounted to £160 3s, which compares well with others elsewhere in the country. The median value of mercers' goods in Kent increased to about £80 by the end of the 17th century, admittedly at a period 80 years before Thomas Harris had his shop. Many rural shops were operating with much lower levels of stock, perhaps valued at only £5.[4]

As we have so few other details of clothing, it is necessary to compare these details with what people were likely to be wearing over the three hundred years covered by the documents. First, we can take a look at the material commonly in use. Mr Harris also stocked 'Printed Cottons'. Cotton was first imported from India by the East India Company towards the end of the 17th century as calico, It became popular, as it could not only be easily washed, but could be printed or painted with patterns. Importation was prohibited from 1701 and later had a tax imposed on it in order to protect British-made fabrics. The prohibition on wearing pure cottons was lifted in 1774 through the efforts of Richard Arkwright of Cromford in Derbyshire, a cotton manufacturer and the inventor of the spinning frame. Until then printers of painted cottons had been forced to make them with a linen warp. Now it could be made as pure cotton and became cheaper when the tax on all printed fabrics was equalized in 1784. Not only that, it was now more attractive, as the cloth was lighter and had a brighter colour.[5] Soon cotton was so popular that women of all classes were wearing it, leading to difficulties of identification according to one 18th-century traveller, who complained that milkmaids looked like 'Strand misses'.[6]

Until the 18th century woollen cloth had been predominant in England in the form of Camblet, 'Tammy' and other cloths such as serge made from worsted yarn. Because they were cheap and hard wearing, woollens continued to be used for under-garments and for the poor in the workhouse well into the 19th century. Mr Harris also stocked lawn (a fine linen), and on nearby shelves were remnants of dowlas (a coarse linen). Regardless of the interesting alternatives available by the 18th century, a preference remained for shirts and shifts to be made from linen through that century and into the 19th, as they were hard-wearing and could be washed more easily than cotton.[7]

Sumptuary laws in the 16th century had tried to restrict what the different classes could wear, people's love of finery leading, it was thought by Queen Elizabeth and her ministers, to less money being spent on hospitality, and even encouraging crime. Various proclamations were made and ignored. Essentially, there was an embargo on gold or silver being used on clothing unless one was a member of the aristocracy; velvet, unless one was a knight's wife or above; and a similar prohibition on anyone lower than a gentleman's wife using satin, damask or 'taffety'. Similar rules applied to men, with the addition that swords were not allowed to anyone below the rank of a Captain 'in her Majesties pay'. Many people might have said at the time 'we should be so lucky', but the fact remained that there was a burgeoning middle class containing newly rich lawyers and merchants who were now able to afford the kind of clothing hitherto restricted to their betters.[8] By the 17th century these rules had gone by the board. The upper classes may have resented anyone dressing above their station, but there was nothing that could now be done about it, and henceforth people were merely restricted by what they could afford.

Of the 27 wills in which clothes are described, 19 are from the 17th century, six from the 18th century and only two from the first half of the 19th. In the main they mention cloth from which to have clothes made rather than ready-made garments. For example, Gwenllian Prosser, a widow of Michaelchurch Escley, left 'cloth to make suits of clothes' in her will of 1670,[9] and, in 1684, Winifryd Phillip, spinster of Clodock, left five yards of cloth to her nurse, five yards of cloth to Mary England and enough cloth to make a waistcoat to Elizabeth Harry. This was probably flaxen cloth, as 12 yards of it appears in her inventory. In 1785 Thomas Watkins, a dyer of Longtown, left his servant enough cloth to make a gown and a petticoat.

The value of the clothing was important, of course, but it did not seem to be the practice to describe it in detail. In the inventories, 'wearing apparel' is almost always at the top of the list and varies from small amounts such as 10s or less for a husbandman, or from £1 to

£2 for a yeoman, whilst a gentleman rarely had clothes worth less than £2. In 1649, at the end of the Civil War, William Walbief, gent, whose wife was the widow of James Watkins, had clothing to the value of £6. James Watkins' clothes had been valued at £5. Generally gentlemen's clothing was not valued at more than about £2 at Ewyas Lacy, in contrast to other wealthier regions where average clothing was valued at between £2 and £3 in the late 17th century. William Walbief and James Watkins were clearly very rich men and their inventories support this.

For an idea of what a wealthy gentleman of Clodock would have been wearing a few years before the Civil War, there is delightful detail in Milo John Miles's will of 1634. He leaves a cloak, a jerkin, two pairs of breeches (one lined with linen), a 'jerkin doublet', a 'new hat', shoes and stockings. At this time, though well into the 17th century, the movement was away from the ruffs, cassocks (worn by both sexes and not just priests), cloaks, doublet and hose. William Harry Thomas Powell of Michaelchurch Escley left his ruff band to his brother, and a ruff to the local vicar in 1619 (together with, rather surprisingly, a short sword). By the end of the 17th century, outfits of coats, waistcoats, breeches and bands (linen collars) or wigs had become the fashion. Details of lace continued to be used throughout the period. By the end of the 17th century white lace of some delicacy was being made at Honiton in Devon and all over Somerset, but Belgian and French lace was still being imported. Thomas Harris lists 'Best Lace' as well as 'Coarse Lace' in addition to remnants of silk, silk muslin and silk handkerchiefs so, by that date, in 1786, the well-dressed in Ewyas Lacy did not have to go far afield.

Changes were not as great for women during the 17th century and they continued to wear gowns, petticoats, stomachers and aprons with only small changes in the detail until the following century. In 1619, Margaret verch Willim of Clodock left her best gown, petticoat, apron and smock to Anne Harry, and four kerchiefs to other relations. Women were always more likely to mention clothes in their wills. It is possible to summon up a picture of what Johan (Joan) Lewis, a widow of Craswall, would have worn as her 'Sunday best' when in 1641 she left to her family what was virtually a total outfit, consisting of her best gown, petticoat, smock, waistcoat, shoes and stockings, a coife (a closefitting cap) and a scarf. Constance Price, also of Craswall, left a half petticoat and an apron in 1648. An apron clearly formed an important part of a woman's outfit. In 1661 Elizabeth Beavan, a well-to-do widow of St Margarets, left a 'Cambrick apron' together with her best silk gown, shoes, stockings, a velvet hood and hat and an unspecified 'margelet'. The combination of a silk gown and the use of velvet in both hood and 'margelet' distinguish her as exceptionally rich.[10] Eight years later, in 1669, Elizabeth Rees Harry of Craswall left no fewer than three half petticoats, together with an under petticoat, a waistcoat, three shirt cloths and one smock cloth. In the same year, another widow, Mauld Hunt of Llanveynoe, left six pairs of shoes.

On only a few occasions are clothes described in any detail. One reason for the absence of women's clothing from inventories and wills may have been due to its legal status; marriage settlements kept a woman's wearing apparel, jewels, bed-linen and plate separate from her husband's estate.[11] However, most women, particularly at the lower end of the social scale, would not have had this protection, as we saw in chapter 7. In one of the few other mentions of clothing, Henry Morgan's inventory includes 'His wife's wearing apparel' and coincidentally (and deeply ironically) the only rolling pin in the inventories.

At St Margarets in 1683, Sible Peate, spinster, left a 'hatt' worth 8d, 'shoos and stockings' valued at 1s 4d and an apron worth 8d. She might have purchased her stockings or her hat at a local shop, but her apron was almost certainly made at home. Sible Peate's stockings would have been the knitted kind first introduced in the early 16th century and made across the country in various local wools. Joan Thirsk says that knitting was mostly confined to pastoral areas but there is no evidence of this craft at Ewyas Lacy.[12]

By the 18th century men were wearing waistcoats, breeches, long coats which flared at the base, square-toed shoes with bows, and possibly a wig if they were wealthy. Thomas Thomas a blacksmith of Michaelchurch Escley in 1719 left his father his best coat and waistcoat, plus two new shirts. Twenty years later styles had not changed very much as William Prosser bequeathed his son almost a complete outfit of his best hat, best coat, a waistcoat and an old silk waistcoat, breeches and a pair of good shoes and boots. Through the century the coat became less voluminous and the knee breeches were worn with stockings and buckled shoes. Buckled shoes were worn by both sexes, with the buckles becoming more prominent and made of all kinds of materials. Sarah James, a widow of Rowlestone, had silver buckles listed in her inventory in 1780.

The dress of a maid in the mid 18th century was probably similar to that worn by many womenfolk of Ewyas Lacy at that time

Three-cornered hats became the fashion for men, whilst women wore mob caps, sometimes topped with large brimmed hats for smart wear. Prints of the time demonstrate that a young girl going to the fair with her beau would be very smartly dressed by today's standards. The couple would both be wearing shoes decorated with buckles.

By the end of the 18th century, gloves, which had been worn since early times, tended to be made of fabric rather than leather, and were often made by women milliners. Gloves were universally worn – even charity schoolchildren were issued with them – and there were many towns throughout the country that based their trade on the making of them. It is instructive to note that Harris apparently did not stock any by 1786, and glovers in Ewyas Lacy (four of them) are found only during the 17th and early 18th centuries. By the 19th century gloves were machine-made.

As the fashion industry of the early 18th century moved on and cottons began to be worn by everyone, a new discovery was made by the elite in the 1780s: muslin, a more delicate woven cotton, usually white.[13] By 1786 it was being sold by Mr Harris, so the wealthy of Ewyas Lacy were keeping pace with the latest fashion. This was accompanied by a quite dramatic change as the heavier, more ornate styles of dress were left behind for a far simpler, lighter style, a move away from hoops to a simple narrow silhouette. France had always been considered the epitome of fashion, but Britain was cut off from French influence by the French Revolution, so turned to other sources of supply. With increasing trade with India and the proliferating industry of the northern mills, people greeted the muslins, and imported cashmere

Fashions in the last half of the 18th century

shawls, with enthusiasm. To the many aristocratic French émigrés this became the *style à l' anglaise*.[14]

By the end of the 18th century men were wearing, as the main piece of their wardrobe, a broadcloth riding coat, single or double breasted, neck-cloths of starched linen (which later turned into cravats) that became ever more of a fashion feature that covered the shirts (usually made at home), while breeches, commonly worn throughout the 18th century, now became pantaloons, the forerunner of the trousers of today. Buckled shoes had been worn with the breeches, but were now ousted by smart knee-length half boots.

'Unmentionables', to use a term Dickens was fond of, by and large literally went unmentioned in the wills and inventories of Ewyas Lacy. It is true that in 1702 the wealthy yeoman William James died leaving, amongst many other items, his four shirts and a pair of drawers – the only drawers mentioned in any of the documents. He probably possessed them because, as an old man, he needed the extra warmth, but they are not named in his will (which does, however, mention his second best suit, which was bequeathed to his manservant). But perhaps surprisingly, 'drawers', as in knickers, were not generally worn by women until late in the 19th century, except by prostitutes or dancers who would be expected to show their legs in an indelicate fashion. To secure some modicum of modesty, women wore a petticoat underneath the open gown, usually of a different colour to create a contrast. This outfit must have made women susceptible to catching cold in our climate and led to the introduction of a pelisse, or coat of velvet or wool. Not soon enough, however, to stop doctors blaming the thin clothing for the levels of consumption that carried so many off during the 19th century.

Shawls, worn from the end of the 18th century, gave extra warmth. Stays, tightly laced in the 18th century, became looser and must have added some element of warmth, together with stockings, made of silk or cotton, attached by garters at about knee-height. Made ubiquitous by Arkwright's cotton machines, these in fine cotton were common wear by 1822 and were so highly esteemed that, ignoring the war going on between the two countries, the Empress Josephine insisted on ordering her stockings from England.

It is also a surprise to learn that 'falsies' created another element of female artifice which we might think belonged only to our own age, and by all accounts they had equal dangers. Although not implants, moulded wax was used to enhance nature. In the early 19th century much quoted were the lines

> Spite of the gibes of wanton wit,
> What emblems can the fair,
> Of their dear tender hearts more fit
> Than waxen bosoms wear?
> Twixt mounts of wax and hills of snow
> How small the difference felt!
> With due degrees of heat we know
> That both will gently melt.[15]

Children were also catered for. Rousseau, that malign influence on morals and poor father to his own children, did some good in advocating that wearing a miniature version of their elders' clothing was unhealthy for children and that boys should be left in frocks for as long as possible. This led to some confusion. There is a delightful woodcut of about the late 18th century showing a tot dressed in a frock whilst behaving in a most boyish manner and driving his mother mad with his noise. The outfit adopted by the 1780s was a short jacket with a shawl collar and ankle-length trousers. These trousers, which were buttoned onto the jacket became the 'skeleton suit', worn until the 1830s when the sailor suit began to be the fashion. Older boys came to wear the trousers and short jacket with a plain collar called the Eton suit that is still worn by boys at that school today.[16]

Although the best wool came from Herefordshire and Shropshire, wool is seldom

A 'skeleton suit' of the type worn by boys from the 1780s to 1830s

mentioned in the Ewyas Lacy inventories. Much was removed from the farm quite quickly unless it was being spun or used locally by the farmer and his family. Much wool was also imported from Ireland, Wales and Spain during the 17th century as English supplies became inadequate for the burgeoning cloth trade. By the early 18th century it was clear that it was cheaper to import yarn, as the cost of spinning in Ireland was cheaper than on the mainland.

Spinning and Weaving

Spinning wheels are the first things that come to mind where textiles are concerned. For such an essential item at a time when it was the responsibility of every married woman to provide her own linen, spinning wheels are mentioned surprisingly little in the Ewyas Lacy documents. Was commercial spinning confined to certain parishes, and did the industry decline over the period as it did in other areas such as Kent and Cornwall?[17] It is difficult to differentiate between those producing yarn for their own use and those engaging in re-sale, but the same decline seemed to apply to both groups.

After the wool had been scoured or cleaned, the spinster carded or combed the wool preparatory to spinning the yarn on her spinning wheel. (Short wool was carded and long wool was combed.) Once spun, the wool was wound onto a spool, and the yarn was then passed to the weaver, who made it up into cloth on a loom. After the cloth was woven it went to the tucker or fuller, who softened, strengthened and thickened the cloth, and thence to the clothier, who dyed it. If this was a notable cloth region, one would expect to find many spinsters, but by the late 17th century the yarn may have been brought in from elsewhere. The charming picture of 'the wheel at night (cheering) the kitchen with its whirring sound, while the family were assembled round the wood-fire hearth' may have held true earlier in the 17th century.[18]

There is a tendency to think of spinning wheels being chiefly in the hands of the women of the family, but they appear in inventories of men as even these were regarded as male property. Rowland Jennings, tanner, in whose inventory are listed one woollen and two flaxen wheels in 1661, would not have had the time to use them. Walter Prichard, yeoman, owned two spinning wheels in 1802. Henry Jenkins, 'bachelor', had one wheel, but several other cloth-making items in 1737.

It is sometimes difficult to tell whether the term spinster means what it says, or is merely describing a woman's status, but the presence of 'three stone of hurds, spun' in the 'spinster' Sarah Davies' inventory in 1751 seems to combine both status and trade. In the parish of St Margarets 70 years earlier, Sible Peate, another 'spinster', had owned 5 yards of cloth and 10 lbs of wool at her death. What, however, can one make of Anne Harry, 'spinster' of Llanveynoe, who left money to her daughter in 1673, or Mary Parry, 'spinster' of Longtown in 1829, who had sons? Even if there is no spinning wheel in the inventory, it is possible that it was hired from someone else, though there is no evidence for this.

There were several widows with spinning wheels whose inventories support the theory that spinning could be a profitable means of support. Elizabeth Prosser, a comfortably off widow, quite clearly was the user of her linen and woollen spinning wheels as she also had linen yarn, 'unspun' flax, hurden yarn and a piece of cloth in her inventory in 1770, but was she producing enough to sell? Her will does not give any evidence of this, while her inventory, valued at over £100, shows that she was also a substantial maker of cheese and owned a fair-sized farm. Another widow, Elizabeth Jenkins of Craswall, who had one of the most interesting and detailed of the inventories, owned one woollen and one linen wheel, 8½ yards of linen at 8d per yard, wool, and 4lbs of hurds (flax or hemp) in 1765. She did not make a will. Hannah Gilbert, widow of Craswall, also had two spinning wheels, three stones of flax and four stocks (for making up the rim for wheels) in 1794. A sad case, she left three small children, for whom her will left a substantial farm stock to sell for their support. It is unlikely that her spinning was any more than for domestic use. Oddly, not every wheel left in a will appeared again in an inventory. Out of eleven wills that mention wheels, only four make an appearance in the inventory that followed.

Spinning wheels do not appear to have been worth very much – linen and wool spinning wheels belonging to Judith Pugh of Walterstone were worth 3s 6d combined in 1791. Looms were worth considerably more, being valued between 13s 4d and 30s for the narrow looms, and at £3 10s for the broad looms. The ones mentioned at Ewyas Lacy were merely called 'looms' and were almost certainly narrow looms. They were evenly distributed across the parishes or townships.

All looms had warping frames on which to create the warp, which comprised two horizontal posts along which pegs were fixed to hold the yarn which was then threaded back and forth between the posts to get it ready for the loom. Women may have done this while the men carried on the weaving. The chain was wound onto the warp beam and placed on the loom, which consisted of two uprights, with the beam at the top and a roller at the base onto which the cloth was wound. The threads were then passed through the harness, or vertical wires, containing the eye for the yarn, and then the harness was alternately lowered and lifted to enable the shuttle to pass through. Weights preserved the tension in the warp (the threads that run lengthways at right angles to the weft).[19]

Weavers could have worked on their own or have employed several people, and thus been a master weaver. William Pugh of Walterstone, a weaver who was probably Judith's son, owned two looms worth 16s in 1811. He left the tools of his trade to his son Elias in his will 'if he will follow the trade'. There is a set of unusually detailed documents for Henry Jenkins of Craswall in 1737, who, though merely listed as a bachelor, is obviously a weaver on quite a substantial scale as he owned two looms, six slayers (or reeds which helped to join the weft to the preceding thread), 'waits [weights] for waying' and a trough for warping. Details from the inventories of other weavers are elusive. Eight years later, Henry Davies, weaver of Craswall in 1745, owned a loom with its 'utensils' worth 10s. Indeed most of his money seemed to be tied up in it as his clothes were worth 6s and his total inventory came to only £4 17s. In 1723, Henry Kite, a weaver from Michaelchurch Escley who appears to be only marginally better off, offers an interesting profile of one of these weavers and the kind of circumstances in which they lived. His looms with 'appurtenances' were worth £3 10s, his clothing only 5s. Seemingly a poor man living at a very basic level, he owned only one bed, two small skillets and 'other trumpery', a cow and calf, an old mare and 'a little pig'. The lease of his 'cott' was worth £5, and his total worth was only £15 17s 6d, out of which had to be paid £14 3s at his death.

Weavers' shops are sometimes mentioned, which seems to indicate more substantial trade. In 1576, Rees Thomas ap Prichard of Clodock left his nephew 'all my wev[r]s shop with all I have belonging to that my said weavers craft' and, over two centuries later, John Williams of St Margarets had 'two looms in his shop' in 1800. Like Rees Thomas ap Prichard, John Williams had a small farming enterprise as a side occupation as his looms were mixed up with a cheese press with a value of £1 15s altogether, and he owned a cow and three heifers, though his total value did not come to more than £17 15s. These appeared to be the only weavers over the 300-hundred-year period of the study; a total of about 22. At Uffculme in Devon, over an 80-year period between 1614 and 1694, 25 looms were listed in the inventories, but that was a cloth-making town.[20] Of course there must have been others who were not picked up in the inventories; wills sometimes tell a different story. There is no inventory for Thomas Williams of St Margarets in 1829, though he is called a weaver in his will.

These workers were at the early stages of the cloth-making process, and generally seemed the least prosperous, as weavers were at the mercy of the clothiers and payment was often late. In Devon in the mid 17th century weavers were amongst the poor, with incomes amounting to £5 or less, whereas master craftsmen such as tuckers and dyers were comfortably off, with annual incomes of £20 or more.[21]

The cloth-making process was taken a step further by the tuckers or fullers, who undertook the fulling process, and clothiers. Outside the Hundred, the nearest village to Clodock was called Pandy, which is Welsh for tucking mill.

Fulling mills

Water played a major part in the development of a cloth industry and Ewyas Lacy was fortunate enough to have a plentiful supply to power her mills. Documentary sources have it that there were two fulling mills in Ewyas Lacy, one on the Olchon Brook and another in Craswall, at Cwm Mill, but others have been identified (with some difficulty). Something listed as a mill could be used for a number of purposes, such as making malt, cider or flour so it can be difficult now to tell whether or not a mill may have been a fulling or tuck mill at some point in the past as they could be turned into grist (corn) mills and back again as required. There is, however, no evidence for a paper mill in the Hundred.

Tuckers may have rented rather than owned a mill. Some of the earliest tuckers are found in the pre-Restoration period, one such being James Madockes, a yeoman of Craswall in 1647, where he owned both a grist and fulling mill. His uncle was a tucker of Michaelchurch Escley where at least two tuckers lived, implying that there was almost certainly a fulling or tucking mill there.

Fulling was the process by which the cloth was softened, strengthened and thickened, the cloth being first immersed in urine (which in cloth-making towns was collected in receptacles along the roadside), soaped in water and then placed in a fulling or tucking mill to be beaten. Fullers Earth was used to absorb any oil or grease used earlier; butter, lard or tallow was often used to make the wool more flexible before carding. Heavy mallets at the ends of beams pounded the cloth as it lay in the fulling trough. Some fullers may have used special boots as we have a mention of 'tucking shoes' (which do not appear in accounts elsewhere in the country) in the inventory of Lodwick David, tucker of Clodock in 1632. Trampling on the cloth was more often done in the Middle Ages before water powered fulling stocks were introduced. John Rice James, a tucker of Michaelchurch Escley, had in 1650 'tucking spurs' in his inventory, together with all the equipment in his 'tucking shop'.

Perhaps the most comprehensive record for any of the mills lies in a bundle of documents held by Hereford Record Office for a tuck mill on the Olchon river. In 1568 a house, lands and a corn mill were held by Morgan Richards of Longtown. By 1719 this had passed to Michael Morgan who, as mortgagee bought the site of 'a decayed tuck mill' on the Olchon in 1721 and proceeded to build a new mill. This passed through various hands until it came to James Hughes in 1782.[22] Is this another mill on the Olchon, besides the corn mill mentioned earlier and owned by John Jenkins?

There is an early mention of a tucking mill at Cwm in Craswall; in 1728, David Nicholls, yeoman, left his niece, Mary Price, 'his messuage, water corn and tuck mills' there. This factory is said to have been established in the early 18th century for the manufacture of a variety of cloths, including flannel, which had originally been made in Abergavenny but began to be manufactured in Ewyas Lacy in the 18th century. During the first half of the 19th century, the tuck mill at Cwm was run by a forceful woman called Elizabeth Phillips for the production of all kinds of cloth, including blankets, carpets and flannel. The place also appears to have been a focus for nonconformity. As we have seen, there was a fulling mill in Craswall much earlier, in 1647, when it was owned by James Madockes, yeoman. Then there was Michaelchurch mill owned and occupied by James Farr in 1840. That tucking mills could be profitable is demonstrated by the will and inventory of Harry Watkin, a tucker of Michaelchurch Escley who died in 1640 leaving a 'mansion house' and a substantial amount of £120 'in money'.[23]

It is perhaps surprising that so few other tuckers are mentioned. There are only about seven over the period of 300 years, though others might be concealed under the status of 'clothworker'. One of the few mentions of tucking equipment turns up in the inventory of 'Clothworker' John Pitt, who lived in Michaelchurch Escley in 1682. He was substantially equipped with a brass furnace, a press and two pairs of tuckers' shears worth £3. He also had an inventory worth £59 13s 10d, with only £5 10s in debts owed him. Forty years earlier, in 1640, Jenkin Harry, a tucker of Clodock, owned a furnace, three shears and two tenterhooks or racks. The inventories of fullers or tuckers in other regions generally include racks, but only these two have been listed at Ewyas Lacy. These racks were used to lay the cloth on in order to dry and stretch it into the required shape. Shearing was the next process, followed by pressing, and, as noted above, the inventories often list both shears and the furnace used for pressing.

In Llancillo in 1712, Walter Baynam, a 'bachelor', left his 'Boiler' to a weaver, William Phillips, who remains in obscurity. Boilers or furnaces were used both domestically and in industry, but can usually be identified as part of a cloth-making business given other clues. Not all would be listed, however, as they might be fixed to the wall and thus part of the freehold. Another one turns up in a Craswall inventory of 1682 (there is no will) of Abraham Watkynes, clothworker, which included a 'Brasse furnace, One Woodden-Wate [weight], Three payre of Sheares and other small Impliments, a wooden vat, and other Necessaryes for the Trade of a Cloth-Worker'. He was clearly someone taking the process further, and was rather better off than those in the first group, leaving a total inventory value of £82 1s 2d, of which debts owed him amounted to £68. The total value of his cloth-making tools amounted to £2 1s 8d. John Pytt of Clodock was another who called himself a clothworker; in 1690 he left his implements of trade worth more than £3. But he also farmed and had a total inventory worth £40.

These workers in cloth seem to have been part of an inter-related community, often leaving equipment to each other. One flaxdresser, John Mills of Newton, was living with a weaver and paying him 2s a week when he died in 1738, making him his residual legatee. John Rice James' wife, Anne, shared the administration of his estate in 1650 with a John William Prichard of Michaelchurch Escley, a 'gent'. Only three years earlier he had appeared in the probate documents of James Madockes, yeoman of Craswall, who owned a fulling mill, as 'John William Prichard, a tucker' – social mobility could be swift in those days!

Feltmakers, Dyers and Tailors

Furnaces were also needed for dyeing, which could be done either before carding or at the cloth stage, but dyers can be included amongst others in the cloth industry involved in the final process, people such as clothiers, tailors, glovers, hatters and feltmakers, such as William Lewis of Michaelchurch Escley, in 1719. (Feltmaking was a simple process by which wool was wetted, pounded or rolled to make a variety of items such as rugs, or even shoes.) There were no wills or inventories for clothiers, which seems to imply that any large scale manufacturing was carried out elsewhere, probably in Abergavenny, only 14 miles away. One of the tuckers, Jenkin Harry of Clodock, had commercial transactions with Thomas Church, a dyer of Hereford, in 1640, which seems to imply that other processes, too, were being undertaken outside the Hundred.

Only four dyers have a surviving will or inventory, including William Pytt of Clodock, who died in 1731, William Price of Craswall, who died in 1745 and Thomas Meredith, dyer of Craswall who left 'tools' in 1784. Another dyer was Thomas Watkins of Longtown, whose inventory of 1785 left no detail save 'Utensils, Impliments and Stock in Trade' worth £7, clothing worth £1, and a small farming enterprise consisting of cows, pigs and a horse – no crops. His cattle and his horse were old, which suggests that he himself was retired, but his will reverses that impression as he leaves to one nephew his freehold estate together with 'all the shops buildings and lands', and to another nephew all his 'implements of trade, stock of goods and colours'. His total inventory was valued at £29 6s. There is the mention of another earlier dyer in 1719, in the will of James Nicholl, in which he leaves £5 to his granddaughter, Elizabeth Pytt, wife of James Pytt, dyer.

There are six men called tailors in their wills, but only two with an inventory: the rather grandly named Bellingham Griffith of Clodock whose inventory in 1634 gives the impression of someone who was anything but grand as his own clothes were worth only 3s 4d, and Walter Davies, tailor of Walterstone in 1711. The bond attached to Walter's papers shows that his son, John, was also a tailor. His inventory was valued at only £2 9s 6d. Much

earlier, in 1594, there is a will for Harry James, tailor of Llancillo. David Prichard of Rowlestone seems to have been more of a farmer than a tailor as most of the value of his inventory (£37 1s 3d) lay in his livestock and crops, though he owned a spinning and a woollen wheel.

Several others emerge indirectly, such as William Miles, tailor, of Craswall, who did not leave a will or inventory but who was bequeathed the sum of 20s in the will of Thomas Perrott, tanner, also of Craswall. A William Perrott of Longtown, for whom no occupation is given, left the sum of £8 to a

Two ladies sewing c.1750. The clothes shown here would have been worn by only the most wealthy in Ewyas Lacy

William Powell, son of William Powell, tailor. Of course, we cannot be sure where the Powells lived. Much later, in 1804, there is John Pritchard, tailor, of Newton, whose will survives but without an inventory (he is an interesting example of the addition of a 't' in the Prichard name by the 19th century). Also of Newton, in 1840, there is Phillip Lewis, tailor, with no inventory but goods sworn to be under £100. None of these allow us a glimpse of the type of equipment they might have used.

Glovers and Hatters

It was quite common for items of clothing to be given at funerals, especially small items such as gloves and hat bands;[24] as late as 1832 gloves were still being given out at funerals by the executors at the bequest of the deceased, so there was still plenty of work for a glover. Thomas Prichard was a glover at Newton in 1668 and Michael Vaughan at Walterstone in 1715, but they are the only ones to turn up among the probate papers. Phillip Walle, a bachelor of Rowlestone, was particularly lavish, asking for 20 pairs of gloves to be issued to his relations at his death in 1741. Walter Watkins, in 1832, asked his executors to give out eight pairs of gloves at his funeral.

Abraham George of Walterstone is the only example of a hatter. Not very well off, his clothes were worth only 5s and his total value amounted to £22 15s 4d, though he was also owed a 'desperate' debt from a Mrs Mary Gabb that was worth almost his total inventory (as we have seen, 'desperate' in contrast to 'specialty' meant that it was without security). He had a small farming enterprise that perhaps kept him off the bread-line, consisting of farming equipment, two ewes and their lambs.

Spinning and Weaving

The art of spinning was part of the normal domestic lives of women, but their primary status in wills and inventories as widows, wives or spinsters makes it difficult to quantify the extent of their involvement in cloth production. However, unmarried girls had a duty to provide a full chest of linen in preparation for their eventual marriage. In an especially interesting and detailed 1680 will of a rich yeoman, Philipp Thomas Price of Michaelchurch Escley, he leaves his favourite granddaughter, Anne 'Pryce' (his inventory shows that the amount she received was greater than any of the other beneficiaries) furniture in various rooms throughout the house, plus the chest in the parlour 'under her own lock and key with all the lynnen, woollen and other goods therein'. He also left another chest in the parlour containing linen and woollen goods to his other granddaughter, Catherine Price, who also had her own key to it. This was necessary to prevent the appraisors listing them with his goods. It seems clear that he was helping towards the eventual setting up of their households.

Any investigation is complicated, as noted earlier, by the fact that what may have been the wife's spinning equipment is likely to turn up in her husband's inventory. However, the amount and type of household linen people owned does say something about them, sheets and napkins being the most prominent items. The value of the linen varied considerably from one inventory to the next, depending on age and whether the item was of flaxen (fine) or hurden (coarse cloth). For instance 20 pairs of 'old' sheets in the 1746 inventory of John Maddocks, gent, of Clodock might be worth only £2 compared with just four pairs of 'fine' sheets valued at £1 owned by Phillip Simon John 80 years earlier in 1666. The latter's eight pairs of 'coarse' sheets were also worth £1. One inventory contained an extra half sheet, maybe for a child's bed. Most of the inventoried people in Ewyas Lacy were sufficiently well off to own at least one pair of sheets, in contrast to Uffculme, where they were considered more of a luxury, even the vicar owning only eight pairs.[25] In Cornwall, unlike Kent (where the amount of bed linen increased in the 18th century), 'for each bed to have only one sheet' was not uncommon, and 'pillowcases were extremely rare'.[26] At Ewyas Lacy most of the inventories listed sheets, sometimes only two or three pairs, but quite often considerably more. James Watkins' mid-17th-century inventory lists not only two damask tablecloths but seven others and 57 napkins, along with eight pairs of fine flaxen sheets. Thomas Price, gent, of Craswall had eight pairs of fine sheets and ten pairs of hurden in 1686. Howell Prees, a yeoman, owned six fine and 22 coarse sheets in 1685, and in 1681 in Llanveynoe, a husbandman, another James Watkins, though his clothing was valued as only worth 6s 8d, owned six pairs of sheets.

It was clearly a matter of pride to own linen of flaxen material and a good supply of sheets and napkins, but very few pillowcases were mentioned, and where they were there was usually only one per household, worth from one to two shillings. They may have been considered so insubstantial as not to be worth mentioning. They are sometimes listed as 'pillowbeers' in the 17th century but this term dies out during the following century. Howell Prees had, besides a large number of sheets worth a total of £3 10s, 'one coverlid' (coverlet), three rugs and six blankets (valued at £1 17s) for only two feather beds, though he did have five bedsteads. Did the five 'bed cases' (bed-covers) listed relate to these?

Tablecloths were rather more in evidence, being mentioned in four out of 23 selected Clodock inventories. Two people had three tablecloths – one was the 'gent', John Maddocks, and one the comfortably off yeoman, Howell Prees. Most people owned napkins, which were almost essential in an age when forks were almost unknown. Generally, those higher up the social scale fared better in the possession of household linen, as one might expect. Oddly, those involved in the production of cloth rarely owned any of it, perhaps because they could not afford to keep any back for their own use.

Various efforts were made, starting in the 17th century, to promote the weaving of hemp and flax as it encouraged the use of small pockets of land that would otherwise go to waste. There was at least one flax dealer operating in Abergavenny, so there would have been an outlet for farmers in the Hundred when they went there to market. Thirsk mentions that the practice of weaving flax and hemp was spreading in Herefordshire from the 17th century, and was a very profitable crop. The final crop might be worth as much as £10 an acre or more, so a good profit could be made, given that the ground could be rented at £3 an acre and the cost of labour and seed might be £2, making a profit of perhaps £5 or £6, so that one acre of flax made as much as 4 to 5 acres of corn.[27] Even so there seems to be little evidence of its being much of an industry in Ewyas Lacy in spite of there being several fields in various parishes called variously 'cae rettin' or 'Linnuck' or 'The Linnux', denoting the production of flax. What little there was is shown as 'filled bags of hemp and flax', or as 'some flax in the house'. One of the rare references to its being grown was in the 1681 inventory of James Probert, gent, of Michaelchurch Escley, which referred to 'hemp in the house and upon the ground' worth only 4s 10d. Over at Clodock in 1685, Howell Prees, yeoman, had 'filled bags of Hemp and Flax' worth 12s, but it is not clear whether this had been grown by him or bought in from elsewhere. In the same parish, Simon John Phillip was growing flax with a value of 5s. (Hemp had been listed in his inventory but was crossed out.) For the cordwainer David Smith of Longtown in 1813, 'flax and hemp' were evidently part of the equipment he needed for lining and sewing shoes; they are listed, together with potatoes, at a value of £1 10s.

Flax certainly appears in small amounts amongst the lists of textiles, indicating that people were spinning and weaving it and using it in sheets and tablecloths for their own domestic use. In 1646, Maude Gilbert, spinster of Craswall, left her daughter 'my worst featherbed and a sheet with so much flax to spin as will make a sheet'. Perhaps its cultivation had declined, as in other areas such as Kent and Cornwall, since Rowland Vaughan identified it in the late 16th century.[28] In neighboring Shropshire, too, linen had been produced. A quarter of its inventories mention hemp or flax between 1660 and 1710 but its appearance decreases markedly thereafter, to only one in ten.[29]

Conclusion

Overall, the inventories do not produce much in the way of evidence to prove that textiles were a major industry in Ewyas Lacy over the period under review. Out of all the parishes there were only 20 post-Restoration individuals who we can be sure were engaged in the production of textiles at their death. In the approximately 100 years of the pre-Restoration probate documents there were nine. Sadly, I had to exclude 'spinsters' as I could not be sure of their status. Many of the wives and 'spinsters' may have been involved in spinning yarn, perhaps mainly for domestic consumption, and any inventory where wheels were mixed with household stuff or lumber as being of little account, or out of use, was discounted. Involvement in textile production is fairly widely distributed around the Hundred, with perhaps a higher proportion in the three parishes of Craswall, Michaelchurch Escley and St Margarets. In view of the evidence of there having been a flourishing textile mill at Craswall in the 19th century it was surprising to find only one tucker there in 1650, a clothworker in 1682, a weaver in 1745 and a dyer in 1784. Clearly, more research needs to be done in this area.

There is only small evidence of any textile production after 1750, except at Cwm Mill. Of the 20 inventories related to cloth production (I have excluded glovers, tailors and mercers here as being involved only with the end product), four were of weavers prior to 1660, 12 were made before the middle of the 18th century, three in the late 18th century with a minor resurgence in the first quarter of the 19th century, as three weavers make an appearance – one at Newton in 1825 (perhaps coincidental with the flaxdresser, John Mills) without an inventory, and two at St Margarets in 1800 and 1829. The first inventory for the latter parish shows that the weaver was also a farmer in a small way, but there is no inventory for the second weaver. Was there a resurgence of textile production in the 19th century at Ewyas Lacy?

It is difficult to make detailed comparisons with other areas in England as scarcely any have inventories surviving after 1750,[30] but other studies have shown that production of textiles was in decline long before this date. At Uffculme in Devon, the trade of clothier or fuller appears to die out by 1702, as the trade moved to larger towns. In Cornwall textile production fell by about 10% by the mid-18th century, and in Kent output fell gradually during the early 18th century. Spinning was especially hard hit, in some places disappearing completely.[31]

Rowland Vaughan was probably correct, then, to say that his neighbours, including those at Ewyas Lacy, were weaving hemp and flax during the 16th century, and they probably continued to do so for some time after that. The conclusion must be that any decline in clothmaking in the west, including in this area, was probably due to the movement of the trade to large urban areas and then to the entrepreneurial efforts of clothmakers in the north of England by the mid to late 18th century. Oddly enough the fortunes made from the industry returned like a tide in the 19th century, as people like the Arkwrights at Hampton Court in Herefordshire ploughed their gains into vast estates in the west.

10 CLERGY AND DISSENT

In late January of the bitter winter of 1664/5, John Delahay, vicar of Clodock, sat writing in his study to Mr Charles Roberts, Registrar of the Church Court in Brecon. He was dealing with the will of one of his parishioners, a yeoman of Clodock, and the purpose of his letter was to ask Mr Roberts to excuse Anne, the widow, from coming to prove her husband's will, she 'not being able to travel by reason of sickness and old age'. He requested that, as her son Hugh was coming instead, he 'deal favourably with him in matter of fees'. This thoughtful man, John Delahay, was almost certainly the son of the previous vicar, Morgan Delahay, himself a kind man and a member of the leading local family from Alltyrynys.

The presence of the clergy is palpable in the probate papers, for they were amongst the small number of educated men in the region and as such they were called upon to act as witnesses, appraisers, writers of letters to, and surrogates of, the archdeacon's court at Brecon, or their bishop in far off St Davids, besides their normal duties as clergy.

As in other border territories, by the time the Revd Delahay was writing his letter, dissent had been active in the Hundred for centuries, and it was incumbent upon clergy officiating there to be on the alert for any nonconformity. Support for Lollardy, a pan-European movement against transubstantiation and tithes (unless given to the poor), and for the idea that anyone could preach, had been strong in this part of the country two hundred years earlier. Sir John Oldcastle knew this region well and was eventually taken prisoner in Powys before being burned at Smithfield in 1417. He and his followers had planned to take over the government, and from their time onwards dissent was seen by the authorities as a double threat – against local order and central government. That the authorities continued to feel unease in the 16th century is evident from the Bishop's Register of St Davids in 1513, which states that the tithes were granted to the king 'for the defence and protection of the Anglican Church ... as well as to allay and extirpate heresies and schisms ... which in these days flourish more than usually'.[1]

Fortunately for them, they had no idea of how much worse things were to become over the next hundred years with the chaos caused by the Reformation. Queen Elizabeth took the reasonable and all-inclusive view that she did not wish to 'look into men's souls' (unless they were Catholic) but there is little doubt that her attitude allowed Puritans to grow in number until they expected their views to prevail. They wanted more simplicity in the church, and had a morbid fear of Roman Catholics, exacerbated by the marriage of Charles I to the Roman Catholic Henrietta of France.

Archbishop Laud tried to impose more order and discipline on the Church of England in the 1630s, insisting that the communion table be returned to the east end of the church, that bishops' 'visitations' be more regular, and that altar rails be in place. He met with a sad lack of success and his unpopularity cost him his life, although some of his reforms – such as the provision of altar rails – survive in Anglican churches to this day.

The Civil War did much to promote dissent, due to the movement of often zealous Parliamentary soldiers across the country. But even before this, attacks on the more traditional clergy had begun. For example, in 1640 a petition by the inhabitants of Mells in Somerset against their minister led to his being arrested. The Bishop of St Davids was attacked by Parliament in the same year, accused of 'Popish innovations', conversing with Papists, and, oddly, 'being Sociable and Jovial'. These attacks gathered pace through the 1640s, when many clergy were replaced by those considered by traditionalists as unsuitable to say the least. 'The learned Mr Gam Chase, B.D. was succeeded at Yarcombe, Devon by two persons; the one of whom could hardly read a Penny Sermon' whilst in Herefordshire, 'a Mr Elmhurst, B.D., who was Sequester'd from Aston-Ingham ... was succeeded by a Justice of the Peace's Clerk ... At Hereford in the course of a single year, they had 'dispossess'd about Threescore of the most worthy Clergymen in that Diocese, including the Cathedral Clergy'.[2]

It is possible that there were no changes at Ewyas Lacy during this time. The livings may even have been left empty, as many were. Information on this subject, though prolific for many other regions, is either sparse or non-existent for the Hundred of Ewyas Lacy. Morgan Delahay was vicar of Clodock from at least 1623 and remained so during the time of greatest upheaval during the Civil War until his death in 1650; there is then a gap in our information. In 1661 John Delahay, who had probably been Morgan's curate, was ordained at Clodock and remained there until his death in the 1680s. Previously the advowson of Clodock and Llancillo had been held by members of the influential Vaughan family.

There is no evidence of neglect in the last half of the 17th century, rather the opposite. An early 20th-century vicar had the impression that Clodock church was 'in good hands from 1620 to 1720' and appeared to have had a re-fit during this time, including new pews, one with a carving of a dragon and the date of 1657, two bells, one of 1649, and a superb three-decker pulpit and gallery. Even the lychgate was replaced, and bore the date 1667. From the end of the 16th century almost all parish churches displayed an hour glass on the pulpit. There was a joke current that one Clodock vicar annoyed his parishioners after an hour-long sermon by turning the glass upside down and saying 'Brethren, let us have another glass!'[3]

John Walker suggests that the vicar in the area who came closest to sequestration was John Rawlins of Cusop, just north of Michaelchurch Escley. By all accounts he had a rough time, being imprisoned at least twice for reading the Common Prayer and baptizing the Royalists' children of the district.[4] At the Restoration in 1660, 16 Herefordshire clergy were ejected and a further seven were ousted in 1662 after the Act of Uniformity, but there are few details.[5]

Before his homecoming, Charles II had raised hopes for religious freedom with the Declaration of Breda – hopes that were soon dashed. Cleverly, all he had done was leave any decisions to Parliament, saying that he would grant toleration to anyone to whom Parliament wished to grant it, so that at his restoration the Church of England was also restored, together with the hierarchy of bishops and church courts.[6] However, some concessions were made, at least initially. Richard Baxter, a prominent Presbyterian, was made a chaplain to the king and also offered the bishopric of Hereford, which he refused as he was convinced that any toleration being shown would soon disappear. He was right. In November 1660 John Bunyan (a Baptist), was imprisoned in Bedford gaol. The fanatical Fifth Monarchist Venner uprising took place in 1661, terrorising London for days and creating a backlash against all the sects, especially the Quakers who refused to take an oath of loyalty. Thousands were imprisoned.[7]

In 1662 the Act of Uniformity was passed, which, as it compelled members of the clergy to accept everything in the Book of Common Prayer, forced hundreds of nonconformist clergy, imposed on the church during the Interregnum, to leave. This created a bevy of clergy roaming about looking for support from congregations, which in turn meant that congregations of dissenters had to support their minister through their own contributions. Baptists and Quakers in particular were quick to establish their own system of registers, charities and burial grounds. This made them independent of the parish clergy and the parish church.[8]

These established conventicles, or meeting houses, declared themselves to be outside the authority of the Anglican Church, and they remained so in spite of persecution. Passing the Act confirmed the severance of the sects from the Anglican Church without hope of reconciliation, whereas previously the Puritan element had been an accepted part of the national church. Persecution continued unabated, with dissenting congregations having to go to great lengths to secure their safety. At Leominster, worshippers supplied themselves with bread and cheese so that if the church authorities broke in on them, they could in an instant turn their meeting into a social gathering.[9]

A further development, after a decade of turmoil and a massive growth of dissent, was the Declaration of Indulgence of 1672, which gave dissenters freedom to worship provided that their meeting places were licensed. In part this was an attempt by Charles to bring in some amelioration of the lot of Catholics, who would be given freedom of worship at the same time. Continued suspicion of Catholics and nonconformists meant that this freedom did not last long.

Finally, pressure by nonconformist groups, and a recognition of the part played by them in the Revolution of 1688, led the new king and queen, William III and Mary II, to approve the Toleration Act in the first year of their reign, 1689, which allowed dissenters to have their own places of worship. However, full rights of university entry and the holding of public office were not granted until the 19th century.

The events of the 17th century, and especially the loss of control during the Civil War, unleashed a welter of differing beliefs which the Anglican Church tried vainly to control at the Restoration whilst the government restored to Royalists their ownership of advowsons, impropriations, tithes and glebes. Under the interregnum, these had been made over to support the poorer parishes, so those hoping for church reform in this respect were disappointed. The sacred and secular were intertwined. Whig reformers in Parliament had little desire to undermine their own stake in church property.[10] In Herefordshire for instance, the Harley family, who traditionally had more sympathy with dissenters than with the Church of England, still acquired church property.[11]

The value accruing from benefices usually comprised three parts. One was the advowson, also known as the donation or collation, which generally went to the local landowner upon whom it conferred the benefit of being able to choose his own clergy, so allowing him to reserve the appointment for a member of his family. Second, the great tithes (and sometimes even the small) usually went to the rector, who was either the landowner (layman) or a clergyman who had bought the advowson, or right of presentation, who 'Impropriated', or took, the tithes. The rector, if a layman, then paid a curate or vicar to act for him out of the income, the curate generally receiving only a very small proportion of the total, possibly as little as £10 p.a. The small tithes usually went to the vicar, who might also have an area of glebe land which varied in size from one parish to another, and for whom a house in good condition was a bonus but by no means a certainty. The amount of glebe land attached to the rectory or vicarage was usually very small. One of the largest in England was about 16 acres, but most were of about half an acre.[12]

The value of the benefices had been reduced in the past by the payment, or a 'tax', of what were known as 'first fruits' and 'tenths', which went to the reigning monarch. The 'first fruits' was a payment made by an incumbent on taking up his living, and the tenths were subsequent annual payments, previously paid to the Pope, but taken over by Henry VIII. During the Interregnum this amount, of about £17,000 per annum across the country, was given to the clergy and schoolmasters, but was retrieved at the Restoration for the Crown.[13]

It is evident that there was jealousy between different parts of the United Kingdom over the levels of subsistence given some of the clergy by the 18th century. In Ireland, in the first half of that century, Dean Swift spoke bitterly of what he saw as the 'comfortable, decently housed English country vicar' compared with his lonely and ill-paid counterpart in Ireland.[14] In Wales there is a telling comment by one Owen Morgan, the rector of Llanwern in Monmouthshire, who writes sourly on his visitation paper, 'the last curate as I had is gone for England, where likely he finds a better maintenance'.[15] How much truth was there in this for the parish and chapelries of Ewyas Lacy?

One of the possible reasons for a falling away of support for the Church was a lack of respect for the clergy. At the turn of the 18th century, clergymen were living at a meagre level and many of them without decent parsonages, many of which were in need of repair. The curate at Clodock, who was responsible for maintaining faith in the other four far-flung chapelries or townships, was paid only £30 p.a. in 1717, and that was quite a respectable amount compared with many others who might be receiving only £13 p.a.

Queen Anne cared about the Church and the poverty-stricken state of many of the clergy. In January 1704, on her birthday, she confirmed a bounty of £16,500 to be used for the support of the poorer clergy, in contrast to the recent use of the clergy's first fruits and tenths to support various unworthy causes such as the upkeep of various bastards of Charles II.[16] The gift came not before time. The system was crying out for reform.

A survey carried out in Somerset in 1705 indicates the problems that the Church faced.[17] Of the clergy who received the questionnaire sent out to each parish in 1705, by order of

Robert Harley as Secretary of State, almost a third did not reply, but of the 59 that did 23 said they had incomes of £30 or more, but a quarter had under £30. In one case the value of the impropriated rectory was £200, out of which the layman paid only £25 to the curate, and in another case, where the great tithes were impropriated, the vicar received only £30. It is not surprising that these church holdings were treated like valuable investments and were traded by all and sundry from the city merchant to the local landowner. In Ewyas Lacy, too, there is one case of a yeoman of Clodock and one of a tradesman owning, or leasing, tithes, in the early 17th century.[18]

It seems ironic that the process of implementing Queen Anne's Bounty should have been started by, amongst others, Robert Harley of Brampton Bryan in Herefordshire, whose family would later become owners of several tithes and advowsons in the Hundred. In 1704 he was Speaker of the House of Commons, and in May he was appointed Secretary of State. The Harleian Papers show that for some time the Harley family had regarded advowsons and tithes as useful property to hold in their portfolio.[19] In July 1720, a few years before the death of Robert Harley, Earl of Oxford, his brother's son, the Hon. Edward Harley of Eywood in Herefordshire (who eventually became the third Earl of Oxford and Mortimer on the death of the son of the first Earl in 1741), acquired many manors and advowsons, including those of Walterstone, and the impropriate rectories of Walterstone and others in Ewyas Lacy on the sale of Nicholas Arnold's estate at Llanvihangel Crucorney. This was property that had anciently belonged to the dissolved priory of Llanthony. The great tithes of corn and grain in Llancillo and Rowlestone alone, when leased out, were worth £50 p.a. to Edward Harley.

In Somerset the diocesan enquiry was sent out and replied to in 1705, but in the diocese of St Davids, and archdeaconry of Brecon, replies to the questions did not appear until 1707, so the questionnaire may have arrived later. Under four columns was listed the name of the parishes, their yearly value, the incumbent's name and the number of families in their 'cure'. (This latter is a most useful piece of information, as population figures are few for this date and region.)

Parish	Yearly value	Incumbent	No. of families
Clodock	£90	Henry Vaughan	175
Michaelchurch Escley	£7	William Allen	60
St. Margarets	£6	William Vaughan	40
Rowlestone	A total of	Ditto	13
Llancillo	£25 for	Ditto	9
Walterstone	these three	Ditto	20

Details from the survey of the diocese of St Davids carried out in 1707, as relating to Ewyas Lacy Hundred

Clodock vicarage, including the chapelries of Craswall, Llanveynoe and Longtown, had the highest yearly value, at £90. The next on the list was Michaelchurch vicarage, which was poorly supported by a yearly value of only £7. The curate in charge had been there for many years, first appearing in 1669, when Elizabeth Rees Harry left him a bushel of rye, (he was called 'Mr Allen vicar' of Michaelchurch Escley), and again in 1671 administering the oath to Edmond Thomas, gent, as 'William Allen, curate of Michaelchurch Escley', together with John Delahay, the vicar of Clodock.

Did the Bounty make a difference? The money was certainly slow to come in. The next investigation seems to have been taken in May 1721, after depositions had been taken at the inn of Thomas Morgan in Hay-on-Wye at a meeting of the local gentry, clergy and churchwardens giving information on their parishes.[20] This time there was nothing under Clodock, only Longtown, a chapelry nearby, which the vicar of Clodock, Richard 'Rice' or Rees and his churchwarden John Powell, affirmed was a chapel of ease within the parish (a chapel built for the convenience of parishioners who lived at some distance from the parish church), while the minister was supported by an annual payment of £16 arising out of 'Certain Tithes'.

Township/Parish	Augmentation	Amount
Craswall	Lot 1728	£14 p.a.
Llancillo	Benefn 1724 £200	£17 p.a.
Llanveynoe	Lot 1735	£13 10s p.a.
St Margarets	Lot 1745	£13 p.a.
Michaelchurch Escley	Lot 1739	£14 p.a.
Rowlestone	Lot 1741	£11 p.a.
Walterstone	Lot 1738 & 1751	£17 p.a.

Details of the amounts paid from Queen Anne's Bounty to augment the clergy's livings in Ewyas Lacy Hundred in 1752

Called to give information on Michaelchurch Escley, two gentlemen, Edward Poskin and William James, stated that the church was a donative, or advowson, with Nicholas Arnold, Esq. as patron, and that the minister was still receiving only £7 p.a. from the small tithes. Not much, considering that the parish contained about 60 families. For St Margarets, John Walters and Thomas Jennings, gent, stated that only £6 arose from the Easter offering and the small tithes. Rowlestone received £4, Llancillo and Walterstone £3 each. The position at Craswall was outlined in more detail. Two gentlemen, William Rogers and William Harries, stated that Craswall was 'a Chappell of Ease' within the parish of Clodock and received £7 for the maintenance of the officiating minister. They explained that the money arose out of the small tithes of the hamlets of Craswall and Newton, and that the chapel of Craswall was at least five miles distant from the mother church at Clodock, making the point that it was essential to have a chapel of ease there. In fact, all but St Peters in Longtown were a considerable distance from Clodock, and each community must have been very isolated when roads were bad, or indeed impassable, in winter. The mention of Newton is also of interest as the manor generally comes under St Margarets and is seldom mentioned at this time.

That left Llanveynoe. Lying in a steep valley under the towering bulk of the Black Mountains, Llanveynoe was one of the most isolated of all the parishes or townships, and was another chapel of ease, receiving, according to William Prosser and Richard Nicholls,

Craswall church

£6 10s from the small tithes and 'from the subscriptions of Inhabitants of the said Hamlet'. They add, firmly, 'which they cannot withdraw at pleasure'. Most of these statements were signed rather than marked, indicating a level of literacy amongst the gentry, and incidentally, the level of control held by the laity over ecclesiastical matters.

The next piece of information on the subject of Queen Anne's Bounty comes in 1752[21] and is here listed in three columns, first the place, then 'when and how Augmented', with the allotment date, and finally the yearly value. This shows that none of the livings were worth more than £20, and most were still well below that. However, the great tithes may have been, and often were, worth a great deal more, generally consisting of the most valuable produce such as grain and wool.

It is possible to get a glimpse of the health of the beleaguered Anglican Church in the Hundred during the last half of the 18th century from the few Bishop's Visitations that have survived.[22] The first one, in 1759, asked how often Divine Service was performed, and if not twice on the Lord's Day, why not? Other questions followed. How often was the Sacrament administered? When were the youth of the parish catechized? Where did the parson or curate reside? What was the latter's name? And finally, did the vicar take services in other churches? At Clodock it emerged that the vicar, Richard Reece the younger, or his curate, John Rowlands, performed Divine Service twice every Sunday, once a month excepted; that the Sacrament was administered four times a year – at Christmas, Easter, Whitsuntide and All Souls Day; and that the youth were catechized every Friday and Sunday in Lent and 'on other Sunday Evenings'. The vicar held the rectory at 'Birch' (Much Birch), closer to Hereford than Clodock, which must have been about a day's ride away, and he lived in Hereford. He does not say where the curate lived. The only other evidence for 1759 comes from the curate of Walterstone and Old Castle, Philip Price, who tells us something interesting about the value of Queen Anne's Bounty and the effect it was having when he says, 'I do not reside personally upon my Cure but do live about a Mile distant from my Church in a house purchased with Queen Anne's bounty allotted to the church of Walterstone.'

More detailed evidence comes in the next Bishop's Visitation of 1762, headed 'My

Reverend Brother ... for my better Information concerning the present state of your Parish I transmit to you the following queries'. These are more detailed, 19 questions this time, asking for information on the extent of the parish, how many villages and houses there were, and whether there were any families of note.

Of interest to a bishop living in mid Wales, but with a diocese extending to,

Rowlestone church. The medieval candle holder is just one of many interesting features for a visitor to the church. Sculptors from the Herefordshire School of Romanesque Sculpture are responsible for the work on the tympanum and capitals to the south doorway, and also the capitals to the chancel arch

and beyond the Welsh borders, was the question of what language was being used for the services. There seems little doubt that at this time the area must have been bilingual, but it was slowly changing. Welsh was being used at the church at Old Castle, right on the border of Ewyas Lacy but in Monmouthshire, whose curate had in 1759 also served at Walterstone in English, and helped his father, another Philip Price, with his cures at Llanthony and Capel-y-fin. Now, possibly in an attempt to rationalize, 'Phil Price, junior' was serving two other cures within the Herefordshire borders at Llancillo and Rowlestone, besides the one at Walterstone, all conveniently within a mile or so of each other, and no longer helped his father at his churches, which were in Wales. None of the churches on the English side of the border were using Welsh for their services.

One of the major problems with this region was the long and often awkward journey required to reach parishioners, especially where the roads were rough and steep, or even non-existent. In fact, travelling clergymen probably quite often didn't use the roads at all. At Clodock the parish stretched for '10 or 12 miles' from Forest Hene, a bleak range of hills dropping down towards Hay, to members of the congregation living just under the Black Mountains. For Phil Price, at Llancillo, the extent of the parish was an easier fairly level seven miles. He served at Rowlestone and Walterstone too, but as there were only 17 houses in Llancillo and the latter two parishes were only a mile from each other, that cannot have been too difficult. He also had the benefit of having a house a mile from his church, and by this time the vicar of Clodock was also living in his parish 'in the House belonging to it'. He does not say whether this was as a result of Queen Anne's Bounty.

Walterstone church

The Hundred begins to get steeper as it ascends past Clodock, and the chapel of ease in Longtown, and by the time Michaelchurch Escley is reached the landscape is one of scattered farms attached to a small hamlet. The 'perpetual' curate there was Thomas Higgins, instituted in about the year 1746, in the deanery of Hay.[23] Although he gives the extent of his parish as about four miles, he served another two miles away at St Margarets, containing 30 houses, the same as Michaelchurch Escley. He had sizeable congregations of 40 people at both places and claimed that there were no papists and no dissenters in St Margarets and just one Quaker in Michaelchurch Escley. (A farm called Quakers today lies between St Margarets and Michaelchurch Escley on the Michaelchurch to Hay road.)[24] He may have had a problem communicating with his fellow clerics, as he was far closer to Hay, to the north, where his post was sent, whereas the rest were closer to Abergavenny and had their

A dragon carving on a pew and the three-decker pulpit in Clodock church

post sent there. He gives no reason for living four miles from his cures and does not tell us where his house was.

A glimpse of the despair and isolation felt by some of the clergy is seen in the sad case of Higgins' predecessor, Thomas Allen, who was presented to the church courts at Brecon in 1729 for neglecting to preach and to catechise children, for drunkenness, and other offences.[25] Not only was he miserably poor, but he had few, if any, educated men to converse with, and the winters must have seemed long. It is hardly surprising that some of the weaker brethren amongst the clergy might have taken to drink.

Services appear to have been held regularly every Sunday in all the parishes, and sometimes twice on Sundays, all except for the little chapel at Llanveynoe, which had to do without a Sunday service once a month, no doubt due to the difficulty of getting there. Craswall, although much further away and in very wild country, was served every Sunday. This may have been because of the constantly perceived threat from the dissenters in such remote places.

By 1762, Clodock's vicar, reporting to the bishop, says he has nearly 150 communicants at all his churches and chapels, and a few papists, but none of note. He admits he has some dissenters: Presbyterians and Anabaptists, but no Quakers. 'The Presbyterians have a licensed Meeting house. They have no paid Teacher,' he says, adding optimistically, 'Their number both Presbyterian and Anabaptist have decreased greatly of late.'

At Llancillo the curate, Phil Price, appears to have had little or no opposition from dissent. He generally had nine communicants, but only seven 'last Easter'. There were no papists, and he notes, proudly, 'We have no Prospiterians nor Dissenters of any denomination whatsoever in the parish'. He also had no school or charitable endowment, nor lands left for the repair of the church. (His father, who was chaplain to the Earl of

Llancillo church

Oxford at Old Castle only a mile or two distant, and preached in Welsh, also said they had no dissenters or papists in the parish, neither did they have a school or charitable endowment 'but the Bounty of Queen Anne and the Great Tyth of our parish which Auditor Harley was pleased to bestow on our Curacy'. Old Castle lies just outside Ewyas Lacy in Monmouthshire; the remains of any castle were noted as 'slight' in 1870, and all traces have now gone. The will of William Gilbarde or Gilbert who lived here and died in 1527 shows he owned land in Ewyas Lacy). At Walterstone, Phil Price the younger had ten or eleven communicants, and there were neither Papists nor Dissenters. There was an 'English School' in the parish, but not supported by subscription or settled endowment.

County borders were notorious for harbouring dissenters, and Ewyas Lacy was no exception in the late 17th and early 18th century, despite the protestations of the Anglican clergy to the contrary. In this sense individual regional studies can be more useful than county studies as boundaries were of little significance to worshippers who needed to find the congregation nearest them. Bishop Ward of Exeter put it in a nutshell in the 1660s when he claimed that Uffculme, in Devon, 'being on the border of three Dioceses as wel as three Counties gives great opportunitie to the Sectaries to play their tricks and escape'.[26] Ewyas Lacy was in a similar situation, with Monmouthshire to the south and Breconshire to the north; its isolation was a great advantage to dissent. Lollardy has already been mentioned as having been strong in this area and at least one 'native of Olchon' in Ewyas Lacy, Walter Brute, is said to have been a supporter of the new movement.[27] The flame was just kept alive until it sprang up again given favourable conditions in the 17th century. Dissent was no less prevalent across the border in Wales. In 1639 there was the First Independent Church in Wales at Llanfaches in Monmouthshire, and in 1649 the first Baptist church in Wales at Ilston, near Swansea, in Glamorganshire.[28] This church, in fact, is said to have been founded by a Newton man, John Miles, after he had replaced an ejected Royalist vicar.[29]

It is possible that, not wishing to worry the bishop unduly, the clergy underestimated or were unwilling to admit to the level of dissent in their parishes. After the 1715 rebellion there was heightened concern over the number of Roman Catholics in the country, and the county archives contain records of a rump of papists living at Walterstone in the 18th century. These included the Watkins family: Thomas Watkins, freeholder, Thomas and William his sons and Mary his daughter; and also another Watkins (George), freeholder, with his son and daughter, George and Anne. There was also Anne, wife of John Pugh, together with John David, a labourer, and Anne his wife.[30] After the severe persecution of the late 17th century, there appears to have been little appetite for Roman Catholicism in the county, though it continued to be feared by church authorities. At the end of that century Herefordshire contained 65,942 conformists, 1,076 dissenters (1.59%) and only 714 'Papists' or 1.05%.[31]

Having sympathetic men in positions of authority was of great importance in the nurturing of dissent. The Harleys of Brampton Bryan were Puritan sympathisers and supporters of Parliament through the Civil War. After the Restoration, the troublesome and closet Catholic Marquis of Worcester doubted whether Sir Edward Harley should command the Regiment of Foot in Herefordshire because he was considered to be a Presbyterian. However, the king did not want him to 'lye by unused' and impatiently commanded the marquis to offer Harley the command without 'more adoe'.[32] There was greater sympathy for dissenters in the county in subsequent decades.

This region does not appear to have been notable for nonconformity compared with elsewhere. Numbers of dissenters tended to be small in the northern counties where Roman Catholicism lingered and populations were scattered and low in numbers. Figures given at the time of the 1689 return at the accession of William and Mary gave the numbers of nonconformists as between 2½ and 5% of the Diocese of St Davids, and at Hereford diocese as under 2½%, compared with over 10% at Canterbury. Nevertheless, in 1676 the Bishop Compton Census gives the number of nonconformists at Longtown as 200 (or 22%). This figure is not as surprising as it may first appear, as the Baptist Church at Ilston, from having only 43 members in 1650, numbered 250 only ten years later.[33]

Nonconformity provided an alternative for those disappointed with their parish church. Many priests or, as they might prefer to call themselves, ministers, had been ejected from livings at the Restoration and others, more conformable, put in their place. In the turmoil, the ejected set up gatherings of their own, supported by some of their old congregations, and called themselves variously, Baptists, Congregationalists, Presbyterians and Quakers. These groups were a cause for concern to the Anglican Church, not least because some sects, such as Quakers, withheld tithes from the church.

This is not the place to enter into the theological beliefs of the various sects, only the practical aspects. Their views can be summarised by saying that they all wanted a return to what they perceived as being the simplicity of the early Church, with the Quakers taking the most extreme stance of ultimate simplicity in dress and behaviour. Apart from the noted Quaker William Penn, early Quakers seem to have been predominantly a rural movement linked to the comfortably-off middling sort and yeomen, property owners or leaseholders of substantial dwellings. This finding seems to have applied to most dissenters.

Like most emerging sects, both Baptists and Quakers attracted bizarre behaviour in their early days until their ideas were properly formulated and discipline established. Baptists were initially associated with the violence of the radical Anabaptists, who regarded the state as a potential enemy and in the mid 16th century had taken over the town of Munster in Germany and installed their own government.[34] Some of the Friends (the name by which Quakers were known) walked naked through the streets or wore sackcloth and ashes, as they wished to disassociate themselves from accepted behaviour. George Fox, founder of the Quakers, began his ministry as a young man in the spring of 1652. His father was a respected weaver who was also a churchwarden, and his mother Mary was of Protestant martyr stock and proud of it. His conversion resulted from reading the Bible and from an inner conviction that salvation came only through a personal experience of the love of God. One of the best connected Quakers was William Penn, whose father, Sir William Penn, Treasurer of the Navy and colleague of Pepys, was influential in the return of the Stuarts in 1660. Charles II and his brother James II were charmed by the Quaker William, who persuaded them, in lieu of repayment of a large loan made by his father, to give him a tract of land in America instead. This was to be Pennsylvania, which Penn hoped would be settled by Quakers and give them the freedom to worship they craved. Charles saw it as a way of getting the troublesome sect off his back.[35] However, to others Quaker views came to be seen as subversive, as Quakers would not doff their hats to anyone, refused to pay tithes and believed that one man was as good as another. As they were honest and hard working, they tended to be very successful; many of the banks started in the 18th century were founded by them.

Mainstream nonconformists like the Presbyterians continued to attend their parish church, as Anglicanism was close enough to their own beliefs, whilst being sympathetic to dissent, especially if they held public office. Thus nonconformity became more a grass roots movement, with support coming in the main from the increasingly confident and prosperous middling sort, particularly the tradesman and the farmer. A list of dissenters in 1715 in Monmouthshire shows that there were 60 gentlemen, 256 tradesmen, 597 farmers and yeomen and 492 labourers, many of whom would have the vote, being amongst the 40s freeholders.[36]

The people of Ewyas Lacy were nothing if not independent; centuries of absent major landowners had ensured this. One of the weapons used to enforce church attendance, the 12d fine for non-attendance, was reintroduced in the 1680s but there is no reference to its having been imposed at Ewyas Lacy; in such tightly knit communities it would have been difficult for a churchwarden to report his relations for absenteeism.

From 1690, the Common Fund set up by Presbyterian sympathisers like Lord Wharton[37] to support Presbyterian and Congregational congregations was giving £5 p.a. for work at Longtown, which confirms that there was an established congregation there. It notes that 'Att Longtowne … is a meeting house lately erected but no minister they can raise £10 per anu towards the maintenance of a Minister they desire help from London, alsoe they desire a minister that may be fitt for the place, and that preach in Welch as well as English.'

Help was soon forthcoming, and from a surprising quarter. Amongst the contributors to the Fund from 1690 were the names of two members of Parliament with close Herefordshire connections: Thomas Foley, Esq. of Stoke Edith and Philip Foley of Whitley Court, who were donating £5 and £10 per annum respectively. Both were members of the prominent and phenomenally wealthy Presbyterian family whose iron-manufactury was said to be the largest in the country. They were also both close associates of Sir Edward Harley, whose 'utter slave' Thomas was accused of being by the writer Richard Steele. Thomas Foley became MP for Weobley in 1691 and for Hereford between 1701 and 1722. Philip Foley was Thomas Foley's uncle, his father a close friend of the Presbyterian divine, Richard Baxter. Philip Foley retained a nonconformist chaplain until 1706.[38]

The dissenters could still vote in elections, in fact their votes were assiduously sought (in 1715 there were 92 nonconformist voters in Herefordshire, and 78 in Breconshire, and no fewer than 690 just over the border in Monmouthshire), but they were otherwise excluded from civil life, being unable to attend university or serve on the Bench of JPs or as MPs. Most of the country clergymen voted Tory.[39]

After the first fervour, decline had set in amongst all sects by the 1730s and did not revive until the end of that decade with the Welsh Revival, which preceded that in England.[40] There was also a decline in the numbers of Quakers by the 1720s which was even more obvious after 1740. So little is known of the state of these congregations in Ewyas Lacy at this time that it is difficult to say with certainty what was happening, especially in such an isolated region where even the local clergy did not seem entirely sure of their flock. However, small congregations of Presbyterians, Quakers and Baptists continued to be set up in some of the parishes and townships from the early to the middle of the 18th century. It is believed that the Baptists were the first to establish meetings in local houses in the Olchon Valley. By 1843 the Baptists had built Salem Chapel in Longtown, which is still flourishing today barely a stone's throw from the Anglican chapel of St Peter's.

There are several cases of individuals leaving bequests to dissenting chapels or ministers at this time. In 1701, Hugh Pugh of Newton, a prosperous yeoman, left 50s to encourage 'a protestant preacher of the Presbyterian or Independent persuasion' to officiate at Newton or St Margarets. This probably worked, as 15 years later Thomas Price of Clodock presented the dwelling house of William Phillips in St Margarets 'to be a place Intended for dissenting protestants to Exercise their Religion'.[41] In 1732, Simon Thomas, yeoman of Cwmbach in Clodock, left £1 annually 'for the use of a dissenting minister' and only eight years later, Morgan Thomas, gent, left the same amount for five years to the first minister to settle 'att the chapell of Longtown'. It seems more than likely that the two men were related. This tradition continued for a further 52 years, as in 1792 James Lewis of Cwmbach left £1 p.a. 'to the Presbyterian Chapel in Clodock known as New Chapel'.

In 1774 money was also left by Elias George, farmer of Llanveynoe to supply copies of John Bunyan's *Pilgrim's Progress* to the 'Baptist Church Meeting in Olchon' and Capel-y-fin (a remote area in Llanveynoe and an adjacent valley). In 1822 Sible Pritchard of Brooks Farm in Longtown mentioned in her will that part of her house was known as 'the meeting house', and that she wished to have a dissenting minister to preach there at her funeral. This is a reminder that many of the early dissenting meetings were held in people's homes and thus were less conspicuous. It is obvious that not only were there different denominations operating outside the Anglican Church, but they were distributed throughout the parishes and townships during the 18th and early 19th centuries.

Even within Anglican circles control of the parishes was by no means entirely in the hands of the clergy. The parishioners even made attempts to control the number, frequency and content of sermons by leaving legacies to that effect. Constant Tomlins clearly had a bee in her bonnet (or a low opinion of her neighbours) in 1766, when she left £9 p.a. to the minister of Clodock 'after he have preached 18 sermons on every Wednesday and Fryday against most vices'.[42]

The Visitations demonstrate that a poor clergyman often lacked the means to fight for the rights of his church against encroachments by the laity.[43] As an illustration of this, Phil Price of Walterstone petitioned the bishop for his advice in connection with a charity made 80 years before by one of the local Delahay family (during John Delahay's time as vicar). The legacy, in former times paid 'without neglect', was now in the hands of a new landowner who was refusing to pay the £6 accruing annually from the estate charged with it. 'The parishioners know not who is the Trustee and has the management of the Charity because they have no copy of the Will which was given ... but are resolved to have a Copy thereof.' Sadly, there is no evidence that the will was ever found and one is left to wonder how often this must have happened, and how many similar charities were lost in this way over time.

At St Margarets and Michaelchurch Escley Thomas Higgins reported that there was no school and he commented that for want of schools 'that duty [of catechizing] is too often neglected'. There was an endowment of £4 for preaching eight sermons a year from a Meredith Maddy, a clerk, and another by a Mrs Elizabeth Widow 'for the teaching of poor Boys and Girls govern'd at present by herself'. One wonders how much of a blessing these endowments were, as he complains again of the want of schools.

There was a school in Clodock parish in 1762, founded by Oliver Maddocks (also spelled Madoke, Madockes, Madock, Madocke or Maddox in various documents and memorials), of which the vicar was a trustee. Earlier, it had been subject to a dispute between a local landowner and the local cleric. In a letter to the bishop in 1754, Sir Henry Howorth of Maeslough pleaded the case of the bearer of the letter, William Bowen, who had kept the charity school in Longtown for 14 years, 'and writes and casts accounts in a Tolerable Manner altho' he is without fingers which were burnt in the fire when he was a child'. The surviving trustee of Oliver Maddocks' Charity of £4 p.a., a Mrs Mary Rees, had appointed Bowen to keep the school, but the letter of appointment had been lost by the landowner. He clearly felt guilty about this, as he goes on to say, 'He is a great object of Charity, and a sober, Carefull honest man, which all the Parishioners will Certifie for him, but Mr Rees the Parson, I find by him has a desire that the Curate should enjoy this Charity, which is, the only thing this Poor man has to support himself.' The parson referred to was the vicar of Clodock, who by this time was the second Richard Reece to serve the parish (see the Appendix), and was paying his curate only £20 p.a.[44] The Maddocks Charity, founded to maintain a Sunday school, or possibly schools, was still in existence in the early 20th century.[45]

Somewhat of a mystery is Webb's charity for the founding of a hospital in Rowlestone in 1674. In the Charity Commissioners' minutes it is noted that a 'Mr Webb gave £27 p.a. towards the maintenance of a hospital in Rowlestone. Payable out of lands in the parish now in the occupation of Chris Landon, widow and Walter Watkins which is constantly paid'.[46] The only other mention of it is in the bond and documents of Thomas Phillips, farmer, in 1833, where his widow's address is given as 'Upper Hospital, Rollston'.

By the mid 18th century the evangelical revival taking place as a counter to the Enlightenment tends to be linked with the arrival of the Methodists under the leadership of the Wesley brothers, Charles and John, but it actually began at Talgarth, near Hay-on-Wye, a few miles from Ewyas Lacy. It was at Talgarth that Hywell Harris preached the sermon that converted one of the most famous hymn-writers in 1737, William Williams, the writer of that hymn beloved of Welsh rugby fans, *Guide Me O Thou Great Jehovah*. William Williams then became an itinerant preacher. Surely it is only too likely that he came over the border at some stage?[47] Not far away, at Hay-on-Wye in 1740, the first Methodist martyr, William Seward, a friend of Charles Wesley and George Whitefield, was battered with stones thrown by a crowd and died a few days later, being buried in the graveyard at Cusop church.[48]

Charles Wesley came to the area in 1749, visiting Garth in the neighbouring county of Breconshire, probably not long before there were groups of Methodists in Herefordshire. By 1767 Methodist preachers numbered 100 nationally and more than 500 by the end of the century,[49] but the Wesley brothers continued to be members of the Church of England. Wesleyanism, or Methodism as it came to be known, was a mainly rural movement that believed in a return to a purer form of Christianity, a personal conversion, the importance of lay preachers, women in the pulpit and that idleness was one of the deadly sins – very similar in most respects to the other nonconformists. A great deal of powerful support came from aristocratic circles, who were able to place their nominees in parochial livings. Amongst these patrons were Lord and Lady Dartmouth, the Duchess of Bedford and Lady Chesterfield, not to mention Lady Huntingdon and her Calvinist Connection, based at fashionable watering places like Bath and Tunbridge Wells. (Lady Huntingdon remained within the Church for decades until forced out in the 1780s.) There was a fear in some quarters that 'the most valuable part of the dissenting interest is likely to be ground to death between enthusiasm [a trait looked down upon by the fashionable world] on the one hand, and luxury and fashion on the other'.[50] However, that was not likely to happen at remote Ewyas Lacy.

In 1795, after the death of their founder, and having gradually drifted from a fragile attachment to the Anglicans over the century, the Methodists became completely separated from them. The Primitive Methodists were a further off-shoot from this break, appearing in the 1820s at Cwm at Craswall, where Elizabeth Phillips gave land for a chapel. Soon there were seven meetings in the Hundred including those at Upper and Lower Maescoed.[51] Several well-known farming families in the district lent their support, including the Gilberts of Blackhill, the Gwilliams of the Wain, the Farrs of Ty Craddock and the Watkins of Middle Cwm, many of whom appear in the wills and inventories.[52]

Wealthy evangelicals who remained within the Church of England deliberately bought up advowsons of parish churches from the mid 18th century in order to install evangelicals within them. Augustus Toplady, writer of the famous hymn *Rock of Ages* and erstwhile friend of Wesley, was one of many evangelical ministers who remained within the Anglican Church. An amusing story about him is that at a large gathering of 40 ministers to celebrate an anniversary at Trevecca, not very far away, at the announcement of the hymn *Blow Ye Trumpets Blow*, the entire edifice on which the ministers were standing collapsed. Fortunately, no-one was hurt.[53]

From the 16th century there had been little music in the Anglican Church, apart from the singing of metrical psalms, long the province of the congregation and associated with Puritans and therefore shunned to some extent by the gentry. Nicholas Temperley, writing about the music of the parish church, suggests that 'the idea was taking root that an English gentleman should have nothing to do with music of any kind' and especially when connected to the 'unsavoury odour of democracy'. This attitude continued until as late as the 19th century. The liturgy was the province of the clergy 'assisted by the parish clerk', thus alienating the congregation. The rare musician amongst the clergy would only be found in a cathedral like Hereford. There were few churches with an organ at the Restoration as they were too expensive for any but the largest cathedrals to afford until towards the end of the century, when town churches obtained them. Not only was there the expense of purchasing an instrument but also of maintaining an organist – beyond the means of all but the wealthiest churches.

All that country churches could do was form choirs and later, bands, reinforced in the early 18th century by children's choirs from the numerous charities being set up. These were a popular attraction, and soon special hymns were being composed for them. The parish choirs were initially expected to lead the singing from the nave, then were eventually provided with pews or a gallery with seats and a place for the psalms and book of music, as can still be seen, unchanged, in Clodock church, which was fortunately left alone by the Victorian 'restorers'.[54] Mr Llewellin, vicar of Clodock in the early 20th century, gives us valuable information on the kind of music played in his church in the mid 19th century, stating that in the fine 17th-century oak gallery there were 'violinists and flautists to lead the singing and the choir sat up there, too'.[55]

It is rare for musical instruments to be mentioned in connection with churches, as most choirs sang unaccompanied or with the aid of a barrel organ through much of the 18th century. (As has been noted, there is also a surprising lack of personally owned musical instruments in the inventories.) Gradually, however, a few musical instruments such as a bassoon or cello were introduced around the mid 18th century. Though the parish band of the west end gallery only came into existence towards the end of the 18th century, galleries had been in existence long before, as at Clodock, to accommodate growing congregations, and many small churches had singing galleries by the early 19th century. By this time the choir were joined by instrumentalists, sometimes as many as eight. These bands, which were of considerable standing in the village, did not consider themselves bound only to the parish church but were very much part of the community, playing at various local occasions such fairs, flower shows and the harvest home. In any case the money for the instruments had probably been raised by the village. It is thus a mystery why almost no musical instruments appear in the lists of people's personal possessions. Maybe the viols, cellos and clarinets for the west end gallery were stored safely in the church as communal property, so would not appear in individual inventories. These west end gallery singers were ousted when the organ became popular in the 19th century, as groups of musicians were harder to control than a single organist, *vide* the Thomas Hardy story in *Under the Greenwood Tree*. It was not unknown for the band to serve both Anglican Church and local nonconformists. Such independence could be of considerable annoyance to the vicar, and the bands were replaced by a barrel organ in most parish churches by the mid 19th century and, gradually, from about 1850, by the harmonium.

Many hymns had been written for the nonconformist churches in the 18th century by people like Newman and Wesley, and there would have been hearty singing in the chapels of Ewyas Lacy, with or without musical instruments. The Anglican church was slower to catch on, probably thinking that it was a step too far to allow the congregation much of a voice, and most of their music had traditionally been written for a choir. But by the 19th century, the Anglican Church could no longer be without music, and treasures of the past were being rediscovered, including the traditional psalm tunes, some dating from the middle ages. Among the first hymn books was the semi-official Church hymnal *Hymns Ancient and Modern*, whose editor-in-chief, and writer of some of the contents, was Henry Williams Baker, the vicar of Monkland church in Herefordshire.[56]

At last this was something that both parties could share. The rise of Methodism had drawn away many Anglican parishioners, attracted in part by the Methodists' lively music. Some of the best hymn writers were nonconformists, among them Philip Doddridge (1702-

51), a dissenting clergyman who was trained at a nonconformist academy and became a tutor at a seminary for nonconformist ministers. He wrote such well-known hymns as *Hark the glad sound*, and *Oh happy day that fixed my choice.* Then there was Isaac Watts (1674-1748), whose father was a nonconformist and sent Isaac to an academy of Independents, which he then joined as tutor in 1693. He wrote a volume of *Hymns and Spiritual Songs* which was published in 1707-9, and many of its hymns are still sung today, such as *Oh God, our help in ages past.* He was early ordained as an Independent pastor and awarded a doctorate in divinity by Edinburgh University. Of Anglican hymn-writers of this time, apart from Charles Wesley, perhaps the best known is John Newton (1725-1807).

In John Rogers, vicar of Clodock, we can see the beginning of a healing process between the Anglican Church and the dissenters, as he received praise for his 'evangelistic and educational effort' from the Methodists. Another vicar who was remembered with affection by all countrymen of the district was the Revd Eagles, who arrived 30 years after John Rogers in the early 1850s. As was fitting for a clergyman, he was known as a 'first class fisherman'. However, in the early 20th century the then vicar, the Revd Llewellin, commented wryly on the disastrous effect that the abolition of the church rate (due to pressure by the nonconformists) had on the churches in the mid-19th century. In spite of the fact that nonconformists could 'still dominate a Parish Vestry ... [and while paying] nothing for the upkeep of the church ... they retained all their previous rights, viz., of a seat in the church, a vote in the parish vestry, and of burial in the churchyard'.

It has been claimed that Queen Anne's Bounty acted as an instrument of reform from early in the 18th century until the 19th century, changing the way the clergy were paid, parishes were organized, and churches rebuilt or repaired.[57] True enough, rationalization of the parishes had also taken place, with county boundaries being observed in addition to efforts to provide houses for the clergy so that they could reside in their parishes. There is no written evidence of Anglican churches being built locally, except in the township of Newton in 1844, and that was mainly due to the efforts of a yeoman farmer rather than the church authorities. However, it could be said that Queen Anne's Bounty provided a temporary refuge from the storm that would descend on the Anglican Church from the mid 19th century when Clodock church, like many others, was out of repair, and in the words of a later vicar ... 'with broken seats, broken floor ... a refuge for birds and bats and no spiritual force in the neighbourhood'. By the early 20th century, due mainly it seems to the efforts of Mr Llewellin, this had been reversed and the advowson was in the hands of an Evangelical Trust.[58]

The latter half of the 18th century shows a clear improvement in the financial status of most, if not all, of the local clergy. According to statements made by the curates of the parishes, all had received money from Queen Anne's Bounty to supplement their livings (the distribution of which ended in the 1840s), and by the end of the 18th century more were in a position to buy their own advowson. In 1803, Phillip Price, vicar of Rowlestone, left his advowsons of 'Rollestone' and Llancillo, 'lately purchased by me of ... the Earl of Oxford', to his wife Elizabeth. Thirty-three years later John Rogers, vicar and now patron of the living of Clodock and the attached chapelries, was able to leave substantial legacies to his large family, which included two sons called Aaron and Moses. (Aaron was also a clergyman but held a living in Bristol.) Rogers, in nominating a curate for the chapelries of Llanveynoe and St Peters, Longtown in 1816, also confirms that both chapelries had been augmented by Queen Anne's Bounty. An early 20th-century vicar stated that the curates in Clodock from 1790 to 1833 received £40 or £50 per annum 'plus surplice fees' (whilst acknowledging that they were still 'underpaid and overworked').[59]

Conclusion

There can be no doubt that the coming of dissent acted as a spur to the Church of England. The Anglican Church, whatever else might be said about it, is so very English. Formed and shaped by an educated elite, it could never match in popularity the warmth of the Catholic Church, with its vividly coloured walls, guilds and jolly, often drunken saint's days. The Puritans first tried to kill off anything that remained of the old worship and then went off to form their own sects. Over four centuries, with one seismic upheaval per century, there were efforts to return to a form of religion that people felt they could embrace with enthusiasm. In the 16th century the changes were top down, with the churches commandeered by the gentry, but by the 19th the changes were from the bottom upwards, with the pressure for change coming from the nonconformist churches until the emergence of the Oxford Movement brought about a revival in the Anglican Church in the 1830s. The Anglican churches were fighting back, after the shaky previous century. Sunday and day primary schools were established. The British and Foreign Schools Society, which was inclined to fraternise dangerously between denominations, was overtaken by the rather pompously named National Society for Educating the Children of the Poor in the Principles of the Established Church. Added to this, by the mid 19th century, any good parish would have a battery of meetings, both secular and spiritual, throughout the week, including a weekly lecture, singing class and parochial library, together with various clubs. The Church was fast becoming more like the medieval church in its compass, but there was a considerable gap between this picture of the Anglican Church and that at Clodock at the end of the 19th century, if Llewellin is to be believed.[60]

Ancient churches like the one at Clodock not only hold the memories, music and memorials of their communities; they are also gathering places where anyone can meet. Most of all they are a witness to a faith in which, by the late 19th century, they were united with the nonconformist chapels to save souls. Ultimately, the body of nonconformists served a useful sociological service in that they were forced to divert their energies outside the mainstream of an otherwise rigid society, producing much of the church music, trade and inventions of the 18th century, viz, the Wesleys in music, the Quaker Cadburys of the Midlands and Quaker Derbys in the confectionery and ironmongering industries.[61]

Much of their support came from women, attracted to these sects partly by the appeal of a religion that gave them a voice at last. Nonconformity also served to channel the rebellious feelings of any who might attack the state and the status quo, to save us from the horrors of the French Revolution. It was felt by many that 'religion was the basis on which civil government rests ... A State is secure in proportion as the people are attached to its institutions'.[62]

11   SIN AND THE CHURCHWARDENS

So far a mainly positive view has emerged of the little community at Ewyas Lacy. We have seen that the makers of wills gave thought (at least conventionally) to spiritual matters, usually via a religious preamble, whether long or short, and bequests to the church and the poor, which preceded the nitty-gritty of what was to be left to whom. But – and some of the wills hint at this – there was a darker side. Beneath a seemingly calm surface, all kinds of resentments and troubles simmered.

Immorality has long been the concern of the Church, and Church courts tried offenders and issued punishments via 'presentments'. Ewyas Lacy was governed by the ecclesiastical authorities in Wales in such matters even when she came under the civil courts of Herefordshire for other crimes, so moral issues were dealt with by the archdeaconry courts at Brecon. The people responsible for making these 'presentments' to the bishop were the churchwardens, who were originally chosen on an annual basis by the parishioners and were answerable to them; only the parishioners had the right to remove them in extreme cases of bad behaviour. The churchwardens were responsible for the fabric and furniture of the nave of the church and for the maintenance of order amongst the parishioners and, somewhat surprisingly, sometimes the clergy.[1]

Illegitimacy

Attitudes to moral issues changed from one century to another; for instance, there was a swing from the lawlessness and immorality of the 18th century to a more moral outlook after Queen Victoria came to the throne and, unlike her uncles, showed an exemplary kind of family life to the nation. Consider illegitimacy. Starting with the 11th century, William 'the Bastard' did not see his illegitimacy as a bar to the throne of England. Queen Elizabeth I could have been considered illegitimate, born whilst the first wife of Henry VIII was still alive. The impression given is that illegitimacy was not frowned on in the 16th and early 17th century. An illegitimate child might inherit in the same way as a legitimate child. In the 16th century there were cases in the Hundred of Ewyas Lacy where little notice was taken of the fact that a child was born out of wedlock. Indeed, one of the earliest owners of the manor in the 16th century, John Arnold, was 'base begotten on the body of Margaret Hore alias Ysam, widow'.[2]

After the Civil War and Interregnum, attitudes seemed to change. Perhaps the years of living under Puritan rule had something to do with it, added to which more people were able to read the Bible and nonconformity was growing, along with intolerant attitudes to sin of any sort. It seems that there were indeed low rates of illegitimacy in the 1650s in England, although numbers rose again in the 18th century.[3] Part of the problem in the latter century may have been economic hardship. If people had to wait to get married until they could afford it, some of them perhaps found they couldn't wait that long, and there is little doubt that what were benignly called 'pre-nuptual' pregnancies were happening regularly. Illegitimacy rates in Ewyas Lacy were probably no higher than anywhere else, given that the community would act as a brake on outrageously licentious behaviour, and such 'by-blows' seem to have been treated responsibly and left sums of money, or even entire estates.

Wills are a good source of this kind of information, and show men and women making provision at the end of their lives for their illegitimate children or grandchildren. In 1582 a leading member of Clodock's community, Griffith Harri, willed to his 'base' son Harry property and land recently purchased from Sir Nicholas Arnold. His legitimate son, John, was to assign land in Olchon obtained from Rowland Vaughan and his wife to another 'base' son, George, 'as he has faithfully promised'.

Class did not seem to matter; from esquire to labourer, these gifts seem amazingly generous, and sometimes even cut out the legitimate in favour of the illegitimate. In 1635 Lyson Thomas, Esq. of Michaelchurch Escley left his 'reputed' son, John Thomas Price, £5 p.a. John Nicholls of the Turnant, a farm in Llanveynoe, left the farm to his 'natural' son, John Nicholls, in 1845. John Griffiths, a yeoman of Newton, when leaving his goods to his grandchildren in 1841, insisted that 'whether legitimate or illegitimate [they should] be divided between them share and share alike'. In his will of 1628 Richard Webb, a prosperous weaver of St Margarets, left his 'reputed son' his weaving equipment. Even the vicar's family was not immune to immorality. In the early 19th century, the vicar of Clodock, John Rogers, left a generous sum of money to his grandson, illegitimate son of his daughter, Sarah.

Some wills were surprisingly explicit in their instructions. In 1631, William Powell Madock of Clodock had two reputed children 'begotten on the body of Christian Morgan'. Some even give the girl's address; unfortunate for the girl, one would think, albeit a way of making sure that the right person was dealt with. William Cecil of Alltyrynys, Esq. names the mother of his illegitimate son, John, as Jane Morgan, daughter of John David Morgan of Llanvihangel Crucorney. Jane Prichard, spinster of Michaelchurch Escley, left a legacy in 1679 to 'Thomas, the bastard who is of Llandeilo bertholea'.

According to canon law, though not in common law, a child born out of wedlock was made legitimate the moment the mother was married to the father.[4] In his will of 1619 Harry Thomas Prees, a yeoman of Clodock, named two illegitimate children who were made legitimate by a later marriage to their mother. They were treated well, the girl inheriting £100 and the boy as if he was his heir, being left freehold land when the rest of the family were left only copyhold land.

On the whole Ewyas Lacy seems to have been fairly well-behaved as far as sexual morality was concerned, but there was no hiding such things in small villages, where many people did not leave the village from one year's end to the next. In 1705 the churchwardens in Clodock, John and James Watkins, presented John Thomas and Elizabeth Parry 'for fornication'. Towards the end of the 1720s there seems to have been an outbreak of this particular sin: at Rowlestone in 1727, when Thomas Prichard William was accused of fornication by the churchwardens; in 1728, when the wardens of Michaelchurch Escley presented Henry Eastland for fornication (and for 'not frequenting his parish church'); and at Llancillo in 1729, when Philip Prichard and Mary Vaughan were presented for the same misdeed. It finally reached Clodock in 1731 when Sybill, the daughter of John Davies/ Lewis, was presented. Rowlestone was again in the news in 1737, when two women, Mary Watkins and Elizabeth Prichard, were each named as having had 'a Base Child'. In this case the fathers were not named. There are two isolated cases of fornication in 1762 when it was reported that Lewis Powell and Catherine Perkins and Job Perrot and Jane Jenkins had fallen into that particular temptation. The main reason for concern, of course, was economic. Unmarried mothers generally cost the parish money.[5] All these presentments were mixed up with complaints about the chancel being out of repair, or a register being missing, or people not paying the church rate.

The church registers for Clodock and Llanveynoe do not mince their words about the status of the child being christened. In June 1752 the 'base' child of Elizabeth Griffiths was christened. The children are also called 'bastard' or 'spurious'. 1765 saw four illegitimate children being baptised. At Llanveynoe the following century the illegitimate births seem to average out at one a year over a ten year period, with most of the babies being born to servant girls. In the event of illegitimacy in a more respectable family it would probably have been dealt with more discreetly, with the man being forced to 'make an honest woman' of the unfortunate girl. The cases we know about may have been only the tip of the iceberg, as some cases must have been hushed up, with the girl sent away for a while.[6]

Defamation

Defamation cases were taken very seriously in an age when one's reputation for probity was vital. Most of the cases revolved round a woman's respectability or otherwise and they often took place in a pub, probably when the people involved were drunk. One reported case involved Timothy Prichard, yeoman, and his wife, Ann versus James Edwards, another yeoman. They were in a pub in Craswall on a Monday night in August 1756 when a row erupted between them. Timothy said to James Edwards in Welsh, according to the witness, John James, 'in an angry, Malicious and invidious manner… 'ni wnelsei neb shwt both ohon of fi ond Bastard'. More Welsh followed between these rather tedious drunks, including the repeated unmistakable word 'Bastard', the indictment continuing with the words translated into English, when James Edwards said 'if I am a Bastard thou dost Nurse some'. Timothy Prichard, on rather rashly asking who they were, was asked about the children of his first wife. James Edwards then went on malign Timothy's second wife, Ann, in the same way, saying 'Bastards what a Divel else will thou make of them', meaning, the witness says, 'that the said Anne was a whore and had been Guilty of Fornication or adultry'.

All this was recorded at the court on 7 November 1757, with the judgment being made and published by 11 April 1758. John Williams, Surrogate of the vicar general and official principal of the Rt Revd Anthony, Bishop of St Davids, 'having heard all the cause between the said parties' said that as James Edwards had taken away the 'good name and Reputation of the said Ann ... by speaking and uttering certain reproachful and defamatory words ... We therefore pronounce and decree that the said James Edwards ought and shall be compelled to retract the said reproachful and defamatory words and to be condemned in the costs of this suit ... and be compelled to make due payment thereof to the said Ann ... which said costs we have thought fit to moderate and tax at the sum of four pounds.'

That seems to have been it on that occasion. However, in 1732, in the case of John Parry against Mary Davids (both of Clodock), John Parry was ordered to appear before morning service in the parish church on 7 January before the minister and parishioners and six of the principal inhabitants, along with Mary Davids 'if she thought fit to be present'. He then had to make a humble apology, saying 'I, John Parry do in the sight of God and the persons here present confess and acknowledge that contrary to the rules of Charity and Christianity I have spoken wickedly against my neighbour, Mary Davids, spinster.' He then had to ask forgiveness of God and Mary Davids and promise to bridle his tongue in future. His defamatory words were in Welsh, as in the previous case, but by 1741 and the case of Martha, wife of David Jenkin versus Margaret wife of James Prichard, the words 'You are a Bastard' were said in English, together with other words implying her adultery and slandering her good name, 'in the presence of many witnesses who well understood the English tongue'.[7]

Incest

Another problem for churchwardens at Michaelchurch Escley and elsewhere was lack of guidance from the Church on the then complex rules regarding degrees of closeness of marriage to a blood relation. They notified the church court in 1705 that they had no table for such degrees and this was a recurring problem for other churchwardens over the years. Some incest did occur, knowingly or not. Ten years later, at Walterstone, the wardens presented Lysent Tranter for marrying clandestinely and marrying his sister. By 1718 Walterstone, Llancillo, and Rowlestone were still without such tables of degree.

Incest occurred both within and outside marriage. One of the worst cases involved the Mabbe/Mabe family of Craswall. Foster Mabbe died in 1697, and so lived to endure the shame of seeing his grandson and namesake being presented for incest by the churchwardens in 1688. The son of Foster the elder was Thomas Mabe, in whose will of 1730 Foster the younger was left only 1s, as was one of Thomas's daughters, Hannah. Enough said. All the other six daughters got reasonable legacies. There was also Mary Borden, presented to the church court at Brecon for having four 'base' children, which was bad enough until the mention of her brother John Borden, 'who was suspected by some to have Delt with her after an Incestious manner'; this was in 1690 at Llancillo, the smallest of the parishes, where there were only nine families at the beginning of the 18th century.[8]

Clandestine marriages were a further problem for the churchwardens. A clandestine marriage was one that had taken place without the prior publication of the banns, or procurement of a licence. The rules were so strict that even the clergy were sometimes caught out. In 1678 a case was brought against William Allen, the curate at Michaelchurch Escley, that he had performed a clandestine marriage, and pardon was asked of the Bishop of St Davids by the minister and parishioners. Hardwicke's Marriage Act of 1753 reinforced the necessity for marriages to take place in a church or chapel where the banns had been published prior to the marriage. However, much earlier, in 1713 or 1714, Lyson Prichard and Anne Prichard of Clodock were accused of having 'noe due regard to the s'd Canons' (of the Church) but at sometime were 'clandestinely married, or joined together in Matrimony

... and call yourselfes husband and wife ... and cohabit and live together at Bed and Board'. The complaint was that they had done this 'without any License or Dispensation first from us obtained or any Banns first allsoe published'. It is possible that this pair were nonconformists who considered that they had already been married in a dissenting church, especially if they were Quakers, the Society of Friends having established their own system of registers and burial grounds. A case occurred in 1739 of a Thomas Harris of Clodock performing a clandestine marriage, again possibly not in the parish church but in a nonconforming one which was not licensed, and in 1750 Sarah Smith of Clodock was also presented for being clandestinely married.[9]

Non-attendance

The offence of neglecting to attend church services was an additional bugbear for the churchwardens, especially as the threat of nonconformity grew in the late 17th and early 18th centuries. The 12 penny fine for such an offence, little used before the 1680s, was brought back into use in some areas, though there is no sign of it at Ewyas Lacy.[10] Reported at Clodock from 1685 to 1686 is a suspiciously long list of people absent from church, including Malachi Jones and his wife, John Roger Howell and Ruth Howell, a widow, Walter Harris and Gwenllian Gilbert. Their absence may be due to quite innocent reasons such as illness, as a Walter Harris of Clodock died in 1686 and a Gwenllian Gilbert died three years later, but the possibility is that some of them were dissenters who were attending their own church or chapel. This was not the only time Malachi attracted the disapproval of the churchwardens at Clodock. On 12 October 1703, 'Henry Vaughan vic: [vicar] there presented Malachi Jones for Christening at Mrs Parry's house and preaching there'. In 1712 Daniel Jones and Alice, his wife, of Craswall were presented for neglecting divine service, and Henry Easeland of Michaelchurch Escley was one of the offenders in 1728/9.[11] There was growing concern about supernumerary preachers. At Clodock in 1714 the wardens complained of the lack of a register in which to note down 'the names of strange preachers' and in 1717 they presented to the court 'one Morgan Thomas a Presbyterian preacher for teaching a school without license'.

Tithes

The reluctance of dissenters to have dealings with the Church of England is probably the reason for a number of cases of non-payment of tithes to the vicar or payment of the church rate, as resentment grew that people were expected to make payments to a church they no longer attended. From 1720 there was a rash of these cases coming up in the church courts but they had begun much earlier. In 1688, two shoemakers (notoriously independent people) named Thomas James and William Powell of Clodock were presented for not paying the church rate. An indication of the hard time they gave the warden is indicated by the note that at the same time several people were presented for abusing the warden. In the same year at Michaelchurch Escley there were three people – Hugh Russell, James Prosser and Anne Lewis (a widow) – who refused to pay the church rate. Sometimes even entire townships were so presented, such as Craswall in the early 1700s. Two highly respected members of the community, 'Mr' William Rogers and 'Mr' Job Gilbert (Lord Abergavenny's steward) were presented in 1725.[12]

In the 1720s, David Jenkins, who was responsible for the collection of some of the tithes, brought several people to the attention of the church. One long-running case was that of John Powell of Turnant Barn in Llanveynoe, but this may simply have been a mix-up over who was due the tithe payment and illustrates the difficulties involved. The tithe in this case was due to the 'improprietor' of the rectorial tithe, once long ago given to Llanthony Priory for its support, which could be leased to anyone prepared to pay for it. (The origin of these tithes is explained in the last chapter – see page 145.) In court it was said that 'Nicholas Arnold, Esq. for several years last past hath claimed or pretended a right but in which of them or in whom the lawful right ... is vested this Rondent [respondent] knoweth not'. In a wordy document laid before the courts it was claimed that Nicholas Arnold,

Tithe list in Clodock church

son of John Arnold the original owner of the tithes, had for some years let the tithes to Meredith Prichard. Powell made an arrangement with Meredith Prichard at the beginning of 1718 for the tithes and again in 1719. In fact, not only were the Arnolds in the process of selling the land to the Earl of Oxford at the time, but it is probable that ownership was not vested in Arnold but in Arnold's mother, Madame Dutton Colt, as her jointure on marriage. The case trailed on for several months, giving, incidentally some information as to the possible amount and use of the land at Turnant, information which is included in the chapter on agriculture – see page 63.[13]

Upkeep of the Chancel

Nicholas Arnold was involved in other disputes too, one of the most common complaints from the wardens being that the owners of the chancels were neglecting to keep them in good repair. This was a particularly sore point, as the owners were the rectors and thus beneficiaries of the greater part of the tithes. Nicholas Arnold was singled out for this over a number of years in the early 18th century, at Clodock, St Margarets and Craswall. In 1702 it was reported from Clodock that the chancel was 'very much out of repair', a complaint that was repeated over the next 18 years with doubtless growing exasperation. In 1708 he was named as the culprit at St Margarets, and at Clodock in 1712 the wardens 'presented the Chancell of the said Church in Decay and that the same ought to be repaired by Nicholas Arnold, Esq.'

All was not perfect in other parts of the church either, but in most cases it was simply a matter of needing a new prayer book, 'an English folio Bible of the New Translacon', or a new account book for the wardens.

The Clergy

There were times when even the clergy were presented for misdemeanours. At St Margarets in 1699 the wardens presented 'Thomas Lewis, clerk for officiating without showing his orders though he has been several times requested soe to do', and at Rowlestone in 1747 the wardens presented 'the Parson for not being resident'.

One of the worst cases coming before the courts in 1728/9 was that of Thomas Allen, the curate at Michaelchurch Escley whose sad tale we came across in the previous chapter. We are told that he was accused by his churchwardens of 'being a drunkard ... and by report adulterer ...'. He had been living at Michaelchurch for several years, probably rooming with some countrywoman, as Francis Kilvert did in nearby Clyro a century later, and would have sought companionship in the many inns and public houses. In 1729 he was brought before the General Court held after Michaelmas for the Archdeaconry of Brecon, in the chapel of St Mary. He was not the first clergyman to have got into bad company. In the next parish, three years earlier, in 1726, the minister of Ewyas Harold was presented for 'being often Drunck'.

Some of Thomas Allen's indictment went as follows (the clerk's abbreviations have been extended): 'By the laws and canons of this Realm it is provided that all persons do live regular and Christian lives in Sobriety and that no Ecclesiastical person shall at anytime other than for his honest Neccesity resort to any Taverns or Alehouses or spend their time in Riot but do forbear Curseing and swearing and Abstain from drinking to Excess and should be Examples to the people to live well and Christian like and teach and Instruct the parishioners and youth of the parish ... Notwithstanding ... you the said Thomas Allen well knowing the same to be true have for two years last past on all or most of the Sundays and Ladydays ... Neglected to preach any sermon within the said Church of MichaelChurch Escley as by law you are obliged to doe and have also ... neglected to teach and Instruct train up and edify the Children and youth of the said parish in Catechizeing them ... and at several times within the said Parish of Michaelchurch Escley ... have been drunk or even overtaken with too much liquor and in that Condition would Commonly swear and Curse and take the Lord's name in vain to the evil Example of others and the great danger of your own soul.' The court hearing took place in February and attached to the indictment was a bill for costs, including the cost of sleeping accommodation and food for the defendant on several occasions up until July 1729.

In Thomas Allen's defence it is worth considering the loneliness of a possibly young man coming from the lively companionship of his peers at university to a place where there were few professional men to associate with, not even the other clerics, as they lived too far away. Sadly, we shall probably never know what happened to him as he then vanishes from the records.[14]

It might be expected that Michaelchurch Escley would have suffered under his careless curacy, but in fact it seldom appears in the churchwardens' presentments at that time, maybe because even the churchwardens had lost heart. However, three years after this event there was a complaint that not only was a Terrier (description of land) missing but, astonishingly, the church had 'no flagon, no paten, no pulpit'.[15]

Churchwardens

The churchwardens themselves did not always uphold honour and decency. Over time, the original ability of the parishioners to elect both churchwardens had been altered, with one churchwarden becoming the 'vicar's warden' and the other the 'people's warden'. In the early 1730s a row broke out between two groups of Clodock parishioners who each claimed to have elected the rightful 'people's warden' for that year. At first sight the affair is so confusing that it is difficult to make head or tail of it, but after reading several accounts of claim and counter-claim it gradually becomes clearer. The case was brought before the court in 1734 by 'Rowland Jennings and John Jenkins, Gentlemen, two of the principall Inhabitants of the parish of Clodock' against Richard Rees, the curate, and John Powell and Walter Morgan, the previous churchwardens of the parish. In the court a year later, Richard Reece, Senior, naturally took the side of his son, the curate, in refuting the claims of Jennings and Jenkins, and said that as vicar of Clodock 'for fifteen years', he was 'well acquainted with the custom of electing wardens' and that it was usual for him on Easter Monday to take morning prayers first at Llanveynoe church where the minister appointed the churchwarden for the whole parish, going thence to Clodock church where 'The Inhabitants of the Township of Longtown only' elected their churchwarden for the year then commencing. On that Easter Monday of 1734, which fell that year on 15 April, the two churchwardens appointed were Philip Parry and John Lewis, Philip Parry being appointed by Richard Rees, curate to the vicar (his father, also Richard Rees) and John Lewis by the parishioners. The reason for the confusion seemed to be partly, as Richard Reece senior went on to admit, that the inhabitants of the parish of Clodock 'had no right from time immemorial nor until about the year of our Lord 1726 ... to elect persons out of the Township of Craswall within the said parish to be Churchwardens'. The pattern was always for the minister to choose a warden out of the inhabitants of Llanveynoe and Newton and for the other warden to be chosen out of the township of Longtown by the inhabitants of the said township. However, from 1726 the minister was allowed to appoint a new warden from Craswall one year and one of the inhabitants of Llanveynoe or Newton the following year. (It seems curious that Craswall had to wait until 1726 to be enfranchised!) After making his position clear, poor Mr Reece senior, claiming that he was 'a perfect Stranger to the whole affair' and that he was not obliged by law to answer or submit to be examined, asked to be dismissed with his costs 'in this Behalf wrongfully charged'. What a to-do, and the kind of thing that breeds ill feeling in a community for years afterwards![16]

By the end of the century some of the earlier difficulties seem to have subsided and the wardens' tasks had become more settled and routine. At Clodock in 1798/9 the account of one of the churchwardens, Thomas Davis shows him, amongst other things, paying for the mending of the chapel lock, the mending of the church gate, the killing of two foxes, repairing the 'great Bell', one and a half hundred of tile for the church and 'two Journeys to Hereford to Buy the Cloth for the Communion Table and Pulpit'. Over at Llanveynoe chapel Thomas Jones, the warden that year, was no less busy. He paid for a 'New coffer' £2 11s, for a ladder 5s, £1 for the 'Clark fees' and added, 'My journey to Brecon - 2s 6d' ... pd for Presentments – 7s ... Cort fees – 5s'.[17]

12   THE MORE RECENT PAST

It is difficult to know whether the hardship endured by the landowners, from taxation and losses in the First World War, was a factor in the decline of farming in the first half of the 20th century but it must have had considerable influence, especially when combined with other factors such as the agricultural depression of the final quarter of the previous century and the departure of many farmers to the Americas. A visitor to the Olchon Valley in the autumn of 1873 could still describe it as very fruitful, with orchards, and full of 'cornfields laden with yellow grain'. Fifty years later, a Mr M'Caw, a more down-to-earth visitor to the Black Mountains region in 1937, concluded that there had been such a 'recession of human population' over the past 50 years that much of the land in the area had become 'indistinguishable from open moor', and more than half the region was not used to its full capacity. His assessment was that it would take 20 years to be restored to the same level as the adjacent Golden Valley. Two years later, the Second World War brought the necessary demand and resources required to bring land back into production.

In the 1850s the size of the average farm had been a mere 58 acres with only about 19 acres of it arable; subsistence farming in other words. To be viable, a farm of this size would have to rely on common grazing.[1] From the mid 19th century, and even earlier if the township of Llanveynoe was anything to go by, the size of some of the farms had been changed by large scale engrossing. Samuel Griffiths, of Olchon House in Llanveynoe, owned a holding of only 47 acres at the beginning of the century, but it had swollen to 260 acres by 1871. There were several other farmers who were taking in the small, unviable farms of 20 acres or so. By the end of the century some of these small farms and cottages were empty or ruinous as farmers left for improved prospects elsewhere. Looking even further into the future, a comment by a farmer, Jim Williams of Longtown, emphasised the changes that had taken place, when he said that his 50-acre farm at Lower Maescoed in 1948 had 'eight scrap houses on it', and as the land was wanted for corn (when, after the war, there was a bread shortage) and no one wanted the stone, they were buried by the bulldozer.[2]

In 1905 every parish included wheat as one of its main crops, followed by oats and barley and in some cases swedes and beans.[3] However one of the comments made by Mr M'Caw after his visit to the region was on the remarkable pasture he found, even in the Olchon Valley at 900 feet above sea level. This was to be the way forward in better times from the 1950s onward, as farmers turned again from growing crops to rearing stock.

The cattle raised on the pastures had gradually become recognizable as the Herefords that, by the mid 19th century, were beginning to be exported all over the world. (The

Hereford can still be seen occasionally today, though foreign breeds have pretty much taken over.) Herefordshire cider had long been famous and could now be transported quickly and safely to new markets as railways and canals took over from the packhorse in the last half of the 19th century. Where earlier, the horse, or mare with her foal, had been as ubiquitous as the pig on the farms, with the coming of the coal industry in south Wales, another outlet for farming in the 19th century was breeding ponies to be loaded onto trains at Pandy station, destined for the coal-pits of south Wales. This practice continued into the following century.

Sheep, however, became the most numerous livestock and a major sheep fair was held each year in Ewyas Harold, and a ram fair in Longtown. Over the years hundreds of sheep were driven down the lanes to the market before being loaded onto the train at Pontrilas. Since the Foot and Mouth outbreak in 2001, Longtown market has gone and some farmers have given up farming altogether. The Ryeland sheep breed has now been replaced, often by a Suffolk cross.

The weekly visits to Abergavenny and other local markets were until recently still remembered with nostalgia by farmers' wives who used to take their produce there. Sadly, most of the local markets have gone now together with the old railway stations. The Second World War brought mechanization to many of the farms, or if not then, soon after.

As far as farmers' wives are concerned, their lives have been transformed since the 19th century. Before women could be free and independent, as has been pointed out three problems had to be overcome: the lack of educational opportunities; the lack of finance; and the necessary legal safeguards to ensure that women were looked upon as equals to men. It was during the 19th century that schools opened their doors to them. At Longtown, the school held in the church in the 18th century became a free National school in 1851 with a master and mistress, then was moved to a purpose-built school built by subscription in 1869 – testimony to the forward thinking of the inhabitants. In 1851, there was a small school for boys and girls in the chapel-of-ease in Craswall. There was no school at Llanveynoe, but

The old school in Longtown, now converted into houses

a National school at Michaelchurch Escley for boys and girls had been erected in 1851. At the same time, Newton proudly stated that it had a new school built adjacent to the church (the latter also a recent acquisition) where 'about 30 children are under instruction' from the church clerk. There was no school at either Rowlestone or Walterstone but the children would have walked to the nearest school. The Education Act of 1870 ensured that elementary education was available to all girls on the same level as boys, and that there was a school in most parishes.In 1881 women were granted degrees from London University for the first time.[4] No longer were marriage or service in some household the only options open to women.

Property rights for women were secured through the Women's Property Act of 1870. This was partially influenced by a pamphlet written by a woman member of the staff at Bedford College, London, together with high profile court cases of men having dissipated their wife's fortune, leaving them destitute. More and more Ewyas Lacy wills can be seen to be protecting the female beneficiaries by making bequests independent of the husbands. In addition there was now a way out of an unhappy marriage by the promulgation of the Divorce Bill of 1857.

More women were managing farms on their own. In the past many widows had been left to run farms after the deaths of their husbands, but in Longtown in 1905, there were nine farms being run by women, some of them single. Both the shop and the post-office were being run by women, and at St Margarets the carrier to Hereford was a woman.

Women were tough and resilient then. One farmer's daughter, Mabel Pritchard, growing up on a farm where they were self sufficient, became a nursemaid after leaving school in the early 1900s, and claimed, jokingly, that she worked until she was 103 'and was then made redundant'. She seemed happy with the current status quo when interviewed, saying, 'life is much easier now. I have everything to hand in the house ... the hard work is gone'.[5]

Many of the larger houses such as Michaelchurch Court and Vedw received a make-over in the 19th century, and others were extended, as the desire grew for greater privacy and with specialization of rooms such as parlours, and dining rooms. Since the 1990s there has been some in-filling by the building of new houses in Longtown.

The keynote throughout the late 1700s was an increase in comfort, with a proliferation of goods from furniture to kitchenware. Furniture, once made of solid oak, was being produced from imported delicate walnut, mahogany and rosewood, though much of the simpler furniture was probably still made locally. A 'tea table' was first listed in an inventory in the early 19th century. From cider being the main drink, tea and coffee drinking was making an appearance, at least Thomas Harris was stocking his shop with coffee and tea at Longtown in 1786, and the richness and variety of goods displayed in his shop are testimony to the prosperity of the area. He also had tea kettles and coffee mills on sale, and had probably sold to the widow Sarah James the small copper tea kettle she had in her inventory in 1780. By 1799 James Thomas, cooper, kept a tin coffee pot in his kitchen. It was the opinion of a Frenchman touring England in 1784 that tea was being drunk not only by the better off, but by peasants 'to the amount of about 4 pounds of tea per person and when they were not drinking tea they were swigging down cider and beer'.[6] The Great Exhibition in 1851 was bound to have stimulated interest in the latest inventions, including those of a domestic nature.

The most dramatic changes came in the 20th century. Until the 1960s, many of the houses were without mains water or electricity. The introduction of these amenities made life far easier, especially for housewives, as they made the introduction of refrigerators, washing machines and other appliances possible and probably did more to emancipate women than anything else.

A reduction in local amenities has been a fairly new development as, people have begun to travel further afield on a regular basis. In living memory there were a number of shops available, including a blacksmith, a butcher, a general store and a cobbler. Back in 1905, Longtown retained, for a population of 970, four mills, five public houses, two post-offices, two butchers, three grocers, four wheelwrights or carpenters, two bootmakers, one mason, one tailor, and a harness maker. By 2013 that totem figure of village life, the blacksmith, has dwindled to one and is called an 'agricultural implement repairer'. A vet was seldom required as farmers reckoned that they were able to deal with most animal ailments themselves and were not averse to using human medicines if necessary. On one occasion a young farm lad, working for his uncle, had been advised to take some proprietary salts for an ailment and had recently bought a pound of them. His uncle, faced with a sick animal needing a drench, and with no drench to hand, mixed his nephew's salts with some water and drenched the beast with it. The nephew remembers that 'Almost immediately the beast made manure and one of the workmen said "My Gosh, them salts are pretty effective". To which my uncle shouted back "It wouldn't work as fast as that if it was electric".'

One service that has, thankfully, been done away with, is that of hanging criminals on the castle green. One story relates tells how people, in the 19th century, were reluctant to buy butter and cheese from Longtown if a body had been known to have been hanging there for a while.[7]

By far the most remarkable change of the 19th century was in matters of faith, from the bitter enmity of the 16th and 17th centuries when people were burned to death for their beliefs to a joint sharing of their common purpose of saving souls in both chapel and church. In part this is the result of a more secular society. Even during the 18th century there had been a reduction in the amount of religious preamble at the start of a will. Also, wills tend to be less interesting and detailed than they were (especially in the 16th and 17th centuries), whilst inventories have been done away with as part of the probate process.

Epilogue

Two World Wars brought change to the region, as elsewhere. After the First World War the greater landowners withdrew, selling off most of the farms to the former tenant farmers; a more recent incoming wave brought active retired incomers who have bought and restored some of the old farmhouses or settled in one of several closes that have been built in the last twenty years or so. Oddly, this does not appear to have added massively to the numbers in the population, in the year 2011 there were still only 438 people on the electoral roll for Longtown with Clodock, a reduction from the 556 people recorded in the 1911 census.

No longer called a Hundred, politically, Longtown and Clodock are now joined with a much larger group called the 'Golden Valley, South Ward' of 15 parishes, including Turnastone and Vowchurch. Across the Ward only 10% of the population are under 18, which is a cause of concern as the number of those aged over 80 grows, though it is a tribute to the healthfulness of the county, if nothing else!

The old shop in Longtown

Hopes, the new shop in Longtown

Today, despite having fewer residents than before, Ewyas Lacy, far from being a sleepy backwater, is an outward-looking power-house of social and community activity. With bus services at a minimum, and the railway lines shrunk drastically, all access to shopping centres, surgeries and hospitals seem far away for those unable to drive. However, one vital facility, a comprehensive shop and post office, was rescued by a local farming family. Hopes of Longtown opened in 2003, three months after the old shop closed.

Six of the Hundred's Anglican churches remain open (St James, Longtown, is now a dwelling and the very isolated St Peters at Llancillo is closed), but with only one vicar. The Baptist chapel has recently lost its minister, and where there were once several Methodist chapels, there is now only one. On another level, there is also the likelihood of substantially improved communication with the rest of the world as by 2016, 90% of Herefordians have been promised 'super fast' broadband, whereas currently as many as 25% do not have access at all.

Always important to the life of a village, there is a flourishing pre and primary school at Longtown (with 52 children in 2006 and 56 in 2013), serving Longtown, Clodock, Lower Maescoed, Llanveynoe and part of Craswall, and another school at Michaelchurch Escley. With mechanisation brought to the farms during and after the Second World War children no longer have to miss school at harvest time or because of the many former debilitating diseases of childhood.

There are fewer pubs, the Crown in Longtown and the Bull's Head at Craswall are still popular, as is the Bridge at Michaelchurch Escley, though the balance is towards food rather than liquid refreshment. Other changes have taken place. The New Inn, once owned by Mr

The Longtown and District Show in 2002

Penry is now the Longtown Outdoor Education Centre, owned and run by Northamptonshire County Council, in tandem with the Mountain Rescue Centre.

The immensely popular and long established Longtown and District Show held in August includes every facet of country life including horse and dog shows, livestock and other classes, demonstration of rural crafts, and family sports.

Cock-fighting and games of Fives at Craswall after Sunday service, are long since gone, to be replaced by television, or football. Concerts for Craswall, held annually in June, draws music lovers from a wide area as does the Eisteddfod later in the year, maintaining the Welsh tradition, and other concerts are held from time to time, not to mention the Young Farmers annual pantomime. Sadly the speaking of Welsh has long since gone but can still be heard in Abergavenny where many people still go to shop.

Local initiatives are represented not only by a flourishing and efficient WI, but Longtown Village Pride, an organisation that lovingly maintains historic features such as the medieval garden next to the castle. Longtown and District Historical Society performs the same function for lovers of history. In Michaelchurch Escley, Escleyside Hall is an important focus for a number of activities.

Tourism is an increasingly important aspect in maintaining and promoting the attractions of the area. Many farms now offer bed and breakfast accommodation or 'holiday lets' and on one farm, Mountain Mayhem is an attraction combining paint-balling and quad-biking.

All these things anchor the residents to the place, as do the Black Mountains, the Black Hill, the river valleys, friends and family. At its core, Ewyas Lacy has not changed all that much. The good things shown in the wills and inventories remain; love and affection between families and children and concern for their future.

Appendix A

The Anglican clergy of Ewyas Lacy

Two things stand out where the clergy are concerned, firstly that they kept livings within the family where they could, passing on benefices from father to son sometimes for several generations and, secondly, they seem to be in a class of their own. In alumni records, instead of being listed as 'pleb' or armigerous, they were 'cler'.

The clerical family of whom most can be discovered were the Reeces/Reeses of Clodock, variously curates and vicars in turn and, confusingly, almost all called Richard. They held office in Clodock for about 65 years, and the musician's gallery in the church was probably built by either Henry Vaughan to celebrate his retirement, or by the incoming vicar, Richard Reece, sometime after 1723.[1] The Bishop's Transcripts show that Richard Reece, or Rees, was the curate of Clodock from 1713. On 9 March 1717/18 a letter was sent to the Bishop of St Davids from Henry Vaughan, then vicar of Clodock, certifying that on 'the 2d day of February last I gave notice in the Parish Church of Clodock yt [that] Mr Richard Reece my curate did design to apply himself to yr Ldship for orders ...'. Another note followed certifying that Mr Richard Reece 'who have been for some years my Curate at Clodock has an allowance of £30 p. annum, and shall be continued there as Curate and have the same sallery allowed him during my life'. Testimonials were signed by not only the vicar, but the vicars of nearby churches.[2] In the register of 1723 Richard Reece signs himself 'vicar' for the first time. He had earlier, in 1719, lost a wife called Elizabeth, probably in child-birth as a burial entry for a John Reece follows hers. By 1723 he was obviously married again as the register entry states that Mary, the daughter of Revd Richard Reece (vicar) of Clodock and his wife Mary was baptized on 12 September. They had a son, John, in 1727, and a third child, Elizabeth, in 1730, another son, William, in 1733, and Delahay in 1735. (This son was eventually to 'inherit' the benefice). Curiously, there was another Elizabeth in 1736, and even stranger was an entry for 24 July 1738, 'Eliz. wife of Rich: Reece, vicar was Buried'. Had his mind slipped, or someone else made the entry? The answer lies in the change of vicars with the same name. In 1736, 'Richard Rees, the Elder, Clerk' had resigned and Richard Rees, the younger, took his place, so she must be the wife of the second Richard. In 1750, another member of the family, also called Richard, was instituted as his curate, in order, no doubt, to succeed him in due course.[3] He does not appear to be another son but was listed in the parish register of St Augustines in the diocese of Bristol as having been baptized on 20 June 1725, the son of William and Mary Reece.[4]

This Richard does not seem to have survived long as in 1758 another letter was delivered to the Bishop of St Davids which said: 'These are to certify to your Lordship that the Reverend Mr Delahay Reece's intentions of offering himself a candidate for the holy order of Priests was by himself proclaimed in the Parish Church of Clodock the thirtieth day of July 1758'.

There followed the names of two churchwardens who made their mark, James Jones and John James. In the meantime Delahay Reece's father, the second Richard Reece, appears to have married again in about 1746 as records show that he married Hanna widow of John Maddox, gent, and had stood as bondsman for the very large sum of £1,000 during her widowhood. By the time of the Bishop's Visitations in 1759, when Richard Reece was questioned about who served the Clodock benefice, he replied that his curate there was a John Rowlands, so what had happened to Delahay? Perhaps he had taken a curacy elsewhere. The use of the name Delahay probably dates from the 18th-century marriage of Bennet Delahay's daughter (name unknown) to this member of the Reece family.[5]

The use of the name Delahay for one of the sons is interesting as it is the surname of another clerical family in the neighbourhood; an armigerous family who came from Alltyrynys in Walterstone, which they had acquired from the Cecil family by marriage.

Morgan Delahay, clerk, of Clodock, was mentioned as a witness of the will of David Phee, yeoman, of 30 June 1630, and he also helped assess the inventory. The inventory shows that Morgan owed the estate £10. Another mention was in the inventory for Harry Williams, dated 1629, when one of those who stood bound as surety was Morgan Delahay of Clodock. He almost certainly had a descendant, possibly his son who is mentioned in his will, follow him into the Church, as a John Delahay, vicar of Clodock, appears in probate documents for 1665, and again in 1671 and 1679, in connection with church administration. A look at the ordination papers confirms that he was installed at Clodock in 1661, but he may have been a curate there before this.[6] There is a tantalizing gap here. What happened to the vicar of Clodock during the Civil War and Interregnum? Morgan Delahay died in 1650 so perhaps his son John, who was to become vicar at the Restoration, then took over as curate. It is interesting to see that Henry Vaughan, who followed John Delahay at the end of the 17th century and later installed Richard Reece, calls himself 'minister' of Clodock. Was this a hang-over from the war years, as all the Reeces called themselves 'vicar'.

In addition to the Delahays and Reeces, there were at least two other families, the Prices of Llancillo and the Higgins of St Margarets and Michaelchurch Escley, who succeeded in keeping livings in the family for long periods. Apart from the Phil Price 'junior', curate at Llancillo/Walterstone in 1759, who helped his father, there was another Phil Price (but 'Mr') at Oldcastle. By 1762 he was still at Walterstone but now served Llancillo and Rowlestone as curate. There was another William Price at Llancillo in 1743. Then in 1803, Phillip Price, clerk, bought the advowson of Llancillo and Rowlestone from the Earl of Oxford. An earlier 'Phillip Price, clerk', probably his father, may have retired to Clodock by 1787.

In 1746, after graduating at Balliol College, a Thomas Higgins was inducted at St Margarets and Michaelchurch Escley, but when he died in about 1770, his son – also named Thomas, and of Jesus College – was ready to take his place.[7] Such a confusing propensity to stick to the same family name!

After an incumbency of over half a century, less tenacious clergy families followed the Reece family at Clodock; the most notable being the much respected Revd John Rogers in 1814. He followed the Revd Thomas Bowen, who died intestate, so presumably suddenly, unmarried and with an estate valued at 'under one hundred pounds'. In sharp contrast, when John Rogers died, like Thomas 'in harness' in 1836, he lists a substantial estate in his will, and the cover sheet notes that his goods chattels and credits were valued at 'less than £2,000'.

Although John Rogers had a son called Aaron in holy orders, he was already established in Bristol, so the Revd Charles Probert took his place.

Vicars were a long-lived lot in those days. Four vicars held office from 1774-1916, an average of 35½ years each, but this was not unusual as there was then no pension meaning vicars and curates usually laboured on until death. Mr Sparkes was curate and vicar from 1774 to 1814, a total of 40 years. His successor, John Rogers, initially his curate, served Clodock for 39 years from 1797 to 1836 and another modern-day Rogers, Frank, served the parish for nearly 30 years.

Appendix B

Stocking Analysis over the 16th to 18th centuries

As we only have records for the last three decades of the 16th century against which to make comparisons, I have compared the last three decades of each of the two following centuries to see if there was evidence of increased numbers of livestock held by yeomen and farmers over the three centuries.

Two problems arose immediately: the makers of the inventories did not necessarily always describe livestock in the same way. Some appraisers might describe the cattle stock in detail – '2 yr old bullocks, weaning calves' etc – whilst others might just list 'young cattle', and similarly with horses and sheep. Thus the only answer was to lump all the cattle together with the exception of Oxen which were clearly defined in all centuries and of interest because they were draught animals. Horses and sheep similarly were treated as single categories, (horses, mares colts and fillies, and sheep ewes and lambs). The results were tabulated:

	Cattle	Av'age	Horses	Av'age	Oxen	Av'age	Sheep	Av'age
16th century, 19 farms	194	10.2	37	1.9	28	1.5	377	19.8
17th century, 25 farms	368	14.7	72	2.9	49	2.0	534	24.2
18th century, 17 farms	277	16.3	61	3.6	23	1.35	497	29.2

A second problem arises from the fact that there are not the same number of farms to consider in each century, and thus from a quick glance at the table it might look as though the stocking level had peaked in the 17th century, but the average of each category shows that the 18th century has the highest level. Was this increase significant or just a chance occurrence? A statistical analysis of the variance shows that this increase can be considered as highly significant and it can confidently be said that there was an increase in stocking level across the centuries. The only exception was with the oxen which, looking at the averages, can be seen to have peaked in the 17th century and declined with a commensurate increase in horses in the 18th century.

Appendix C

Longtown and District Historical Society's website

In 2004 the Committee of the Society decided to set up a group to explore the possibility of collecting information on the whereabouts of scattered archival material relating to the Hundred of Ewyas Lacy and publishing this information on a website for use by researchers.

Three record Offices, Hereford Record Office, Gwent Record Office and Powys Record office were trawled and details of information gleaned was collected. Professional assistance was sought for the design and implementation of the fully searchable website (www.lhsarchive.org.uk) on which this information is available.

When it came to the probate papers these were obtained in three phases. First, a lottery grant through the Local Heritage Initiative was obtained for the purchase of the 1,047 local sets of photocopies of post Restoration documents held at the National Library of Wales at Aberystwyth, then work commenced on the transcription and précising of them for the website. This task has been on-going since then, the wills being completed first in 2007. The inventories continue to be put on-line.

The second phase was the collection by my husband, over a series of visits to the National Archive, Kew, of the details of appropriate probate documents from the Prerogative Court of Canterbury which he completed by the end of 2009. The third phase has been the collection and transcription of the earliest local probate documents from 1553 to 1652 held at the National Library of Wales, also carried out by my husband and the results published on the website.

In transcribing and précising the documents we have tried to ensure that every name mentioned in a document with their legacy, if any, has been included, as well as the names of all debtors and creditors, witnesses and assessors.

An index to the probate papers on the website has been produced in two booklets, copies of which can be requested from the Longtown and District Historical Society.

Appendix D

Glossary

Andirons – pair of movable iron plates to contract the fire grate.
Andogg – pair of horizontal bars, supported on short legs. Used to support a spit or logs in the fireplace.
Beetle – heavy wooden hammer. Came in various shapes depending on what it was used for.
Bell metal – an alloy of several metals.
Broach – iron pin which pierced the meat.
Chattels – any kind of movable property
Chattel lease – the remaining part of the lease held by the deceased
Cobbs/Cobberts – long bars with hooks to lean against the front of the fireplace at angle of 45 degrees. On the hooks revolved spits or broaches.
Copyhold – type of tenure for which the tenant had to produce, when required, a copy of the court rolls
Cordwainer – shoemaker
Corvisor – shoemaker
Coverlid – bedcover
Fuller – one who shrinks and mills cloth to make it thicker and stronger.
Gavelkind – Welsh system of inheritance whereby all the children inherit an equal share.
Holograph will – will in the testators own hand.
Hurden – a coarse fabric, often used in sheets.
Holland – fine linen, used for sheets, shirts and table napkins.
Leasows – open land which could be used either for grass or arable crops.
Moiety – half.
Muncorn – a mixture of half wheat and half rye (regarded by a traveller in Shropshire as making wretched bread). It was more or less phased out by the mid 18th century.
Nuncupative – an oral will made before witnesses.
Pillowbere or beer – a pillowcase.
Pikel – a pitchfork.
Posnet – a metal pot used for boiling.
Posset cup – a cup with a lid and handles, and a spout to drink from.
Trind – a wooden tub, or container. Often found in the brewhouse or dairy.
Wain – a large farm wagon.
Yeoman – usually a freeholder, he had a higher status than a husbandman

Appendix E

Meaning of Welsh words in place names

Allt – hillside or wood
Blaen – source of river
Bryn – head of the valley
Bras or brass – fat, or flourishing (as in Brass Knoll)
Cae – field (as in Cae Croon, a round field)
Caer – wall (as in a castle or city)
Canol – middle
Cefn – back or ridge
Celyn – holly
Coch – red
Cwm – valley
Dan – under
Derw – oak
Dwr – water
Ffynon – well
Glan – bank
Glas – green
Groes – cross
Gwern (or Wern) – marsh or bog with alder trees
Gwrlod – meadow
Gwyn – white
Hafod – summer pasture

Hen – old
Heol – road
Hendre – main or winter home, or old house
Hir – long
Isaf – lowest
Llan – enclosure (s in Llanveynoe)
Llwyn – bush
Maerdy – dairy
Maes – field
Mynydd – mountain
Nant – stream
Pandy – fulling mill
Parc – field
Pen – top
Pont – bridge
Pwll – pool
Quarrelly – quarry
Rhyd – ford
Tre – homestead
Ucha or uchaf – highest
Ynys – island (as in Alltyrynys)
Ysgubor – barn (as in Skybor barn)

Bibliography

Abbreviations used

GRO   Gwent Record Office, Cwmbran
HMC   Historical Manuscripts Commission records
HRO   Herefordshire Record Office, Hereford
Longleat   The archives of the Marquis of Bath
NLW   National Library of Wales, Aberystwyth
ODP   Olchon Development Project
PRO   Powys County Archives, Llandrindod Wells
TNA   The National Archive, Kew

Manuscripts

GRO   Abergavenny Leases and Releases etc, D1583, 2, 3,12, 35, 36, 229.002-008, 238.10
          and others
          Sir Trevor Williams Survey of Ewyas Lacy, article 5
          Baker-Gabb Collection, Miscellaneous
Hereford Cathedral Archives   Charity Report
Herefordshire Council   Sites and Monuments Record
HMC   Portland Papers (1901), Vol. 29
HRO   Harleian Papers, Methuen & Co [1902], bundle 16, 17
          M26/6/104-206, Scudamore Correspondence
          J91/1-4, Manor of Ewyas Lacy, Court Books
          AF 57/5/8, Sir George Cornwall, Correspondence
          J56/III/106, Moccas Collection, Correspondence
          A95/V/W/e/13 and 216
          Scudamore Papers M26/6/107
          G 71/6 'Roade Book'
          T24/2 Bundle of Deeds relating to Farms called Caitack and Tykennol in Longtown
          G 71/1, Churchwarden's Accounts, 1798 -1846
          BB2/21-39, Olchon Deeds, 1752-1875
          M26/6/83. Conditions of sale of Timber
Longleat   DU/ VOL XVII Rental of Ewias Lacy on the behalf of Robert Dudley, Earl of Leicester
          (Transcribed by Dewi Williams)
NLW   Schedule of the Baker-Gabb Papers, Deeds and documents. No. 134
          Lord Oxford's tithe estate, 'Schedule of contract, lands in Jointure to Madam Colt, wife of
             John Dutton Colt, Esq.'
          The records of the Brecon Probate registry for Ewyas Lacy.
          SD/CCB(G)/664; SD/PDM, no. 62; SD/P/1139; SD/P/2780 and 2781; SD/QA/180;
             SD/QAB/(A)/29; SD/QAB/(A)/38; SD/QA/180; SD/RC/19
          Bishop's Visitations. SD/QA/181
          Bishop's Transcripts - Swansea and Brecon, Clodock Parish Registers
          SD/CCB(G)/344, 468; Schedule of Baker-Gabb papers, no. 138, 'Schedule of contract,
             lands in jointure to Madam Colt'
          Bishop's and Archdeacon's Visitation. Abstracts of Presentments, Brecon, 1699-1727;
             1728-1749 and 1750-1789; SD/CCB/various

ODP   Local History report

PRO   Bx/23/84; RD/JGW/35/98-99. 5th April 1813. Estate of Thomas Higgins, 1800-1820, 'Sale conditions of oaks on Brazenolls estate, Llanveynoe'.

TNA   The records of the Prerogative Court of Canterbury

Unpublished Theses and Research papers

Fisher, R.   'A study of political allegiance among members of two related West Country families: the Balles and the Cookes during the 17th Century' (1995)

Flower-Smith R.P.   'Landowners on The Devon and Somerset Border: 1660-1715', (PhD Thesis, University of Exeter, 1996)

Bowen Williams, Dewi   Unpublished material from the Longleat Collection

Published material

The Concise Dictionary of National Biography (OUP)

Kelly's Directory

Addy, John   *Death, Money and the Vultures* (Routledge, 1992)

Andrews, C.B. (ed)   *The Torrington Diaries* (1954)

Arkell, Evans and Goose (eds)   *When Death do us part* (Oxford, reprint 2004)

Aubrey, John   *Brief Lives* (The Cresset Press, 1949)

Baker-Gabb, R.   *The Families of Bailey Baker and Baker Gabb* (Abergavenny, 1903)

Barry, J.   *Introduction to Bristol Probate Inventories, Part III*, George, E. and S., (eds) (The Bristol Record Society, 2008)

Barry J.   'The Seventeenth and Eighteen Centuries' in *Unity and Variety*, Nicholas Orme (ed) (Exeter Studies in History No. 29, University of Exeter Press, 1991)

Bate, F.   *The Declaration of Indulgence* (1672)

Bates Harbin, E.H.   'History of the Manor of Newton Surmaville' in *Somerset Archeological and Natural History Society*, Vol. 56 (1910) pt. 2

Beale, C.   *Champagne and Shambles* (Gloucestershire, 2006)

Bebb, E.D.   *Nonconformity and Social and Economic Life, 1660-1800* (Philadelphia, 1935, reprint 1980)

Best, G.F.A.,   *Temporal Pillars* (CUP, 1964)

Bowden, P. (ed)   'Economic Change, Wages, Profits and Rents, 1500-1750', in Thirsk (ed) *The Agrarian History of England and Wales,* Vol. v

Brears, P.   *Food and Cooking in the 17th century* (English Heritage, 1985)

Browning, Andrew (ed)   *English Historical Documents 1660-1714*, Vol. VI

Burnett, D.   *Longleat* (1979)

Bush, R.   *Somerset* (The Dovecote Press, 1994)

Campbell, B. and Overton, M.   'A New Perspective on Medieval and Early Modern Agriculture' in *Past and Present*, 141 (1993)

Campbell, M.   *The English Yeoman* (The Merlin Press, 1983)

Charters and Hay, (eds)   *English Rural Society, 1500-1800* (Cambridge, 1990)

Chisolm, K.   *Wits and Wives* (2011)

Clark, J.   *A General View of the Agriculture of the County of Hereford* (1794)

Coates, S.D., and Tucker, D.G.   *Water-mills of the Monnow and Trothy* (Monmouth District Museum Service, Gwent, 1978)

Collier, J.P. (ed)   *The Egerton Papers* (The Camden Society, 1840 (reprint))

Copplestone-Crow, B.   *Herefordshire Place Names* (1989)

Cox, J. and N.   'Probate 1500-1800: A System in Transition' in Arkell *et al* (eds), *When Death us do Part* (Oxford, reprint 2004)

Crook, J.M. (ed)   *Bedford College* (2001)

Cruickshanks, Handley *et al* (eds)   *The History of Parliament, The House of Commons, 1690-1715* (CUP, 2002)

Defoe, Daniel   *A Tour of England and Wales*, Vol. II (The Folio Society, 1983)

Ditchfield, G.M.   *The Evangelical Revival* (UCL, 1998)

Dodds, J.P.   'Hereford Agriculture in the Mid-Nineteenth Century' in *Transactions of the Woolhope Naturalists' Field Club* (1980)

Downing, S. J.   *Fashion in the Time of Jane Austen* (Shire Books, reprint 2011)

Duncumb, J.   *Collections towards the History and Antiquities of the County of Hereford* (Hereford, 1812)

Eisel, J. and Bennet, F.   *The Pubs of Hay-on-Wye and the Golden Valley* (Logaston Press, 2005)

Elliot, N.   *Dore Workhouse in Victorian Times*

Ellis, M.   *Using Manorial Records*, PRO Publications (revised edition, 1997)

Erickson, A.L.   *Women and Property in Early Modern England* (Routledge, 1995, reprint 2005)

Faraday, M.A. (ed)   *Herefordshire Militia Assessments of 1663* (Royal Historical Society, 1972)

Fletcher, C.R.L.   *An Introductory History of England*, Vol. II (1907)

Glendinning, V.   *Jonathan Swift* (1998)

Gordon, A.   *Freedom After Ejection* (Belfast, 1917)

Green, D.   *Queen Anne* (History Book Club, reprint 1971)

Gritt, A.J.   'The Census and the Servant: A Reassessment of the Decline and Distribution' in *The Economic History Review*, new series, vol. 53, No. 1 (Feb., 2000)

Gwilym-Jones, Rev. D.B   *The Parish Church of Sant Clydawg* (privately printed)

Hainsworth, D.R.   *Stewards, Lords and People* (CUP, 1992)

Hillaby, J.   'Hereford Gold: Irish, Welsh and English land' in *Transactions of the Woolhope Naturalists' Field Club*, Vol. XLV

Hoskins, W.G.   *The making of the English Landscape* (Leicester, 1950)

James, D.   'Dendrochronology in Herefordshire' in *Essays in Honour of Jim and Muriel Tonkin*, Rosalind Lowe (ed) (Woolhope Naturalists' Field Club, 2011)

Jenkins, P.   *The Making of a Ruling Class, 1640-1790* (1983)

Jones, E.L.   'Agricultural Conditions and Changes in Herefordshire, 1660-1815' in *Transactions of the Woolhope Naturalists' Field Club*, Vol. XXXVII (1961-63)

Jones, J. (ed)   *Monmouthshire Wills, 1560-1601* (South Wales Record Society, 1997)

Kussmaul, A.   *A General View of the Rural Economy of England, 1538-1840* (CUP, 1990)

Langford, P.   *A Polite and Commercial People* (OUP, reprint 1990)

Latham, J.   *Happy Families* (1974)

Laurence, A.   *Women in England* (1995)

Llewellin, Revd F.G.   *The History of St Clodock, British King and Martyr* (Manchester, 1919)

Longtown and District Historical Society   *In the Shadow of the Black Mountains*, Vol. II

Marshall, G.	'The Occupation of lands in the Golden Valley, Ewyas and Clifford and their motte and bailey castles' in *Transactions of the Woolhope Naturalists' Field Club* (1936-38)
Matthews, A.G.	*Walker Revised* (Oxford, 1948)
Matthews, A.G.	*Calumy Revised* (Oxford, 1934)
McInnes, A.	*Robert Harley* (1970)
Mingay, G.E.,	*The Gentry, the Rise and Fall of a Ruling Class* (1976)
Mingay, G.E.	*Agrarian History*, VI, 1750-1850, (CUP, 1989)
Morrill, S.	'Poor Law in Herefordshire, 1836-1851' in *Transactions of the Woolhope Naturalists' Field Club*, Vol. XLI (1974)
Morris, M.G.R. (ed)	*Romilly's Visits to Wales, 1827-1854* (Llandysul, 1998)
Newman, R.	'Sir Ralph Hopton- Lord Hopton, Ist Baron of Stratton', www.newman-family-tree-net
Oman, C.	*Nelson* (The Reprint Society, 1950)
Overton, M.	'A New Perspective on Medieval and Early Modern Agriculture, Six centuries of Norfolk Farming, c.1250-c.1850' in *Past and Present*, No. 141 (Nov., 1993)
Overton, M.	*Agricultural Revolution in England*, (CUP, 1996)
Overton, M. (ed)	*Production and Consumption in English Households* (Routledge, 2004)
Page, W. (ed)	Victoria History of the County of Hereford (1908), vol.1
Peare, C.O.	*William Penn* (1959)
Plant, D.	'Biography of Sir Ralph Hopton', British Civil Wars and Commonwealth website
Prior, M.	*Women in English Society, 1500-1800* (Methuen, 1985)
Purcell, M.	*From Bury to Bromham* in National Trust, Houses and Collections Annual, 2010
Raymond, S.A.	*Words from Wills* (The Federation of Family History Societies 2004)
Richardson, R.E.	*Mistress Blanche, Queen Elizabeth's Confidante* (Logaston Press, reprint 2008)
Roberts, S.K.	*Recovery and Restoration in an English County* (Exeter, 1985)
Robinson, C.J.	*A History of the Mansions and Manors of Herefordshire,* (Logaston Press, 2003)
Roscoe, E.S.	*Robert Harley, Earl of Oxford* (Methuen, 1902)
Rose, K.	*The Later Cecils* (1975)
Rouse, A.L.	*The England of Elizabeth* (reprint, 1953)
Smith, L.A.J.	*Goods by the Mrs* (privately printed, 2005)
Sparrow, T.	*A Brief History of Badsey and Aldington* (Badsey Society, 2002)
St. Clare Byrne, M. (ed)	*The Lisle Letters*, (The University of Chicago Press, 1983)
Stanadic N.	'Middle Rank Consumers & Domestic Culture in Edinburgh and Glasgow, 1720-1840' in *Past and Present*, Nov. 1994)
Stanes, R. and Wyatt, P. (eds)	*Uffculme, A Peculiar Parish* (Exeter, 1997)
Stanes, R.	*The Old Farm* (Devon Books, 1990)
Steer, F.W.	*Farm and Cottage Inventories of Mid Essex, 1635-1749* (2nd ed. Phillimore & Co. Ltd, 1969)
Stephens, M.	*Book of Wales: an Anthology* (Harper Collins, 1989)
Stone, L.	'Social Mobility in England, 1500-1700', in *Past and Present*, 33 (1966)

Stone, L. and Fawtier Stone, J.	*An Open Elite* (OUP, 1986)
Styles, J.	*The Dress of the People* (Yale University Press, 2nd ed. 2010)
Temperley, N.	*The Music of the Parish Church* (CUP, 1979)
Thirsk, J. (ed)	*Agrarian History of England and Wales, Vol v, pt I 1640 to 1750*, (CUP, 1985)
Thirsk, J.	*The Rural Economy of England* (1984)
Thompson, D. (ed)	*Change and Tradition in Rural England* (Cambridge, 1980)
Thoresby-Jones, P.	*Welsh Border Country* (Face of Britain series, Batsford, 1938)
Tonkin, J.W.	'The Goods and Chattels of our Forefathers, 1660-1760', and 'An Introduction to the Houses of Herefordshire', in the *Transactions of the Woolhope Naturalists' Field Club*, Vol. XXXIX (1968, part II)
Tonkin, J.W.	'The Goods and Chattels of our Forefathers, 1660-1760', in *Transactions of the Woolhope Naturalists' Field Club*, Vol. XLV (1985/87)
Tonkin, M.	'Herefordshire Toll-Houses – Then and Now' in *Transactions of the Woolhope Naturalists' Field Club*, Vol. XLVIII (1996)
Trinder, B.	'Food in Probate Inventories, 1660-1750' in *The Local Historian*, Vol. 38, No.1 (February 2008)
Turner, M.	*The Economic History Review*, 2nd ser. Vol. 35, no. 4 (Nov. 1982)
Vincent Evans, E.	*Episcopal Register of St Davids*, vol. 2 (1397-1518)
Vipont, E.	*The Story of Quakerism, 1652-1952* (reprint 1955)
Walker, J.	*An Attempt towards recovering an Account of the Numbers and Sufferings of the Clergy of the Church of England* (1714)
Webb, J. and T.W.	*The Civil War in Herefordshire, vol.1* (1879)
Wedell, N.	*Ewyas Lacy and the Origin of Longtown* (privately published, 1998)
Whitehead, D.	'Holme Lacy House', in *Essays in Honour of Jim and Muriel Tonkin*, Rosalind Lowe (ed) (Woolhope Naturalists' Field Club, 2011)
Whiteman, A. (ed)	*The Compton Census of 1676* (1986)
Yellings, J.A.	*Agricultural History Review* (1973)
Young, D.	*The Origin and History of Methodism in Wales and the Borders* (1893)

.

References

Preface

1. Tonkin, J.W. 'The Goods and Chattels of our Forefathers, 1660-1760', *Woolhope Transactions*, vol. XLV, 1985/87, pp.13-35.
2. Overton, Mark, *Agricultural Revolution in England*, (CUP, 1996), p.131.

Chapter 1 The Early History of Ewyas Lacy

1. Church leaflet by Gwen Moore; '9th century Tombstone from Clodock', *Transactions of the Woolhope Naturalists' Field Club*, (1959), p.239.
2. Keith Ray in *The Early Church in Herefordshire* (ed. Leominster History Study Group, 2000); Watkins, Alfred *The Old Standing Crosses of Herefordshire* (1930), p.49; Flower-Smith, P. Llanveynoe church leaflet.
3. Llewellin, F.G. *The History of St Clodock, British King and Martyr*, (Manchester, 1919), p.53.
4. National heritage site, Scheduled monuments; *Tonkin*, Herefordshire p.172; Shoesmith, Ron, *Castles and Moated Sites of Herefordshire*, (Logaston Press, 1996), pp.7, 9, 12, 220, 221; Hillaby, Joe, 'Hereford Gold: Irish, Welsh and English Land, Part 2', *Transactions of the Woolhope Naturalists's Field Club*, (1985), pp.193-270.
5. Shoesmith, *Castles*, pp.169,173,174; Tonkin, J.W., *Herefordshire*, (1977), pp.172,173
6. Llewellin, p.74.
7. Pevsner, p.241, 242; Ellis, P., 'Longtown Castle. A report on Excavations done by J. Nicholls, 1978', *Transactions of the Woolhope Naturalists's Field Club*, (1997), p.78; Shoesmith, *Castles*, pp.33, 35, 37, 39.
8. Hutchison, Carole, The order of grandmont, www.. newadvent.org/cathen/06725c.
9. Llewellin, p.99.
10. Webb, J. & T., *The Civil War in Herefordshire*, Vol. 1, (1879), pp.7-10.
11. I have drawn on several sources here including the Local History report for the Olchon Development Project, Nina Wedell's *Ewyas Lacy and the Origin of Longtown* and my own introduction to the Longtown History web site (see www.lhsarchive. org.uk. For the Norman period and the De Lacys the reader is directed to Joe Hillaby's paper in the *Transactions of the Woolhope Naturalists Field Club*, 'Hereford Gold: Irish, Welsh and English land', Vol. XLV: 193-270.
12. Webb, *The Civil War in Herefordshire*, pp.197, 231.
13. Duncumb, John, *General View of the Agriculture of the County of Hereford*, (1805), p.66.
14. Mingay, G.E. *Agrarian History*, Vol. VI, 1750-1850, p.174; Thompson, Denys (ed) *Change and Tradition in Rural England* (Cambridge, 1980), pp.91, 92.
15. HRO. Harleian Papers, Methuen & Co (1902), bundle 16, p.3.
16. Llewellin, pp.89, 69.
17. Delorme, Mary, 'A Watery Paradise; Rowland Vaughan and Hereford's Golden Vale' *History Today*, 39: 7 (1989, July) pp.38-43.
18. I am grateful to my husband for drawing my attention to this will and for transcribing the wills from the National Archives, some of which were used in this study.
19. Overton, Mark, 'A New Perspective on Medieval and Early Modern Agriculture, Six centuries of Norfolk Farming, c.1250-c.1850', *Past and Present*, no. 141 (Nov., 1993), pp.38-105.
20. Mingay, *Agrarian History*, Vol. VI, 1750-1850, p.854.
21. Kussmaul, Anne, *A General View of the Rural Economy of England*, 1538-1840 (C.U.P. 1990) p.72.
22. Mingay, *Agrarian History*, Vol. VI, 1750-1850, p.337
23. Thirsk, J*., Agrarian History*, Vol. VI, I, p.228; Overton, 'A New Perspective', *Past and Present*, pp.38-105.
24. Mingay, *Agrarian History*, Vol. VI, p.315.
25. Mingay, *Agrarian History*, Vol. VI, pp.270-1; Jones, E.L. 'Agricultural Conditions and Changes in Herefordshire, 1660-1815', *The Woolhope Club Transactions* XXXV11 (1961-63), pp.32-55.
26. Kussmaul, *A General View*, pp.88, 113.
27. Jones, 'Agricultural Conditions', p.35.
28. Jones, 'Agricultural Conditions', p.33.
29. Faraday, M., 'Herefordshire taxes in the reign of Henry VIII', *Transactions of the Woolhope Naturalists Field Club*, vol. 53 (2005), p.11.
30. Cwmbran Record Office. Abergavenny Leases, D1583, 3, 35, 36.
31. Jones, Judith, (ed), *Monmouthshire Wills, 1560-1601,* South Wales Record Society (1997).
32. My thanks to Dewi Williams for this quote; Webb, J and T. *The Civil War in Herefordshire, vol.1* (1879), p.11.

Chapter 2 Probate

1. In all probability he was the Earl of Oxford's steward (ref. HRO.Harleian Manuscripts, Bundle 17).

2. Erickson, Amy, 'Using Probate Accounts', in T. Arkell et al (eds), *When Death us do Part* (Oxford, reprint 2004), p.104.

3. Stanes, R. and Wyatt, P. (eds), *Uffculme, A Peculiar Parish* (Exeter, 1997) p.6.

4. Erickson, Amy, *Women and Property in Early Modern England* (reprint, 2002), p.27.

5. Cox, Jeff and Nancy, 'Probate 1500-1800: A System in Transition' in Arkell, *When Death us do Part,* p.20.

6. Ibid., pp.20, 21, 36, 107; Erickson, 'Using Probate Accounts', p.103.

7. Morris, M.G.R.(ed) Romilly's *Visits to Wales, 1827-1854* (Llandysul, Ceredigion, 1998), p.63.

8. Cox, Nancy and Jeff, 'Probate Inventories', part one and part two, in *The Local Historian* (August 1984, vol. 16, nos 3 and 4), p.133.

9. Spufford, Margaret in Charters and Hay, eds, *English Rural Society, 1500-1800* (Cambridge, 1990), pp.144, 145, 146; Cox, Jeff and Nancy, 'Probate' in *When Death do us Part,* pp.32, 30.

10. Overton, Mark, 'Prices from Probate Inventories' in *When Death do us Part,* p.125.

11. Erickson, *Women and Property,* p.33.

12. Arkell, 'The Probate Process', in *When Death do us part*, p.12.

Chapter 3 The Landowners of Ewyas Lacy

1. The steward, by the 18th century, was usually a local solicitor or attorney. Earlier, there are accounts of a Welsh attack on the castle at Clodock in 1146. This was almost certainly the castle at Pont Hendre. FN. Duncumb, p.277 (1818); Wedell, Nina, 'Ewyas Lacy and the origin of Longtown', p.20 (privately published, 1998). A lane called 'King Street' close to another castle at Ewyas Harold may have been the route taken by Henry to Clodock.

2. Llewellin, F.G., *The History of St. Clodock, British King and Martyr* (Manchester, 1919) p.94.

3. Copplestone-Crow, Bruce, *Herefordshire Place Names* (1989); Hillaby, Joe, 'Hereford Gold, Welsh and English Land', Part 2, pp.193-270; Marshall, George, 'The Occupation of lands in the Golden Valley, Ewyas and Clifford and their motte and bailey castles', *Transactions of the Woolhope Naturalist Field Club*, 1936-38, pp.141-158. FN. Duncumb, John, *Collections towards the History and Antiquities of the County of Hereford* (Hereford, 1812) p.270; Richardson, Ruth Elizabeth, *Mistress Blanche, Queen Elizabeth's Confidante*, (Logaston Press, reprint 2008) pp.13, 14; *Dictionary of National Biography*, p.2162.

4. Debrett's *Peerage, Baronetage, Knightage and Companionage* (1919) p.20; Cunningham, Peter,

Letters of Horace Walpole (Edinburgh, 1906), Vol. VIII, p.412. The Braose family originally held the title, but did not use it as it was a lesser title than their other title, Lords of Brecon. Once again heiresses come into the picture when one of their heiresses brought the castle of Abergavenny to Sir William Cantelupe, who was then created Lord Bergavenny by Henry III in the 13th century. However the title fell into disuse again until it was conferred on Sir William Beauchamp in 1392 in the reign of Richard II. Elizabeth, his granddaughter, another heiress, took the title and half the manor of Ewyas Lacy to the Neville family on her marriage to Sir Edward Neville, though they were not fully in possession until a petition to HenryVIII restored the lordship to their grandson, George Neville (1440-1492). His son, Edward, became the 3rd Baron Bergavenny and fought for Edward IV. FN. Luminarium Project, 'Wars of the Roses'; Thomas Moule, *English Counties Delineated*, Vol.2. Monmouthshire (1837)

5. St. Clare Byrne, Muriel (ed), *The Lisle Letters* (1983) pp xviii, 390, 410.

6. Burnett, David, *Longleat* (1979), pp.15, 16, 17, 19.

7. Rowse, A.L., *The England of Elizabeth* (reprint, 1953), p.369.

8. Williams, Dewi, 'Rental of Ewias Lacy on the behalf of Robert Dudley, Earl of Leicester', Longleat DU/VOL. XVII, pp.40, 41, 42, 43.

9. Bush, Robin, *Somerset*, p.238.

10. Plant, David, 'Biography of Sir Ralph Hopton, British Civil Wars and Commonwealth website, pp.1-3; Newman, Richard, 'Sir Ralph Hopton-Lord Hopton, Ist Baron of Stratton', www.newman-family-tree/net; see 'Rental' of 1653.

11. Cruickshanks, Eveline, et al (eds), *The House of Commons, 1690-1715*, Vol. 4, pp.481, 482; HRO, BB2/21-39, Olchon Deeds, 1752-1875.

12. Duncumb, *Collections*, pp.292, 293.

13. Duncumb, *Collections,* p.291; Richardson, *Mistress Blanche*, p.14.

14. Duncumb, *Collections*, p.298.

15. It was probably the Vaughans who owned it first, then the Reeces.

16. NLW, Schedule of the Baker-Gabb Papers, Deeds and documents. No. 134; Duncumb, *Collections,* pp.279, 280, 284.

17. NLW, Baker-Gabb papers, ref. no. 196; The title of Earl of Oxford became extinct in the 19th century on the death of the 6th earl in 1853.

18. Jenkins, Philip, *The making of a ruling class, 1640-1790* (1983), pp.125, 127-9, 137-8; HRO. Harleian Papers, Bundle 17 and 16; Parliamentary History, Members, v. IV, pp. 233, 276. HMC vol

29 (1901); NLW, Schedule of Baker-Gabb papers, no.138; Laurence, Anne, *Women in England, 1500-1700* (1995), p.231.

19. *Concise Dictionary of National Biography*, Vol. 1 (O.U.P., 1992), p.74.

20. McInnes, Agnes, *Robert Harley* (1970), p.175.

21. Jones, E.L., 'Agricultural Conditions and Changes in Herefordshire, 1660-1815', *Transactions of the Woolhope Naturalists Field Club*, 1961-63, pp.32-49.

22. Baker-Gabb, R., *The Families of Bailey Baker and Baker Gabb,* Abergavenny (1903), p.49; see deposition, when Job Gilbert was 57 years old, BR/1734/9. In the early 19th century the steward was Baker Gabb, gent. FN. HRO. Manor of Ewyas Lacy. Court Books J91/1-4.

23. Hainsworth, D.R., *Stewards, Lords and People* (C.U.P., 1992), pp.27-45.

24. This was an old Saxon term for a district containing ten households.

25. Ellis, Mary, *Using Manorial Records*, PRO Publications (revised edition, 1997), pp.48, 49.

26. HRO, Manor of Ewyas Lacy Court Books, J91/1-4.

27. Longleat DU/VOL. XVII. Rental of Ewias Lacy on the behalf of Robert Dudley, Earl of Leicester. My thanks are due to Dewi Williams for this information.

28. HRO, Court Rolls J91/1 and 2.

29. Gwent Record Office, Abergavenny Leases, D.1583.2.12.

30. Gwent Record Office, Sir Trevor Williams Survey of Ewyas Lacy, article 5; HRO, Court Rolls J91/1 and 2.

31. Hainsworth, *Stewards*, pp.207, 226.

32. Hainsworth, *Stewards,* p.240.

33. HRO, M26/6/83. Conditions of sale of Timber; M26/6/107.

34. Andrews, C. Bruyn, (ed), *The Torrington Diaries* (1954), pp.203, 204.

35. Oman, Carola, *Nelson* (The Reprint Society, 1950), p.439.

36. Powys Record Office, RD/JGW/35/98-99. 5 April 1813. Estate of Thomas Higgins, 1800-1820. Sale conditions of oaks on Brazenolls estate, Llanveynoe. (A 'maiden' oak was a standard that had not been coppiced.)

37. *Transactions of the Woolhope Naturalists Field Club,* 1936, pp.33, 34.

38. Page, William (ed), *Victoria History of the County of Hereford* (1908), vol.1, p.410.

39. Fisher, R., 'A study of political allegiance among members of two related west country families: the Balles and Cookes during the 17th century', unpublished study (1995), pp.190, 191.

40. Duncumb, *Collections*, p.291.

41. NLW, Baker Gabb catalogue of Abergavenny lands, p.91, no.138.

42. NLW, Lord Oxford's tithe estate, 'Schedule of contract, lands in Jointure to Madam Colt, wife of John Dutton Colt, Esq.'

43. Gwent Record Office, Abergavenny Releases, Renewals, etc., 1583.229.002-008.

44. Duncumb, *Collections*, Part I of Vol. II, p.291.

45. HRO, Sir George Cornwall, Correspondence, AF 57/5/8.

46. HRO, Moccas Collection, Correspondence, J56/III/106.

47. Historical Manuscripts Commission Reports, Portland Papers (1901), Vol. 29, pp.xvii, 323, 377.

48. HRO, Harleian Files, Bundle 9; Duncumb, *Collections*, p.294.

49. HRO, Scudamore Correspondence, M26/6/104-206.

50. Gwent Record Office, Baker-Gabb Collection, Miscellaneous.

51. Fisher, R., pp.223, 225; Henning, III, p.72.

Chapter 4 The Gentry

1. Mingay, G.E, *The Gentry, the Rise and Fall of a Ruling Class* (1976), p.2.

2. Jenkins, Philip, *The Making of a Ruling Class* (1983), p.30.

3. Flower-Smith, P., 'Landowning on the Devon and Somerset Border, 1660-1715', PhD. Thesis, University of Exeter, 1996, p.10; Mingay, *Gentry*, p.5.

4. Bates Harbin, E.H., 'History of the Manor of Newton Surmaville', SAHNS, 56 (1910), pt 2, pp.1-30.

5. Faraday, M.A. (ed), *Herefordshire Militia Assessments of 1663*, Royal Historical Society, 1972, p.50.

6. Stone, Lawrence and Fawtier Stone, Jeanne, *An Open Elite* (O.U.P., 1986), p.6.

7. Roberts, S.K., *Recovery and Restoration in an English County* (Exeter, 1985), pp.72-8.

8. Tonkin, J, 'The Goods and Chattels of our Forefathers, 1660-1760', *Transactions of the Woolhope Naturalists' Field Club,* 1985/87, pp.13-35.

9. Stone, L. & F., *An Open Elite*, p.180; Robinson, Charles J. (Revd), *A History of the Mansions and Manors of Herefordshire* (Logaston Press, Herefordshire Family History Society, 2003), p.322.

10. Robinson in *A History of the Mansions,* adds that in 1652 the chief owners in Walterstone were John Delahay, gent and the Earl of Salisbury, son of Sir Robert Cecil, younger son of Lord Burleigh.

11. Rose, Kenneth, *The later Cecils,* (1975), p.5.
12. Hoskyns, a canon of Hereford and vicar of Ledbury, is mentioned by John Aubrey in *Brief Lives*, p.201.
13. Robinson, *Mansions and Manors*, p.322.
14. HMC reports, vol. 29 (1901) VII, *Portland Papers*, p.471.
15. Hereford Cathedral Archives, Charity Report, pp.259, 260.
16. Verch means 'daughter of', and vach means 'small', in Welsh.
17. This is one of only a handful of inventories surviving for the area at the National Archives, Kew.
18. I am grateful to Dewi Bowen Williams for this reference.
19. Stone, L., 'Social Mobility in England, 1500-1700', *Past and Present*, 33 (1966), pp.16-55.
20. Stone, *Open Elite*, pp.61, 56.
21. There is an account of this in the 'Sin and the Churchwardens' chapter.

Chapter 5 Agriculture

1. Defoe, Daniel, *A Tour of England and Wales*, V.ii (The Folio Society, 1983) p.186; Webb, Revd J. and T.W., *Memorials of the Civil War between King Charles I and the Parliament of England*, Vol.i (1879), pp.2-8; Jones, E.L. 'Agricultural Conditions and Changes in Herefordshire, 1660-1815', *Transactions of The Woolhope Naturalists' Field Club*, vol. xxxvii (1961-63), p.32-50; Clark, John, *A General View of the Agriculture of the County of Hereford* (1794), pp.33, 51; Page, William, *Victoria History of the County of Hereford*, (1908), p.413; Emery, *The Agrarian History of England and Wales*, V. chap.12, pp.393-426.
2. Olchon Development Project, Local History Report (2) Field name Survey. This useful survey also produced several names denoting flax production.
3. Duncumb, John, *Collections towards the History and Antiquities of the County of Hereford*, p.173.
4. Thirsk, Joan (ed.), *The Agrarian History of England and Wales*, V, 1640-1750 (Cambridge, 1985).
5. Emery, Frank, *Agrarian History*, chap. 12, pp.393-426.
6. Longtown and District Historical Society, *In the Shadow of the Black Mountains,* Vol.ii (2008).
7. Clarke, *General View*, pp.51-2; Page, *Victoria History*, p.413; Webb, *Memorials*, Vol.i, pp.6-7.
8. Tonkin, Muriel, 'Herefordshire Toll-Houses – Then and Now (1996), pp.398-433, *Transactions of the Woolhope Naturalists' Field Club*, Vol. XLVIII, 1996, part III; Tonkin, J.W., *Herefordshire*, (1977), p.164.
9. I am indebted for information on this subject to Mildred Campbell's *The English Yeoman* (The Merlin Press, 1983).
10. Gritt, A.J. 'The Census and the Servant: A Reassessment of the Decline and Distribution'. *The Economic History Review*, new series, vol.53, No.1 (Feb., 2000), pp.84-106.
11. Olchon Development Project and the Local History report 2.
12. Dodd, J. Phillip, 'Herefordshire Agriculture in the Mid-Nineteenth Century', *Transactions of the Woolhope Naturalists' Field Club*, 1980, p.210.
13. Page, *Victoria History*, p.412, and Overton, M., p.126
14. Bowden, Peter (ed), 'Economic Change, Wages, Profits and Rents, 1500-1750, *The Agrarian History of England and Wales*, Vol.V, p.201; Page, *Victoria History*, p.413.
15. Tonkin, J.W., 'Houses of Herefordshire', *Transactions of the Woolhope Naturalists' Field Club*, 1968, Part II, pp. 186-197; Thirsk, J.,*The Rural Economy of England*, pp.376, 384, 393-6.
16. Cwmbran Record Office, Baker-Gabb Collection, D7. Misc. Letter of 25 Sep. 1861.
17. I am grateful to the Longtown History Society and the 'Olchon Development Project' for this information on p.21.
18. Thirsk, *Agrarian History*, p.228; Campbell, Bruce and Overton, Mark, 'A New Perspective on Medieval and Early Modern Agriculture', *Past and Present*, p.80.
19. Page, *Victoria History*, p.409.
20. Duncumb, *Collections*, pp.311, 177; Mingay, *Agrarian History of England and Wales*, V1, 1750-1850, pp.164, 165; Jones, 'Agricultural Conditions, p.36.
21. A 'bucke' was a basket.
22. A coule was an open tub used for cooling in brewing or butter-making.
23. Mingay, *Agrarian History*, pp.270, 271. Mingay gives a figure of 14s per hogshead set by dealers in Hereford in 1784.
24. Clarke, *General View*, p.41.
25. Obtained from the *Mid Wales Journal*, 25 Feb. 2000, and quoted in *Welsh Border Country*, Face of Britain series (Batsford, 1938).
26. Clarke, *General View*, pp.18, 20, 69; Michael Turner, *The Economic History Review*, 2nd ser. Vol.35, no.4 (Nov. 1982) pp.489- 510; Yellings, J.A., *Agricultural History Review*, (1973) pp.18-34.
27. NLW, SD/CCB/G 468 (a-b), David Jenkins, farmer of tithes of Turnant barne, v. John Powell of Longtown.
28. Bowden, *Economic Change*, pp.189, 190, 197.
29. Bowden, *Economic Change*, pp.211, 230.

30. Jones, 'Agricultural Conditions', p47; *The Hereford Times*, Thursday, 17 August 2006.
31. Bowden, *Economic Change*, pp.214, 235.
32. Clarke, *General View*, pp.27, 28.
33. Jones, 'Agricultural Conditions', p.21; Gwent Record Office, Cwmbran, under Lord Abergavenny's Leases.
34. Bowden, *Economic Change*, pp.19, 191; Langford, Paul, *The Excise Crisis*, pp.23, 4.
35. Page, *Victoria History*, p.410.

Chapter 6 Tinker, Tailor ... Hammerman

1. Arkell, T. et al, *When Death Us Do Part* (Oxford, reprint 2004), p.84.

2. Jim Tonkin in his report of 1999, and the Royal Commission for Historic Monuments
3. Coates, S.D. and Tucker, D.G., *Water-mills of the Monnow & Trothy (*Monmouth District Museum Service, Gwent, 1978), pp.5-30 This is an invaluable guide to the mills of the region.
4. Coates and Tucker, *Water Mills*, pp.40-47.
5. Arkell, *When Death Us Do Part*, p.81.
6. Wikipedia / *Tanning*.
7. Cruickshanks, E., Handley, S., Hayton, D.W. (eds) *History of Parliament*, vol. 111, p.1058.
8. A bark mill was used to crush the oak bark for the tanning pits, and was probably driven by a horse.
9. Hereford Cathedral Archives, Charity report.
10. NLW, SD/CCB(G)/764.
11. Eisel, John and Bennett, Frank, *The Pubs of Hay-on-Wye and the Golden Valley* (Logaston Press, 2005), p.5.
12. Eisel and Bennett, *The Pubs of Hay-on-Wye*, pp.88, 92, 93.
13. Eisel and Bennett, *The Pubs of Hay-on-Wye*, pp.93, 94.
14. Eisel and Bennett, *The Pubs of Hay-on-Wye*, pp.93, 96-97.
15. Powys County Archives, RD/JGW/ 98-99.

Chapter 7 Women, Wives and Widows

1. Laurence, Anne, *Women in England*, (1995), pp.144, 165.
2. Laurence, *Women in England,* pp.165, 166.
3. Langford, Paul, *A Polite and Commercial People* (OUP, reprint 1990), p.110.
4. Laurence, *Women in England*, p.244.
5. Laurence, *Women in England*, p.251.
6. Chisolm, Kate, *Wits and Wives*, (2011), p.23.
7. Prior, Mary, *Women in English Society, 1500-1800*, p.10.
8. Laurence, *Women in England*, p.167.
9. Chisolm, *Wits and Wives*, p.31; Laurence, *Women in England,* p.169.

10. Erickson, Amy Louise, *Women and Property*, (2005), p.192.
11. For further reading on Blanche see Richardson, Ruth, *Mistress Blanche, Queen Elizabeth I's Confidante* (Logaston Press, reprint 2008).
12. I am grateful to Dewi Williams for this reference which is in the papers of Robert Dudley, Earl of Leicester, held at Longleat, p.16, fol.52, p.19, fol.54.
13. Erickson, *Women and Property*, p.25.
14. Laurence, *Women in England*, p.28.
15. Laurence, *Women in England*, pp.78, 79, 30, 35, 85.
16. HRO, A95/V/W/e/13 and 216.
17. HRO, Scudamore Papers M26/6/107.
18. Erickson, *Women and Property*, p.15.
19. Erickson, *Women and Property*, p.200.
20. Gwent Record Office, Abergavenny Catalogue D.1583. 238.10.
21. Erickson, *Women and Property*, p.125.
22. In the 1851 census there was a blacksmith called Samuel Jones living there so perhaps she was his widow. Eisel, John and Bennett, Frank, *The Pubs of Hay-on-Wye and the Golden Valley* (Logaston Press, 2005), p.102.
23. The National schools were founded in 1811 by the Anglican Church, British Society schools by the nonconformist churches.

Chapter 8 The Houses of Ewyas Lacy

1. Hoskins, W.G., *The Making of the English Landscape* (Leicester, 1950); Whitehead, David, 'Holme Lacy House', in *Essays in honour of Jim and Muriel Tonkin*, (Woolhope Naturalists' Field Club, 2011), pp.69-92.
2. Arkell, Tom, 'Interpreting Probate Inventories', in Tom Arkell, Nesta Evans, and Nigel Goose, (eds,) *When Death Do Us Part* (Oxford, re-print 2004), pp.72-102.
3. James, Duncan, *Essays in Honour of Jim and Muriel Tonkin,* (Woolhope Naturalists' Field Club, 2011), p.68, fn.98.
4. HRO, G 71/6 'Roade Book'.
5. A cockloft was the space between the ceiling and the roof, perhaps an attic.
6. Erickson, A., *Women and Property in Early Modern England*, p.42; Steer, F.W., *Farm and Cottage Inventories of Mid Essex,1635-1749,* p.8; Tucker, M., 'Houses, Furnishings, and Household Equipment' in P. Wyatt and R. Stanes, (eds), *Uffculme, A Peculiar Parish* (Exeter, 1997).
7. Overton, M., 'Rooms and Room Use', in *Production and Consumption in English Households,* pp.121-136.

8. Tonkin, J.W., 'The Goods and Chattels of our Forefathers, 1660-1760', pp. 13-35; 'An Introduction to the Houses of Herefordshire', *Transactions of the Woolhope Naturalists' Field Club*, vol. xxxix, 1968, part II, pp.186-197.

9. The Herefordshire Council's Sites and Monuments Record.

10. Arkell, T, 'Interpreting Probate Inventories', in *When Death Do Us Part,* (reprint, 2004), pp.72-102.

11. Overton, M., 'English probate inventories', in *Production and Consumption in English Households*, pp.15-16.

12. Stanes, R. and Wyatt, P. (eds) *Uffculme, A Peculiar Parish* (Exeter, 1997), p.87.

13. Overton, M., 'The material culture of consumption', in *Production and Consumption in English Households,* pp.91, 92.

14. Steer, *Essex Inventories*, p.19 and Tucker, 'Houses, Furnishings and Household Equipment', p.87.

15. Overton, *Production and Consumption*, pp.91, 92.

16. Tonkin, J., 'The Goods and Chattels of Our Forefathers', *Transactions of The Woolhope Naturalists' Field Club*, vol. xlv, 1985. part I, pp.13-35.

17. Overton, *Production and Consumption*, p.143.

18. Purcell, Mark, 'From Bury to Bromham', in National Trust, Houses and Collections Annual 2010, pp.18-25.

19. Tucker, 'Houses, Furnishings, and Household Equipment', pp.89, 90.

20. In the 16th century seamen carved their own knives out of hardwood. Examples can be seen in the Mary Rose Museum; Brears, Peter, *Food and Cooking in the 17th century,* (English Heritage, 1985), p.22.

21. Chitterlings were the boiled intestines of the pig, cut into small pieces, seasoned and fried with onions and breadcrumbs. Stanes, Robin, *The Old Farm* (Devon Books, 1990), p.59.

22. Trinder, Barry, 'Food in Probate Inventories, 1660-1750', in *The Local Historian*, February 2008, vol. 38, no. 1, pp.35-48; Elliot, Nancy, *Dore Workhouse in Victorian Times;* Morrill, Sylvia, 'Poor Law in Herefordshire, 1836-1851', in *The Transactions of the Woolhope Naturalists' Field Club*, vol. xli (1974).

23. Kaye-Smith, Sheila and Stern, G.B., *Talking of Jane Austen* (1944), pp.41, 42, 43.

24. Brears, Peter, *Food and Cooking in 17th century Britain* (English Heritage booklet, 1985), p.22.

Chapter 9 Clothing and Household Linen

1. For Uffculme see Mary Fraser's study of costume in chapter 7 of *Uffculme, a Peculiar Parish;* W. Steer, *Farm and Cottage Inventories of Mid Essex, 1635-1749*, pp.44, 45.

2. A mercer sold mainly textiles but also a variety of other goods.

3. This was stout quality cotton or silk tape. See Raymond, Stuart A., *Words from Wills*, an invaluable source of information.

4. Overton, M., *Production and Consumption in English Households*, pp.55, 56.

5. The resulting popularity made Arkwright a fortune which his heir invested in land, including Hampton Court in Herefordshire.

6. Andrews, C. Bruyn (ed), *The Torrington Diaries*, vol.1, p.xvi.

7. Styles, John, *The Dress of the People* (Yale University Press, 2nd ed. 2010). I have drawn some of my material from p.109, then pp.126-31. Another excellent source, and of inestimable value for an understanding of the cloth industry, has been the late Peter Newton's chapter, 'The Woollen Cloth Industry in Uffculme', in Wyatt, P. and Stanes, R., (eds) *Uffculme: A Peculiar Parish*, (Exeter, 1997), pp. 40-68. I also drew on Mary Fraser's study of costume, in chapter 7, pp.96-110, in the same volume.

8. Collier, J. Payne, (ed), *The Egerton Papers* (The Camden Society, 1840 reprint), pp.247-256.

9. Fraser, Mary, in *Uffculme, A Peculiar Parish,* p.93.

10. Styles, *The Dress of the People*, p.34.

11. Amy Louise Erickson, *Women and Property in Early Modern England* (Routledge, London and New York, 1995), p.26.

12. Thirsk, J., *The Rural Economy of England*, (1984), pp. 235-244.

13. Styles, *The Dress of the People*, p.127.

14. Downing, Sarah Jane, *Fashion in the Time of Jane Austen* (Shire Books, reprint 2011), p.9.

15. Downing, *Fashion*, pp.13, 24, 42, 43.

16. Smith, Laurence, *Goods by the Mrs* (privately printed, 2005); Downing, *Fashion*, p.39.

17. Overton, *Production and Consumption*, p.48.

18. Webb, Revd John, *The Civil War in Herefordshire*, vol.1, p.6.

19. Newton, *Uffculme A Peculiar Parish*, pp.42-68.

20. *Uffculme*, pp.51, 50.

21. *Uffculme*, p.61

22. HRO, T24/2 Bundle of Deeds relating to Farms called Caitack and Tykennol in Longtown.

23. Coates, S.D., and Tucker, D.G., *Water-mills of the Monnow and Trothy* (Monmouth District Museum Service, Gwent, 1978), p.36.

24. *Uffculme,* p.99; In the will of Phillip Walle, bachelor, he leaves 20 pairs of gloves 'to my nearest relations'.
25. *Uffculme*, p.86
26. *Production and Consumption*, p.110.
27. Thirsk, *Rural Economy*, pp.209-213.
28. *Production and Consumption*, p.46.
29. Arkell, Tom et al, *When Death us do Part* (Oxford, 2000), p.81.
30. Past and Present, no.145 [1994] pp.122-156. Nina Stanadic's 'Middle Rank Consumers & Domestic Culture in Edinburgh and Glasow, 1720-1840'.
31. *Uffculme*, p.41; *Production and Consumption*, p.48.

Chapter 10 Clergy and Dissent

1. *Episcopal Register of St Davids*, vol.2 (1397-1518) p.789.
2. Walker, John, *An Attempt towards recovering an Account of the Numbers and Sufferings of the Clergy of the Church of England*, (1714), pp.16, 98.
3. Llewellin, F.G., *The History of Saint Clodock* (Manchester, 1919), pp.140, 148, 156, 157, 158; Gwilym-Jones, Revd D.B., *The Parish Church of Sant Clydawg* (privately printed).
4. Matthews, A.G., *Walker Revised*, (Oxford, 1948), pp.194-5.
5. Matthews, A.G., *Calumy Revised*, (Oxford, 1934), p.xii.
6. Fletcher, C.R.L., *An Introductory History of England*, Vol. II (1907), p.509.
7. Bate, Frank, *The Declaration of Indulgence,* 1672, pp. 8-16.
8. Flower-Smith, P., 'Landowning on the Devon and Somerset Border, 1660-1715', PhD Thesis, University of Exeter, 1996, p.178.
9. Bate, *The Declaration,* pp.8, 9, 15, 16, 52.
10. Best, G.F.A., *Temporal Pillars* (CUP, 1964), pp.3, 11.
11. Roscoe, E.S., *Robert Harley, Earl of Oxford*, pp.42, 100.
12. Dunning, R.W., 'Some Somerset Parishes in 1705', pp.71-92, in SANHS Proceedings, vol. 112 (1968).
13. Best, *Temporal Pillars*, pp.22, 23.
14. Glendinning, Victoria, *Jonathan Swift*, (1998).
15. NLW. SD/QA/180-181.
16. Green, David, *Queen Anne* (reprint 1971, History Book Club), pp.124, 125.
17. Dunning, 'Some Somerset Parishes in 1705', pp. 71-92; and for an interesting discussion of what was happening in Devon and Cornwall see the chapter on 'The Seventeenth and Eighteen Centuries' by Jonathan Barry, in *Unity and Variety*, (ed) Nicholas Orme (Exeter Studies in History No. 29, University of Exeter Press, 1991), pp.81-108.

18. William Symont. Will dated 6 Feb. 1622, pr. 27 Feb 1622. (mfs_clo_1107). He also owned part of the lease of the tythe corn of the parish of Grysmont (Grosmont), Monmouthshire which he left to his brother, David, and also wills that 'the lease of the tieth of Llansilloe' shall be passed to his wife for the unexpired term of the lease.
19. HRO, Harleian Papers, Bundle 16, 72.
20. NLW, SD/QAB/(A)/29.
21. NLW, SD/QAB/(A)/38.
22. NLW, SD/QA/180-1.
23. NLW, SD/P/1139.
24. A 'perpetual' curate usually served a remote parish or district not served by a rector or vicar and their income was not from tithes but from the diocese. 'Perpetual' because they could only be removed by the bishop.
25. NLW, SD/CCB(G)/664.
26. Flower-Smith, 'Landowning', p.154.
27. Young, David, *The origin and history of Methodism in Wales and the borders*, (1893), chapter 2. Walter Brute was a member of a family who were later well-known as stone masons in the area and were connections of the Gunter family of Walterstone.
28. *A Book of Wales* (Collins, reprint 1971).
29. http:baptisthistoryhomepage.com/myles.
30. HRO, SD/RC/19.
31. Browning, Andrew (ed.), Douglas, David C., *English Historical Documents*, Vol. VIII, p.414.
32. Portland MSS, vol. III, p.306.
33. Bebb, E.D., *Nonconformity and Social and Economic Life, 1660-1800* (Philadelphia, 1935, reprint 1980), pp.32, 33, 34; Whiteman, A., (ed), *The Compton Census of 1676* (1986); www.baptisthistoryhomepage.com/myles. I have Jenny Houston to thank for the latter reference.
34. wwww.exlibris.org/nonconform/engdis/anabatists.
35. Vipont, Elfrida, *The Story of Quakerism, 1652-1952* (reprint 1955), pp.15-1; Pearc, Catherine Owens, *William Penn* (1959).
36. Unfortunately there was no information on Hereford or Brecon. Bebb, Appendix V, p.179.
37. Flower-Smith, 'Landowning', p.170.
38. Gordon, Alexander, *Freedom After Ejection* (Belfast, 1917), pp.48, 305; Eveline Cruickshanks, Stuart Handley et al. (eds), *The History of Parliament, The House of Commons, 1690-1715*, (CUP, 2002), pp.1080-1087.
39. Bebb, *Nonconformity*, Appendix VII, pp.182, 183; Ditchfield, G.M., *The Evangelical Revival* (UCL, 1998), p.41.
40. Bebb, *Nonconformity*, pp.35-39.
41. NLW, SD/PDM, no. 62.
42. NLW, Bishop's Visitations. SD/QA/181.

43. Best, *Temporal Pillars*, p.14.
44. NLW, Licences/SD/SM; SD/598.
45. Llewellin, F.G., *The History of St Clodock* (Manchester, 1919), p.209.
46. HRO, F44/1/70.
47. BBC Wales History; Wikipedia.
48. Sparrow, Terry, *A Brief History of Badsey and Aldington*. I am very grateful to Jenny Houston for this and some of the other references to early Baptists and Methodists.
49. Bebb, *Nonconformity*, pp.54, 93.
50. Langford, Paul, *A Polite and Commercial People* (OUP., reprint 1990), pp.253, 256.
51. Powys Record Office, Bx/23/84.
52. This is taken from a talk given at Llanrosser Chapel by Jenny Houston on the history of Primitive Methodism.
53. Temperley, Nicholas, *The Music of the Parish Church* (CUP, 1979), pp.205; 207; Langford, *A Polite and Commercial People*, pp.250, 251.
54. Temperley, *The Music of the Parish Church*, pp.86, 88, 97, 104.
55. Llewellin, *The History of Saint Clodock*, pp.151, 152.
56. Temperley, *The Music of the Parish Church*, pp.297, 298; Wikipedia. Hymnary.org/person/Baker
57. Best, *Temporal Pillars*, p.4.
58. Llewellin, *The History of Saint Clodock,* pp.18, 189, 190.
59. NLW, SD/P/2780 and 2781; Llewellin, *The History of St Clodock*, p.187.
60. Best, *Temporal Pillars*, pp.146, 155.
61. Bebb, *Nonconformity,* pp.50, 53.
62. Best, *Temporal Pillars*, p.145, quoting the social theorist of the day Robert Southey.

Chapter 11 Sin and the Churchwardens
1. NLW, Bishop's and Archdeacon's Visitation. Abstracts of Presentments, Brecon, 1699-1727; 1728-1749 and 1750-1789, SD/CCB/various.
2. HRO, Harleian Catalogue, bundle 17, grant of seisen 1629.
3. Laurence, Anne, *Women in England, 1500-1760* (1995), p.34.
4. Laurence, *Women in England,* p.82.
5. NLW, Bishops and Archdeacons Visitation. Abstracts of Presentments, Brecon, 1699-1727, 1728-1749 and 1750-1789, SD/CCB/various.
6. NLW, BT Swansea and Brecon, Clodock Parish Registers.

7. NLW, SD/CCB/59. Clodock cases from 142.
8. NLW, SD/CCB/55.
9. NLW, SD/CCB(G)/79, 427, 847, 954.
10. Flower-Smith, P. 'Landowning on the Devon and Somerset Border' (Exeter Ph.D thesis, 1996), p.176.
11. NLW, SD/CCB(G)/344; SD/CCB/55.
12. NLW, SD/CCB/55.
13. NLW, SD/CCB(G)/344, 468; Schedule of Baker-Gabb papers, no. 138, 'Schedule of contract, lands in jointure to Madam Colt'.
14. NLW, SD/CCB(G)/664, 664a. There is no record of Thomas Allen on the Church of England database.
15. NLW, SD/CCB/56 folio 1.
16. NLW, SD/CCB(G)/764.
17. HRO, G 71/1, Churchwarden's Accounts, 1798-1846.

Chapter 12 The More Recent Past
1. May Newsletter for the district, quoting an article written by 'a Merthyr Pilgrim'; 'Black Mountain land use', *Transactions of the Woolhope Naturalists Field Club*, 1937, pp.xlv-xlvii; Dodd, J. Phillip, 'Herefordshire Agriculture in the Mid-Nineteenth Century', *Transactions of the Woolhope Naturalists Field Club*, 1980, pp.203-222.
2. Longtown & District Historical Society, Oral History Group, *In the Shadow of the Black Mountains* (2008, Longtown), v. ii, p.11. I have been grateful to be able to draw material from this excellent booklet.
3. Kelly's Directory, 1905.
4. Crook, J.M. (ed.) *Bedford College* (2001), pp.14, 20.
5. *In the Shadow of the Black Mountains,* pp. 4-5.
6. Latham, Jean, *Happy Families,* (1974), p.165.
7. *In the Shadow of the Black Mountains*, p.16.

Appendix A The Anglican clergy of Ewyas Lacy
1. Llewellin, Rev. F.G., *The History of Saint Clodock* (Manchester, 1919), pp.186, 187; NLW. SD/QAB(A)29.
2. NLW. SD/O/246.
3. NLW. SD/P/2657; NLW SD/O/598.
4. NLW. SD/O/598B.
5. Robinson, *A History of the Mansions and Manors of Herefordshire* (Logaston Press), p.322.
6. NLW. SD/P/567.
7. NLW. SD/ P/1139, 1140, 1141.

Index of People

John, vicar of Clodock, 1665
41, 181
Mary, wife of Thomas 43
Morgan, vicar of Clodock
13, 181
Walter 10, 14, 41, 145, 146,
150, 159
Delahays of Walterstone 39
Doddridge, Philip 162
Dudley, Robert, Earl of Leicester
26
Dukes, Anne, widow, 1815 94
Duncumb, John 45
Dutton Colt, Madame 170

Eagles, Revd, vicar of Clodock
163
Eastland/Estland, Henry, 1728
21, 61, 167
Edward 3rd Earl of Oxford 29
Edwards, James, accused of
defamation, 1756 167
Elizabeth I, Queen 165
Elmhurst, Mr B.D. 146
Emery, Frank 45
England, Mary, 1684 131
Eustance, Thomas, carpenter,
1725 70
Evans, David, 1729 80
Thomas at the Bryn 89
Exton, James of Michaelchurch
Escley, 1774 121
William, yeoman, of
Craswall 1711 92, 110

Farr, James, mill owner of
Michaelchurch Mill, 1840
75, 139
Farr family of Ty Craddock 161
Fiennes, Celia 86
Foley, Paul, MP, of Stoke Edith,
1697 33, 78
Philip, of Whitley Court,
1690 158
Sarah, of Whitley Court 29
Thomas, Esq, of Stoke Edith,
1690 158
Foley family, iron masters 77
Fox, George, 1652 157
Francis, Richard, yeoman, 1679
20
Robert, smith, 1803 73

Gabb, Mrs Mary, desperate
debtor, 1710 141
Gegg, Thomas, yeoman, 1632 91
George, Abraham, hatter of
Walterstone, 1710 66, 141
David, yeoman, 1636 59
Elias, farmer of Llanveynoe,
1774 119, 159
John, of Bilbo in Clodock,
1772 110
William 20
Gilbert family of Blackhill 161
family of Clodock 38
family of Clodock, Craswall
and Llanveynoe 41, 43
Gwenllian widow of
Craswall, 1689 112, 114
absent from church,
1685-86 169
Hannah, widow of Craswall,
1794 64, 88, 95, 137
Job, presented for refusing to
pay church rate, 1725 169
Job, gentleman of Craswall,
1749 14, 30, 44, 119
John, 1659/60 90
John, gentleman of Brass
Knoll 40, 43
Judith his wife 42, 44
Lewis of the Brynn 42
Lewis, 1686 89
Lewis, bailiff 30
Mary, 1830 87
Maud, spinster of Craswall,
1646 143
Gilbert, Phillip, 1796 57
Thomas, gentleman, 1657 59
William yeoman, 1731 49
William, 1737 80
William, yeoman, 1804 87
William, mason, 1816 70
William, boy, 1825 68
William, 1825 91
William, yeoman, 1839 62
Zachary, 1666 64
Gregg Thomas,yeoman, 1632 91
Griffith, Bellingham, tailor of
Clodock, 1634 140
Giles, 1663 75
Griffiths, Edward, smith, 1681 71
Elizabeth, baptism of her
base child, 1752 167
John, of Olchon 32

John, yeoman of Newton,
1821 166
Philip, 1640 20
Philip, 1799 33
Samuel, of Olchon House,
Llanveynoe, 1857 114,
173
Gunter, Catherine, 1746 73
Gurney, Mrs 97
Gwatkin, Julyan of Pontrilas 40
Gwillim family of The Wain 161
David, the older, 1832 97
John, yeoman of Longtown,
1797 73
Margaret, spinster of
Rowlestone, 1814 67
Robert of Wain Herbert,
Newton, miller, 1798 73
William, farmer, 1781 46,
64, 65
Gwyn, Nell 86

Hamilton, Lady 32
Hamilton, Sir William 32
Harley family 33, 36, 149
Brilliana 86
Edward of Brampton Bryan 28
Hon. Edward of Eywood 28,
149
Lord 35
Robert, Secretary of state,
1705 149
Harrie/Harri, Griffith, mill owner,
of Clodock, 1582 75, 88, 166
Harries, William, gentleman of
Craswall 150
Harris, Henry Thomas 44
Henry, shopkeeper 80
Hywell, preacher 160
Miss Maud of Gilbertstone 80
Mr, agent to Lord
Abergavenny 55
Thomas 44
Thomas, mercer, 1786 34,
80, 112, 127, 128-130,
132, 175
Thomas, of Clodock accused
of carrying out
marriages, 1739 169
Walter, absent from Clodock
church, 1685-86 169
Harrison, Major General Thomas
27

Index of Places

209

General Index

Rushlight 122
Rye 46, 62, 63, 64
Ryeland 8, 46, 57, 174

Sailor suit 135
Salt box 122
Salt cellar 123
Saltstone 111, 123
Scarf 132
Scudamore family of Kenchurch
    28, 32
Serge 131
Servants 67
Settle 111, 114, 116
Sewage disposal 105
Shawls 134, 135
Shears 139
Sheep 45, 46, 47, 50, 51, 53, 56,
    57, 68, 174
Sheep farming 8, 56
Sheets 130, 142, 143
Shirt cloths 132
Shoemakers 69, 71, 77
Shoes 130, 132, 133, 134, 143
Shopkeepers 69, 70, 75, 80, 127
Shops 69, 81, 127, 178
Shutters 105, 113
Silver 43
    plate 118
Singing galleries 43, 162
Sites and Monuments register for
    Herefordshire (SMR) 99
Skeleton suit 135
Skimmer 122
Slayers 137
Smock 132
Smoking chambers 123
Snuff 124
Spinners 71
Spinning wheels 136, 137
Spinster 85, 88, 94, 96; 131, 133,
    136, 142, 143

Spit 121
Spoons 118, 122, 123, 126
St Davids diocese 2
Standards 13, 111
Stays 127, 130, 135
Steward 30, 44
Stomachers 132
Study 106, 109
Sugar 124
Suit 130, 131, 134, 135
Sumptuary Laws 131
Surrogates 145
Sway 121
Sword 131, 132

Table linen 130
Table of degrees 168
Table cloth 142, 143
Tailor 130, 140, 141, 144
Tallow 122
Tanners 53, 69, 77, 78, 79, 80
Tanning 77, 79
Tea table 114, 175
Tenants 27, 30, 31, 33, 35, 36
Tenterhooks 139
Tenths 148
Timber 32, 33, 35
Tithes
    great 148, 149, 151
    small 148, 150, 151
    non-payment 169
    of Rowlestone 29
Trough for warping 137
Tuck mill 138, 139
Tucker 136, 138, 139, 140, 144,
Tucking
    shoes 138
    spurs 139
Turners 70
Turnips 47
Turnpike roads 46, 48, 49, 68
Turnpike Trust, the, 1782 81

Uniformity, Act of 146, 147

Venner, Fifth Monarchist
    uprising 147
Victualler 58
Violin 43

Waistcoats 131, 132, 133
Waste 66, 68
Water grist mill 73
Weaver 69, 71, 136, 137, 138,
    140, 144
Welsh acre 27
    herefordshire dialect 10
    language 11, 153, 156
    measure 9
    mines/coal pits 56, 174
    surnames 9
    the 25
Wheat 46, 47, 51, 58, 60, 62, 63,
    64, 65
Wheel 95
Wheelwrights 69, 70
WI 178
Widows/widowhood 85, 86, 87,
    88, 92, 93, 94, 95, 96
Wig 132, 133
Wilkins family of Maeslough,
    Breconshire 28
Wills 12, 13, 14, 16, 17, 20, 23
Witnesses 145
Wives 86, 89, 91, 92, 93, 94, 97
Wool 46, 48, 57, 91, 95
Worsted 131

Yarn 136, 137, 144